GREAT BRITISH WEEKEND ESCAPES

70 Enticing Weekend Getaways

David Hampshire

King's College, Cambridge

CITY BOOKS

City Books • Bath • England

First published 2021

City Books, c/o Survival Books Limited
Office 169, 3 Edgar Buildings
George Street, Bath BA1 2FJ, United Kingdom
+44 (0)1225-422884, info@survivalbooks.net
citybooks.co, survivalbooks.net and londons-secrets.com

British Library Cataloging in Publication Data
A CIP record for this book is available
from the British Library.
ISBN: 978-1-913171-21-6

Printed in China via D'Print Pte Ltd

Acknowledgements

The author would like to thank the many people who helped with research and provided information for this book. Special thanks are due to Gwen Simmonds and Richard Todd for their invaluable research; Susan Griffith for editing; Grania Browning for final proof checking; John Marshall for desktop publishing and photo selection; David Gillingwater for cover design; Jim Watson for the maps; and the author's wife for the constant supply of tea and coffee. Last, but not least, a special thank you to the many photographers – the unsung heroes – whose beautiful images bring the destinations to life.

The Author

David Hampshire's career has taken him around the world and he lived and worked in many countries before taking up writing full-time. He's the author, co-author or editor of over 30 titles, including *London's Green Walks*, *London's Village Walks*, *London's Monumental Walks*, *London's Waterside Walks*, *Hidden London*, *Quirky London*, *Peaceful London* and *London Escapes*. David was born in Surrey and lived and worked in London for many years and still considers himself a Londoner. Nowadays he divides his time between London and Bath (Somerset).

The Publisher

City Books is an imprint of Survival Books, which was established in 1987 and by the mid-1990s was the leading publisher of books for expats and migrants planning to live, work, buy property or retire abroad. In 2000 we published the first of our London books, *Living and Working in London*, and since then have published over 20 additional London titles, including a series of walking guides. We now specialise in alternative London and UK guidebooks for both residents and visitors. See our websites for our latest titles.

Readers' Guide

- **Address:** The city or town's postcode (usually the town or city hall) and tourist website are listed. You can enter the postcode to display a map of the location on Google and other map sites or, if you're driving, enter the postcode into your satnav.

- **Getting there:** The nearest airport (distance in miles), railway station (and main service provider) and major roads are listed.

- **Highlights:** These may include notable buildings (e.g. cathedral, castle, guildhall, etc.), harbour/port, waterways, museums & galleries, parks & gardens, markets, theatres, nightlife, etc. Many museums and galleries offer free entry, as do notable national collections and those run by local councils, while National Trust and English Heritage sites are free to members (otherwise there's usually a hefty fee). Some cathedrals levy an entrance fee, while others solicit donations (usually at least £5 per person) for their upkeep.

- **Nearby:** A selection of nearby interesting places and attractions is listed, with those featured in this book shown in **bold**.

- **Sleep:** Three recommended hotels (or B&Bs) are listed for each entry, one each in the categories of luxury, moderate and budget; most are located in city/town centres but a few are out of town. Note that in some popular tourist towns budget-priced hotels are rare, while in many towns and cities real 'luxury' hotels are non-existent. Rates depend very much on the time of year and local demand; when demand is high a budget hotel can cost as much as a luxury hotel in a quiet period! **Always shop around for the best rate.**

- **Food & Drink:** Recommended eateries are listed for all cities and towns. It isn't always necessary to book (telephone numbers are listed), although you usually need to book well in advance for popular and first-class restaurants; if you wish to visit a particular restaurant it's advisable to book before planning a trip. A rough price guide is included: £ = inexpensive (< £20 for two courses), ££ = moderate (£20-40), £££ = expensive (over £40). Most recommended restaurants fall into the inexpensive and moderate categories, although we have also included many 'fine dining' establishments. **Note that opening times may vary from those listed due to the uncertainty wrought by the covid epidemic.**

Contents

Disabled Access

Many historic public and private buildings don't provide wheelchair access or provide wheelchair access to the ground floor only. Wheelchairs are provided at some venues (although users may need assistance) and you may also be able to hire a mobility 'scooter'. All museums, galleries and public buildings have a WC, although it may not be wheelchair accessible. Contact venues directly if you have specific requirements. The Disabled Go website (disabledgo.com) provides more in-depth access information for many destinations.

Castlefield Conservation Area, Manchester (see page 58)

Introduction

Britain offers a wealth of options for memorable weekend breaks, from exciting historic cities and charming towns to magnificent architectural gems and fascinating overlooked cities, stunning countryside to beautiful coastline. Whether you're looking to discover a new city, indulge in a cultural or foodie weekend, enjoy a ramble in the countryside or experience an exhilarating coastal break, you'll find them all in *Great British Weekend Escapes*' 70 enticing getaways.

If your chosen destination is within a few hours by road you simply need to throw a few things in the car and off you go, although many destinations can also be reached via domestic flights and most have excellent rail connections. Don't let the weather deter you as every season has its attractions: the enchanting renewal of spring, summer's long balmy days, autumn's ravishing golden landscapes and the invigorating frosty days of winter. There's also a lot to be said for a break outside the most popular times – such as public holiday weekends and peak holiday periods – when hotels are usually less expensive and you can avoid the crowds.

Whether your passion is for architecture, culture, gastronomy, nightlife, green spaces, shopping or adventure, it's covered in *Great British Weekend Escapes*. From the delightful tourist hotspots of Bath and Cambridge, Edinburgh and Oxford, to the architectural treasures of Durham and Salisbury, Chester and Wells, and the unexpected pleasures of Bradford and Nottingham, Coventry and Rochester. If country pursuits are more your thing, then head for delightful Bakewell or Buxton for the magnificent Peak District and Derbyshire Dales, historic Cirencester in the enchanting Cotswolds, beautiful Beaulieu in the New Forest or captivating Kendal in the Lake District, while coastal lovers can take their pick from Brighton and Ramsgate, Falmouth and Southwold, Conwy and Whitby – and many more.

Bear in mind that it's often impossible to see and do everything in a few days, so you'll need to do some research and draw up a 'must-see' list. You may also wish to time your visit to take in a particular celebration, festival or fair, such as Edinburgh's Fringe or Hogmanay, the Isle of Wight (music) Festival or Cowes Week, York's JORVIK Viking Festival or London's celebrated Notting Hill Carnival.

So, why not escape the rat race for a few days and explore the exciting world just a few hours from your doorstep? We trust that you'll enjoy discovering it as much as we did.

David Hampshire
July 2021

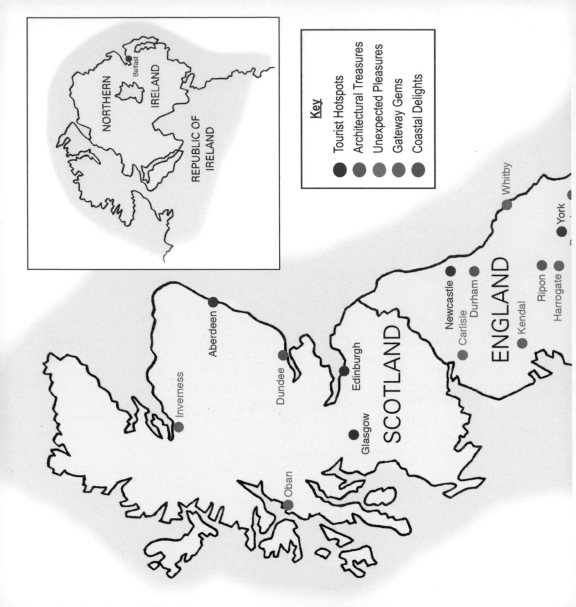

Roman Baths, Bath (see page 15)

1.
Tourist Hotspots

The UK's tourist hotspots attract millions of visitors annually from around the globe and include many of the country's great historic cities, such as Belfast and Cardiff, Edinbugh and Glasgow, Liverpool and Manchester. They also include the UNESCO World Heritage city of Bath, the ancient university cities of Cambridge and Oxford, the Bard's birthplace, Stratford-upon-Avon, and regal Windsor and its majestic royal castle. What all 20 cities and towns have in common is a wealth of attractions, from stunning ancient and contemporary architecture to world-class museums and galleries, beautiful parks and gardens to outstanding hotels, restaurants and shopping. Bear in mind that it's often impossible to see everything in a weekend, so you'll need to decide your priorities.

Aberdeen

Address: Aberdeen AB10 1AR (visitabdn.com)

Getting there: air (Aberdeen, 6mi), rail (Aberdeen, Scotrail), road (A90/A92)

Highlights: granite architecture, St Machar's Cathedral, Mariscal College, Sir Duncan Rice Library, Maritime Museum, riverside parks, waterfront walks, City beach, seafood restaurants

Nearby: Cairngorms, Peterhead, Speyside, Stonehaven

- **Luxury:** Marcliffe Hotel & Spa (5*), N Deeside Rd, Pitfodels, AB15 9YA (01224-861000).
- **Moderate:** Chester Hotel (4*), 59-63 Queen's Rd, AB15 4YP (01224-327777).
- **Budget:** Mercure Caledonian (4*), 10-14 Union Ter, AB10 1WE (0871-376 9003).

Scotland's third most populous city and the county town of Aberdeenshire, majestic Aberdeen lies on the River Dee in northeast Scotland. The friendly 'granite city' and its surrounds offer the perfect balance between vibrant city life, sandy beaches and spectacular countryside, and is considered one of the top ten places to live and work in the UK.

The modern city grew up as two separate burghs: Old Aberdeen, the university and cathedral settlement at the mouth of the River Don (north of the modern city), and New Aberdeen (from the 12th century), a fishing and trading settlement where the Denburn waterway enters the Dee estuary. The modern city was constructed between the mid-18th and mid-20th centuries, mostly using local grey granite – hence it being dubbed the 'Granite City'. Today, the traditional industries of fishing, papermaking, shipbuilding and textiles have been overtaken by the oil industry, following the discovery of oil under the North Sea in the '70s.

Aberdeen boasts a wealth of beautiful architecture, including **St Machar's Cathedral Church** in Old Aberdeen, built by the Normans in 1132, although little remains of the original building, the present church mostly dating from the 15th-16th centuries. The cathedral has a stunning interior, particularly its striking wooden heraldic ceiling. Among the city's oldest churches is the **Kirk of St Nicholas** (the patron saint of Aberdeen) – the mother church of the city – built in 1151 and enlarged in the 15th century. Another must-see is

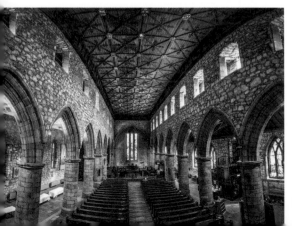

St Machar's Cathedral

King's College Chapel (1495) – containing the most complete medieval church interior in Scotland – the centrepiece of the **University of Aberdeen** campus, which is complemented by grand **Elphinstone Hall** (1931) and the **Quadrangle of King's College**.

Sir Duncan Rice Library

After visiting Old Aberdeen take a walk along Union Street – Aberdeen's sparkling Granite Mile – home to many notable buildings (or located close by), including **Provost Skene's House** (1545); the **Old Aberdeen Town House** (1789); **Aberdeen Music Hall** (1822); majestic **Mariscal College** (1837), the second-largest granite building in the world, now the Aberdeen City Council's HQ; Flemish-Gothic **New Town House** (1870s); and **His Majesty's Theatre** (1906), with twin domes, designed by acclaimed architect Frank Matcham. The theatre forms a handsome row of buildings that include **St Mark's Church** (1892), with a dome modelled on St Paul's Cathedral (London), and the **Central Library** (1892). More recent buildings include award-winning **Sir Duncan Rice Library** (2012), an imposing cube-shaped building that's the main academic library of the University of Aberdeen; the interior is even more impressive, with curved floors around a central atrium.

Aberdeen has a number of museums, including the striking glass-fronted **Aberdeen Maritime Museum,** which poignantly illustrates the decline of the oil and

Food & Drink

• **Café 52:** rustic café service light bites, tapas and modern British dishes (52 The Green, AB11 6PE, 01224-590094, noon-midnight, Tue 6pm-midnight, closed Sun-Mon, £).

• **Moon Fish Café:** Cosy, chic bistro offering creative British-Scottish cuisine (9 Correction Wynd, AB10 1HP, 01224-644166, noon-10.30pm, Sun noon-6pm, closed Mon-Tue, £-££).

• **Silver Darling:** Light-filled restaurant specialising in local fish/seafood dishes (Pocra Quay, AB11 5DQ, 01224-576229, noon-2pm, 5.30-8pm, Fri-Sun, noon-8pm, ££).

gas industry since its '70s heyday**; Aberdeen Art Gallery,** one of Scotland's finest art galleries recently redeveloped; the **Tolbooth Museum**, set in one of the best-preserved 17th-century gaols in Scotland; while

Mariscal College

close by (in Castle Street) is the 17th-century **Mercat Cross** (market cross). Other museums include the **Gordon Highlanders Museum**, which tells the history of one of Scotland's finest regiments, the hands-on **Aberdeen Science Centre** and the vast, eclectic **University of Aberdeen's Collections**.

If you fancy stretching your legs or just relaxing, Aberdeen – the floral capital of Scotland – is home to some fourteen public parks and gardens. These include the lovely **Union Terrace Gardens** (currently being rejuvenated) in the centre of town and **Duthie Park** (44 acres) on the banks of the River Dee, which incorporates the **David Welch Winter Gardens**, one of Europe's largest indoor gardens and Scotland's third most visited garden. To the west of the city centre is 180-acre **Hazlehead Park**, with woodland walks and a maze, while in Old Aberdeen is beautiful **Seaton Park** (adjacent to St Machar's Cathedral), just south of which is gorgeous 11-acre **Cruickshank Botanic Garden** on King's College campus. While wandering around the city, keep an eye out for striking murals and painted doors, a unique local art form (see nuartaberdeen.co.uk).

When you need a break from sight-seeing, Aberdeen has a host of excellent eateries – it's particularly noted for its superb seafood and Scottish restaurants – and is

> An enjoyable 5-mile walk takes you along the Esplanade (seafront) and sandy beach past the Art Deco Beach Ballroom, inland along the River Don, over the ancient Brig o' Balgownie and back to town via the Old Town and university.

one of Scotland's largely unheralded foodie hotspots. If you fancy a spot of retail therapy, then look no further than Union Square Shopping Centre, with over 50 top stores plus some 30 (mainly chain) restaurants and a ten-screen cinema. The brutalist circular muralled Indoor Market building on Market Street has some independent shops on two levels and a few good eating places, such as the Sushi Box and Madame Mew's Thai Café.

With a student population of over 50,000, Aberdeen has a vibrant nightlife, from theatres and cinemas to an abundance of pubs (Brew Dog was founded here), bars, comedy, live music venues and nightclubs, some of which occupy disused churches such as the 'Gothic' Slains Castle pub and Triple Kirks nearby. The city stages some interesting cultural festivals such as a 10-day jazz festival in March and the Sound Festival of new music in October.

If you have some spare time, you may wish to sample some malt whiskies in Speyside, go hiking/skiing in the Cairngorm Mountains or river fishing for salmon, cycle along the Deeside Way to Crathes Castle or enjoy outstanding fish and chips after a bracing beach walk at Stonehaven.

Brig o' Balgownie

Bath

Address: Bath BA1 5AW (visitbath.co.uk)

Getting There: air (Bristol, 19mi), rail (Bath Spa, SW trains), road (M4/M5, A46)

Highlights: Georgian architecture, Bath Abbey, Roman Baths, Holburne Museum, American Museum, Royal Victoria Park, Thermae Bath Spa

Nearby: Bradford-on-Avon, **Bristol**, Castle Combe, **Cotswolds**, Dyrham Park, Lacock

Sleep

- **Luxury:** Bath Priory (5*), Weston Rd, BA1 2XT (01225-331922).
- **Moderate:** The Ayrlington (5*, B&B), 24/25 Pulteney Rd, BA2 4EZ (01225-425495).
- **Budget:** Parade Park Hotel (3*), 8-10 N Parade, BA2 4AL (01225-463384).

Set in the rolling countryside of the River Avon valley in North Somerset, beautiful Bath – the only city in the UK designated a UNESCO World Heritage Site (since 1987) – is located 97 miles west of London and 11 miles southeast of Bristol. Famous for its natural hot springs and ravishing Georgian architecture – built from local honey-coloured Bath stone (limestone) – a stroll around Bath is a journey through centuries of architectural delights. These include splendid 16th-century **Bath Abbey**, noted for its fan-vaulting, tower (which you can climb) and lovely stained glass windows;

the majestic **Royal Crescent** and inspired **Circus**. Don't miss the **Assembly Rooms**, the social hub of Georgian Bath, or a stroll along grand Great Pulteney Street and across **Pulteney Bridge**, inspired by Florence's Ponte Vecchio, one of only four bridges in the world lined with shops.

Roman Baths

Built for pleasure and relaxation – it was the centre of fashionable life in England during the 18th century –

Pulteney Bridge

Bath has been a spa destination since Roman times. The waters remain a big draw, both the ancient **Roman Baths** (*Aquae Sulis*) and the modern **Thermae Bath Spa** (see box), the only natural thermal hot springs in Britain where you can still wallow in the waters. Restored in 2011, the Roman Baths are now a museum and include the Great Bath, Roman statues and a temple, comprising one of the finest historic sites in Northern Europe. The city's unique thermal springs rise here and the Baths still flow with natural hot water, while interactive exhibits and computer-generated reconstructions illustrate their importance to our Roman ancestors.

If it's culture you seek, Bath offers plenty of options, including the impressive **Holburne Museum** (home of the eclectic private collection of Victorian art enthusiast Sir William Holburne); the **Fashion Museum** at the Bath Assembly Rooms; the museum of Georgian life

Parade Gardens

at **No 1 Royal Crescent**; classic and contemporary art at the splendid public **Victorian Art Gallery**; Bath's **Old Theatre Royal**, opened in 1750, now home to the excellent **Masonic Museum**; and the **Jane Austen Centre**, which celebrates one of Britain's favourite authors who lived in Bath from 1801 to 1806. A short way out of town is the **American Museum**, set within 125 acres of beautiful grounds, home to the finest collection of Americana outside the United States. Bath also offers an abundance of commercial art galleries and antiques shops, such as Beaux Arts and the Rostra Gallery.

If you wish to stretch your legs, Bath has some beautiful parks and gardens, including the expansive **Royal Victoria Park** (57 acres) and **Botanical Gardens**, the bijou riverside **Parade Gardens**, charming **Henrietta Park** and delightful **Sydney Gardens** straddling the Kennet & Avon Canal. A short walk from the centre, **Alexandra Park** offers spectacular views over the city, while a bit further afield is magnificent **Prior Park** (National Trust), an 18th-century landscape garden created by Bath entrepreneur Ralph Allen (1693-1764).

Thermae Bath Spa

Although you can no longer take the waters at the Roman Baths, you can enjoy the same natural hot spring water at the award-winning Thermae Bath Spa, which brings the spa into the 21st century, with luxurious treatments and a rooftop pool offering panoramic views over the city (thermaebathspa. com).

Royal Crescent

Food & Drink

- **Circus Restaurant:** award-winning restaurant serving modern British cuisine (34 Brock St, BA1 2LN, 01225-466020, Mon-Sat 10am-11pm, closed Sun, ££).

- **Pump Room Restaurant:** elegant restaurant housed in the splendid Georgian Pump Room (13 Abbey Churchyard, BA1 1LZ, 01225-477785, 10am-5.45pm, breakfast, lunch, afternoon tea, ££).

- **Sotto Sotto:** popular Italian restaurant in atmospheric 18th-century barrel vaults (10 N Parade, BA2 4AL, 01225-330236, noon-2pm, 5-10pm, £).

When it's time for some refreshments, the city is overflowing with places to eat and drink – it has a well-deserved reputation as a foodie destination – and also offers some of the best independent shops and boutiques in the UK (particularly for fashion), along with the indoor **Guildhall Market**, a weekly farmers' market, and regular antiques fairs and markets. Come the evening Bath offers plenty of entertainment options, including no less than five theatres, three cinemas, live music and comedy, numerous pubs, bars and clubs and a casino – along with a comprehensive programme of concerts, fairs, festivals and sports events.

Bath Panorama

Belfast

Address: Belfast BT1 5GS (visitbelfast.com)

Getting there: air (Belfast, 13mi), rail (Great Victoria St, NI Railways), road (M1/M2, A20/A24)

Highlights: Docklands, Titanic Belfast, St Anne's Cathedral, Belfast City Hall, Ulster Museum, Crumlin Road Gaol, Botanic Garden, St George's Market, seafood restaurants

Nearby: Bangor, Carrickfergus, Larne, Lisburn, Lough Neagh

Sleep

• **Luxury:** Merchant Hotel (5*), 16 Skipper St, BT1 2DZ (028-9023 4888).

• **Moderate:** Bullitt Hotel (4*), 40a Church Ln, BT1 4QN (028-9590 0600).

• **Budget:** The Crescent Townhouse (3*), 13 Lower Cres, BT7 1NR (028-9032 3349).

The capital of Northern Ireland, Belfast stands on the banks of the River Lagan on the east coast of Northern Ireland. The city has undergone rapid expansion and regeneration since the late '90s and is now one of the UK's most vibrant cities and a major tourist centre.

The city developed into a major settlement in the 17th century after being established by Sir Arthur Chichester and was initially settled by Protestant English and Scottish migrants. A major port since the early 19th century, during the Industrial Revolution it was the largest linen producer in the world ('Linenopolis') and by the time it was granted city status in 1888 had the world's largest shipyard (Harland and Wolff), which built the *RMS Titanic* in 1912 and many other famous ships. Following Ireland's partition in 1922, Belfast became the capital of Northern Ireland, which remained part of the United Kingdom. The city was heavily bombed during the Second World War and also suffered greatly in 'The Troubles', the sectarian violence between Roman Catholics and Protestants, which ended in 1998 with the Good Friday Agreement (although the city is still divided along sectarian lines by the so-called 'Peace Lines' or 'Peace Wall').

A visit to Belfast wouldn't be complete without visiting the **Docklands** and **Titanic Belfast** – you can cross over the River Lagan via the Lagan Weir footbridge and stroll along the riverside – northeast of the city centre. Housed in an iconic,

Belfast City Hall

Titanic Belfast

futuristic building shaped like a ship's bow, the museum tells the story of the world's most famous ship, which hit an iceberg and sank on its maiden voyage to New York in 1912 with the loss of over 1,500 lives. Nearby is the **SS Nomadic**, Titanic's sister ship built at the same time, now refurbished as a visitor attraction, while to the north is **Titanic Studios**, where scenes from the legendary *Game of Thrones* TV fantasy drama were filmed.

Returning to the city centre, a tour of some of the city's impressive architecture is in order – you can take a walking tour with tips-based Belfast 'Free' Walking Tours (belfastfreewalkingtour.com) – taking in beautiful **St Anne's Cathedral** (1904), a Romanesque Anglican church constituting the heart of the Cathedral Quarter

St George's Market

St George's is the last surviving Victorian (1890-96) covered market (Fri-Sun) in Belfast, with some 250 traders selling everything from artisan foods to flowers, vinyl records to vintage jewellery (with live music at weekends).

(noted for its colourful murals); **Belfast City Hall** (1906) – a Baroque Revival masterpiece with a grand marble hall (outside is the poignant Titanic Memorial Garden); the **Grand Opera House** (1895), an innovative design by Frank Matcham with a breathtaking auditorium; and **Ulster Hall** (1859), which has a superb English pipe organ (Mulholland Grand Organ). To the south of the city is Queen's University, where the **Lanyon Building** (1849) is a majestic Tudor-Gothic, red-brick building famous for its Hogwarts-esque character, while north of the city is **Belfast Castle** (1870), a fairy-tale fortress at the foot of Cavehill, which is close to **Belfast Zoo**. Six miles east of the city centre is the handsome Neo-Classical **Stormont Parliament Building** (1932), home to the Northern Ireland Assembly.

Belfast Castle

If museums and galleries are your thing, then don't miss the **Ulster Museum**, located in the Botanic Gardens, which explores 9,000 years of Irish culture and has a rich collection of art, history and natural sciences. The city has many interesting smaller museums and visitor attractions, including the haunting **Crumlin Road**

Gaol (the 'Crum'), a notorious former Victorian prison that closed in 1996 after 150 years. Also worth a visit is the impressive **Metropolitan Arts Centre** (MAC) – an award-winning cultural centre (visual art, theatre, dance, etc.) housing three major art galleries – and **W5**, a science and discovery centre with over 250 interactive exhibits.

If you fancy some exercise, Belfast has over 40 public parks and gardens, including the magnificent **Botanic Garden** (1830) in the Queen's Quarter centred on the University; lovely **Ormeau Park** (1871), the city's oldest municipal park; **Sir Thomas & Lady Dixon Park** (128 acres) to the south of the centre, home to the ravishing International Rose Garden and Japanese and walled gardens; and **Victoria Park** (close to Titanic Belfast), a dramatic park almost surrounded by water, with pleasant walks, viewpoints and abundant birdlife.

Belfast's fashion hotspots are the Victoria Square and Castle Court shopping centres, plus a host of independent boutiques, not forgetting historic **St George's Market** (see box on page 19). When you're hungry you'll find Belfast has enjoyed a culinary renaissance in recent years and is home to a profusion of first-class restaurants, with some of the UK's best fish and seafood. After the sun goes down the place to be is cobbled Hill Street in the Cathedral Quarter, the buzzing heart of the city's vibrant nightlife and *craic*. Belfast has

Food&Drink

- **Darcy's:** classic Belfast dishes with a contemporary twist (10 Bradbury Pl, BT7 1RS, 028-9032 4040, Mon-Thu 4-9.30pm, Fri-Sun 1-9.30/10pm, £).
- **Deanes Love Fish:** Stylish and bright fish and seafood restaurant (28-40 Howard St, BT1 6PF, 028-9033 1134, noon-3pm, 5-10pm, Sat noon-10pm, closed Sun, £-££).
- **James St:** highly rated bar and grill specialising in chargrilled aged steaks (19-21 St James St S, BT2 7GA, 028-9560 0700, see website for times, ££).

a bounty of pubs – don't miss the ornate **Crown Bar** in Great Victoria Street – bars, clubs and music venues, plus a variety of theatres and cinemas.

If you have some spare time, Northern Ireland offers many attractions, historic towns (e.g. Derry/Londonderry), beautiful countryside and a dramatic coastline, including the stunning **Giant's Causeway** (below) on the north coast (60mi), Northern Ireland's only UNESCO World Heritage Site.

Giant's Causeway

Birmingham

Address: Birmingham B1 1AA (visitbirmingham.com)

Getting there: air (Birmingham, 14mi), rail (New Street/Grand Central, West Midlands/Virgin), road (M5/6)

Highlights: Jewellery Quarter, Museum & Art Gallery, Barber Institute of Fine Arts, Gas Street Basin, Library of Birmingham, National Exhibition Centre, Sutton Park, Indian restaurants, Bullring

Nearby: Cadbury World, **Coventry**, Dudley Zoo, Edgbaston, **Lichfield**

- **Luxury:** Hyatt Regency (4*), 2 Bridge St, B1 2JZ (0121-643 1234).
- **Moderate:** Bloc Hotel (3*), 77 Caroline St, B3 1UG (0121-212 1223).
- **Budget:** Rowton Hotel (3*), 145 Alcester St, B12 0PJ (0121-627 0627).

At first glance Birmingham – England's second largest city (home to 1.1 million people) in the Midlands – may not appear to be the ideal place to spend an enjoyable weekend, but the city has undergone a remarkable transformation in recent decades. Today, it's a dynamic, multi-ethnic cultural and social hub, as well as being the financial and commercial heart of both the East and West Midlands.

A market town in the medieval period, Birmingham grew rapidly in the 18th-century 'Midlands Enlightenment' and subsequent Industrial Revolution, and by the early 19th century was hailed as 'the first manufacturing town in the world'. A combination of entrepreneurial spirit and engineering excellence made the city the manufacturing powerhouse of Britain throughout the 19th and most of the 20th centuries.

Birmingham is home to many world class museums and galleries, including the celebrated **Birmingham Museum & Art Gallery** opened in 1885. It

Gas Street Basin

Library of Birmingham

boasts over 40 galleries of art, applied art, social history, archaeology and ethnography, including the most important collection of pre-Raphaelite art in the world, the Anglo-Saxon Staffordshire Hoard and a magnificent collection of Baroque art. Also of note is the **Barber Institute of Fine Arts**, an art gallery and concert hall housed in a handsome Art Deco building, containing an internationally-acclaimed collection of artworks spanning the 17th-20th centuries. The city is also home to a number of excellent contemporary art galleries, like the RBSA Gallery in the Jewellery Quarter. Other museums – many celebrating the city's industrial heritage – include **Thinktank** (Birmingham's Science Museum), the **National Motorcycle Museum**, the **Lapworth Museum of Geology**, the **Museum of the Jewellery Quarter**, the **Pen Museum** and the **Coffin Works**, dedicated to the manufacture of coffins! Also worth a visit is the city's striking futuristic **Library of Birmingham** (2013), the largest public cultural space in Europe.

The Birmingham metropolitan area is one of the UK's greenest regions, boasting over 500 parks and gardens – more than any other European city – and although it doesn't have a river it more than makes up

for it with its vast network of canals (see box). **Sutton Park** in the north of the city covers 2,400 acres and is the largest urban park in Europe, while the city's **Botanical Gardens** in Edgbaston (est. 1829) and the nearby **Winterbourne Botanic Garden** – a rare surviving example of an early 20th-century Arts and Crafts garden – are a treat for garden lovers. Other popular parks include **Cannon Hill Park** (120 acres) – home to **Birmingham Wildlife Conservation Park** – **Sheldon Country Park** (over 300 acres), **Lickey Hills Country Park** (500 acres), **Handsworth Park** and lovely **Martineau Gardens**. Popular attractions for kids include the **National Sea Life Centre** aquarium and **Cadbury World** (a real-life Willy Wonka chocolate factory), while just a short train ride away the **National Exhibition Centre** (NEC) hosts nationally important trade fairs and shows like Crufts Dog Show.

Birmingham's Canals

An enduring legacy and the lifeblood of the city's industrial supremacy, Birmingham's intricate canal network extends to over 100 miles – some claim it's larger than that of Venice! – the hub of which is the bustling city centre junction of Gas Street Basin. Here colourful boats (you can take a canal trip) and historic canal architecture sit alongside vibrant restaurants, cafés and bars, at the heart of the city's cosmopolitan nightlife and shopping districts.

Birmingham provides one of the UK's best shopping experiences, including the new **Grand Central** shopping centre above the station, while celebrated **Bullring** is home to the Open Market (Tue-Sat) and the futuristic

Selfridges

Food & Drink

- **Adam's:** Michelin-starred, contemporary fine dining British restaurant (16 Waterloo St, B2 5UG, 0121-643 3745, noon-2pm/7-9pm, closed Sun, ££-£££).
- **Lasan:** excellent Indian restaurant offering the finest nouveau Indian cuisine (James St, St Paul's Sq, B3 1SD, 0121-212 3664, noon-2.30pm, 5-10pm, Sat noon-11pm, Sun noon-9pm, £-££).
- **Tapas Revolution:** Spanish restaurant chain specialising in tapas (Grand Central Station, Stephenson Pl, B2 4XJ, 0121-643 6381, Mon-Fri noon-9pm, Sat-Sun to 10pm, £-££).

scene – it was the birthplace of heavy metal – where you can hear the latest bands at the O_2 Academy and Institute, plus a multitude of smaller venues. Don't neglect to take in the city's lively street life, not least in the Gay Village (the city's LGBT quarter), with its eclectic mix of bars and cabaret clubs.

Selfridges building. Elsewhere in the city, the preserved **Jewellery Quarter** and the regenerated **Custard Factory** in Digbeth (the city's cool artsy district) host lots of quirky shops and cafés. When you're peckish or fancy a drink, Birmingham caters for every palate, with a host of restaurants, pubs and cafés offering everything from Michelin-star cuisine to fast food and take-aways. It's one of the UK's finest gastronomic centres, noted for its superb Indian cuisine and authentic Chinese food in the Chinese Quarter.

Birmingham offers a variety of theatres and music venues to while away the evening, including a world-class symphony orchestra (and Symphony Hall), ballet company and repertory theatre. The city's nightlife is among the liveliest in Britain with a vibrant live music

New Street Station

Bristol

Address: Bristol BS1 5TR (visitbristol.co.uk)

Getting there: air (Bristol, 8mi), rail (Bristol Temple Meads, GWR), road (M5/M4/M32)

Highlights: harbour, Cathedral, Bristol Museum & Art Gallery, SS Great Britain, M Shed, Clifton Suspension Bridge & Clifton village, Cabot Tower, Banksy murals, St Nicholas Market

Nearby: Bath, Chepstow, **Cotswolds**, Mendips, South Wales, Weston-super-Mare

Sleep

- **Luxury:** Bristol Harbour Hotel & Spa (4*), 53-55 Corn St, BS1 1HT (0117-203 4445).
- **Moderate:** Hotel du Vin (4*), The Sugar House, Narrow Lewins Mead, BS1 2NU (0117-403 2979).
- **Budget:** Victoria Square Hotel (2*), 29-30 Victoria Sq, Clifton, BS8 4EW (0117-973 9058).

One of the UK's most popular tourist destinations, vibrant Bristol – some 120 miles west of London – was named the 'best city in which to live in Britain' by the *Sunday Times* in both 2014 and 2017 (and was awarded 'European Green Capital' status in 2015). Founded in the 11th century, the city received its royal charter in 1155 and from the 13th to 18th centuries was one of England's richest cities and most important ports, although it was surpassed by Birmingham, Liverpool and Manchester during the Industrial Revolution. Today, Bristol's economy is based on the creative media, electronics and aerospace industries, while the city's docks have been redeveloped as centres of heritage and culture.

The best place to start a visit is with a stroll around the historic city centre and harbour – if you aren't up to walking then there's a hop-on hop-off ferry (waterbus) service serving most of the city's harbourside attractions. The once neglected harbour area has been re-invented as a tourist destination, with the former warehouses and wharves transformed into museums, galleries, shopping

Bristol Harbour

If you've kids in tow, delightful **Bristol Zoo Gardens**, the world's oldest provincial zoo (1836) is a great day out, while in the city centre there's **Bristol Aquarium**.

and entertainment centres. Don't neglect to visit historic Clifton village and Brunel's stunning **Clifton Suspension Bridge** and **Clifton Observatory**, which offers panoramic views of the bridge and city.

If you love ancient buildings then don't miss **Bristol Cathedral** (founded 1140), the **Lord Mayor's Chapel** (opposite the cathedral) – the only remaining building of the 13th-century Hospital of St Mark founded in 1220 – and **St James Priory** (open Mon-Fri), founded in 1129 as a Benedictine priory and the oldest building in Bristol. The city offers a number of interesting museums and galleries, including the **Bristol Museum & Art Gallery**, **M Shed** (Bristol's social history museum), **We the Curious** (a Science Museum with a planetarium), **Aerospace Bristol** (home to Concorde) and the **Georgian House Museum,** an 18th-century sugar merchant's home. Brunel's *SS Great Britain* – Bristol's premier attraction – and **Being Brunel Museum**, explore the life and legacy of Britain's greatest engineer,

Bristol Marina

Balloon Fiesta

Isambard Kingdom Brunel (1806-1859). Brunel built bridges, tunnels, railways and ships that were longer, faster and bigger than anything seen before, including the *SS Great Britain*, the first iron steamer to cross the Atlantic (in 1845) and the world's longest passenger ship from 1845 to 1854.

The city also offers some splendid galleries, including the **Royal West of England Academy** (RWA), **Arnolfini** – Bristol's international centre for contemporary arts – and **Spike Island** (contemporary artists' studios and gallery). The city is also famous for its street art – it's **Banksy's** home town – where you'll find beautiful works of art on buildings throughout the city (you can join a 'street art tour' – see wherethewall.com/tours)

If you fancy a stroll and some fresh air, Bristol is home to over 400 parks and gardens, from handsome **Queen Square** (5.9 acres) in the city centre to the sprawling **Ashton Court Estate** (great city views) to the west of the city, an 850-acre country park (and mansion), laid out by Humphry Repton. Other highlights include **Castle Park** (and the ruins of St Peter's Church),

Food & Drink

- **Casamia:** Michelin-starred British restaurant that has been called 'the best restaurant outside London' (8 The General, Lower Guinea St, BS1 6FU, 0117-959 2884, casamiarestaurant.co.uk, Wed-Fri 6-10pm, Sat noon-4pm, 6-10pm, closed Sun-Tue, £££).
- **Pasture:** highly-acclaimed upscale steakhouse – carnivore heaven! (2 Portwall Ln, Redcliffe, BS1 6NB, 07741-193445, noon-3pm, 5-11pm, Fri midnight, Sat noon-midnight, Sun noon-6pm, ££).
- **Spiny Lobster:** superb seafood restaurant serving the best fish in Bristol (128-130 Whiteladies Rd, BS8 2RS, 0117-973 7384, 10am-5pm, closed Sun-Mon, £-££).

Brandon Hill (and 105ft **Cabot Tower**, built in the 1890s to commemorate the 400th anniversary of John Cabot's voyage from Bristol to the New World), **Clifton Down** (just north of Clifton village) and the University of Bristol's **Botanic Garden**.

Bristol caters for all pockets and tastes, from the Broadmead Shopping Centre to Clifton Village, Gloucester Road and edgy Stokes Croft to **St Nicholas Market's** (est. 1743) maze of quirky stalls in the heart of the old city. When you need a break, Bristol is a foodie's dream destination with something to suit every palate and budget, from Michelin-starred restaurants to street food (and everything in between).

SS Great Britain

Bristol can more than hold its own in the entertainment stakes, with a plethora of clubs, live gigs, bars/pubs, speakeasies, comedy, karaoke and theatres (including the famous **Bristol Old Vic** and **Bristol Hippodrome**) – enough to keep you amused until the small hours. The city also has a thriving LGBT scene, with hubs in the Old Market Quarter and West End gay villages. Bristol also stages a comprehensive programme of festivals, particularly in summer, with St Paul's Carnival, the Harbour Festival, the Downs Festival and the spectacular Bristol International Balloon Fiesta in August.

Clifton Suspension Bridge

Cambridge

Address: Cambridge CB2 1BY (visitcambridge.org)

Getting there: air (Stansted airport, 30mi), rail (Cambridge, Greater Anglia, etc), road (M11, A14)

Highlights: university colleges, King's College Chapel, medieval churches, Fitzwilliam Museum, Kettle's Yard, River Cam, Botanic Garden, Jesus Green, historic pubs, market, restaurants

Nearby: Bury St Edmunds, Ely, Grantchester, Newmarket, Saffron Waldon, St Ives

The county town of Cambridgeshire, captivating Cambridge lies on the River Cam 50 miles north of London, just south of the low-lying coastal wetland known as the Fens. An important trading centre during the Roman and Viking periods, its first town charters were granted in the 12th century, although modern city status wasn't officially conferred until 1951. Quintessentially English – possibly the most archetypal English city – with a rich history, charming streets, stunning architecture, bucolic riverside walks, lovely open parkland and handsome pubs. Cambridge is difficult to beat for a city break.

King's College

Sleep

• **Luxury:** Gonville Hotel (4*), Gonville Pl, CB1 1LY (01223-366611).

• **Moderate:** Lensfield Hotel (3*), 53 Lensfield Rd, CB2 1EN (01223-355017).

• **Budget:** Fenners Hotel (2*), 144-146 Tenison Rd, CB1 2DP (01223-360246).

The city is synonomous with world-class **Cambridge University** (cam.ac.uk), founded in 1209, although the oldest existing college, Peterhouse, wasn't established until 1284. It has much in common with Oxford University (see page 65) – from ancient colleges to a shared affection for flat-bottomed pleasure boats known as punts – but has more green space, less traffic and is much prettier than its academic rival.

A tour of the majestic university colleges is a must and the highlight of any visit. There are 31 colleges – founded between the 13th and 20th centuries – each with its own separate grounds and gardens, accommodation, chapels, dining halls and lecture rooms. A visit to any college is worthwhile, but among the most popular are **King's College** (and its magnificent chapel), **Trinity**

Bridge of Sighs, St John's College

St Mary the Great

College (whose glorious library was designed by Sir Christopher Wren), **Peterhouse**, **St. John's** – famous for its romantic Bridge of Sighs – and **Queen's College**. The latter features the splendid wooden **Mathematical Bridge**, so called because it was built without nails, relying for its strength on meticulous calculation (although today's version is a 1905 reconstruction).

Cambridge is home to a treasure trove of beautiful medieval churches, which include the **Church of St Mary the Great**, aka Great St Mary's or GSM, at the north end of King's Parade. Built in the 15th century – a parish church and the university church of Cambridge University – it has a fine interior and a tower dating

from 1608. Also of note is **Little St Mary's Church** (St Mary the Less, 1352), which has beautiful stained-glass windows, and the **Round Church** (aka Church of the Holy Sepulchre), built around 1130 and one of only four Norman round churches in England. Other historic churches worth a visit include St Bene't's (ca 1020) – the oldest building in Cambridge, with Anglo-Saxon features – St Clement's (1225) and St Botolph's (ca 1350).

Kettle's Yard

The city's many museums – eight cultural and scientific museums are run by Cambridge University alone – include splendid **Fitzwilliam Museum**, whose world-class collections of art and antiquities span centuries and include masterpieces by Titian, Modigliani and Picasso, along with ancient artefacts from Egypt, Greece and Rome. Another must-see collection is **Kettle's Yard**, the former home of one-time Tate curator

---

College Visitor Information & Fees

For college opening times and fees (if applicable), see cambridge-news.co.uk/news/cambridge-news/cambridge-university-colleges-free-visit-13810784.

Fitzwilliam Museum

Jim Ede, and the adjacent modern art gallery, housing a major collection of 20th-century and contemporary art, including works by Ben Nicholson, Barbara Hepworth, Henry Moore, Joan Miró and Constantin Brancusi. Other museums include the **Museum of Cambridge**, the **Museum of Archaeology & Anthropology**, the **Museum of Classical Archaeology**, the **Sedgwick Museum of Earth Sciences**, the **Polar Museum**, the **University Museum of Zoology**, the **Whipple Museum of the History of Science**, the **Cambridge Museum of Technology** and the **Centre for Computing History** (phew!).

> When you've had your fill of academia, a punting trip along the River Cam is a splendid way to explore the city on a summer's day, perhaps culminating in a picnic on the Backs, the meadows bordering the willow-shaded Cam.

If you fancy a walk (or bike ride) after all that culture, Cambridge offers dozens of green spaces, including magnificent riverside parks, tranquil water meadows and ravishing gardens. The natural fen landscape flows gently through the city centre along the **River Cam**, with cows grazing within sight of glorious **King's College Chapel**, and the beautifully manicured college

River Cam at Jesus Green

grounds, fellows' gardens and the university's lovely **Botanic Garden** (est. 1831). The city's public parks and commons are a paradise for children and include **Jesus Green** (close to Jesus College), where the river laps its northern edge and an avenue of London plane trees provides a leafy canopy, while adjoining **Midsummer Common** is an ancient area of grassland bordered by the Cam, where you can watch the rowers on the water. In the city centre to the east of Christ's College is **Christ's Pieces**, a splendid Victorian park with ornamental trees and flower beds, while a short distance away is **Parker's Piece**, a 25-acre common regarded as the birthplace of the rules of association football (soccer).

Christ's Pieces

Punts on River Cam

Food & Drink

- **Cambridge Chop House:** Popular restaurant just 50m from King's College Chapel (1 King's Parade, CB2 1SJ, 01223-359506, Mon-Fri 11.30am-8.30/9pm, Sat 10am-9.30pm, Sun 10am-5pm, £-££).

- **The Eagle:** 17th-century Greene King pub, perfect for a traditional pub lunch (8 Bene't St, CB2 3QN, 01223-505020, 11am-11pm, midnight Thu-Sat, Sun 10.30pm, £).

- **The Senate:** cheery bar and bistro with all-day Mediterranean menu (1 St Mary's Passage, CB2 3PQ, 01223-315641, Mon-Wed & Sun noon-4pm, Thu-Sat noon-9/10pm, £-££).

range of real ales. If shopping is your bag, Cambridge has more than enough shops and boutiques to satisfy the most dedicated shopaholic, plus a general market (Mon-Sat, 10am-4pm) and a Sunday arts and crafts market.

When it comes to entertainment, Cambridge offers something for everyone, including an exciting theatre and performance scene encompassing drama, dance and family entertainment, and a wide range of music, from pop to classical, jazz to rap, not forgetting the sublime choir of King's College Chapel; Trinity, Selwyn, St. Johns and many other colleges also have notable choirs. Finally, with over 20,000 students, Cambridge has plenty of student theatre, particularly at the ADC Theatre, comedy and concerts.

When you need a break from sightseeing, Cambridge caters for all tastes and pockets, from Michelin-star cuisine (it's a gourmet's paradise) to tasty street food (see foodparkcam.com). It's particularly noted for its pubs, from traditional to trendy, city or river views, traditional pub grub to gastro fare, along with a wide

Newnham College

Mathematical Bridge, Queen's College

Canterbury

Address: Canterbury CT1 1YW (canterbury.co.uk)

Getting there: air (n/a), rail (Canterbury, Southeastern), road (M2/A2)

Highlights: Cathedral, St Augustine's Abbey, Westgate, Beaney House, medieval streets, River Stour, Westgate Gardens, Marlow Theatre

Nearby: Faversham, Isle of Thanet, Kent Downs, Margate, **Ramsgate**, Whitstable

One of England's most attractive cathedral cities, Canterbury in east Kent is 61 miles southeast of London astride the River Stour. The area has been inhabited since prehistoric times and was the capital of the Celtic Cantiaci and the Jute Kingdom of Kent in the 1st century AD, when it was captured by the Romans and named *Durovernum Cantiacorum*. Today Canterbury is a beautiful city whose charming alleyways and lanes still follow its medieval street plan, with the River Stour meandering through its centre. It's a city where it's a pleasure to wander aimlessly, with something to delight around every corner and where street names – from Butchery Lane to Iron Bar Lane – reflect their original purpose. A boat trip on the Stour

(aka Great Stour) is also a treat not to be missed. **Canterbury Cathedral** is a gem – a UNESCO World Heritage Site since

1988 – and the centre of English Christianity since St Augustine, its first bishop, converted the Saxons here in 597. You enter the cathedral precinct via the monumental **Christ Church Gate**, built

Canterbury Cathedral & Cloisters

St Augustine's Abbey

to celebrate the marriage of Arthur, Prince of Wales, to Catherine of Aragon in 1502; Arthur died a few months later and the gate wasn't finished for another 20 years, while Catherine subsequently married Henry VIII in 1509 (whose divorce led to the Reformation). Vast, beautiful and inspiring, the cathedral's history is intrinsically linked to that of England; as the seat of the Archbishop of Canterbury, leader of the Church of England, it's the most important Christian site in the country.

After you've explored the cathedral and its cloisters and gardens, you can visit the ruins of 6th-century **St Augustine's Abbey** (English Heritage) just outside the **City Walls**, where St Augustine and King Ethelbert (550-

St Martin's Church

616) are buried. Also worth a visit is **St Martin's Church** (a short walk from St Augustine's), the first and oldest church in England, recognised along with the cathedral and abbey as part of the city's World Heritage Site. St Martin's was founded as the private chapel of Queen Bertha of Kent in the 6th century, before Augustine even arrived from Rome.

Canterbury isn't particularly noted for its museums and galleries, although it has a number of important collections, including the engrossing **Beaney House of**

Christ Church Gate

Thomas Becket

Canterbury Cathedral is infamous as the place where Archbishop Thomas Becket was murdered in 1170, an event memorialised in TS Eliot's play *Murder in the Cathedral*, which was premiered at the cathedral. A journey of pilgrims to Becket's shrine served as the basis of Geoffrey Chaucer's 14th-century classic, *The Canterbury Tales*. You can discover more at the **Canterbury Tales Visitor Attraction** in St Margaret's Street.

The Old Weavers House

Food&Drink

- **The Corner House**: fine dining British restaurant in 16th-century coach house (1 Dover St, CT1 3HD, 01227-780793, Mon-Thu 5-10pm, Fri noon-2pm, 5-10pm, Sat noon-10pm, Sun noon-3pm, 5.30-10pm, £-££).
- **Goods Shed Restaurant**: excellent restaurant that's part of the Goods Shed food emporium (Station Rd W, CT2 8AN, 01227-459153, Tue-Thu 9am-6pm, Fri-Sat 9am-10pm, Sun 10am-4pm, closed Mon, £-££).
- **Pork & Co**: popular fast food outlet noted for its pulled pork. (25-27 Sun St, CT1 2HX, Mon-Thu 11am-8pm, Fri/Sat to 9pm, Sun 11am-5pm, £).

Art and Knowledge, the city's central museum, library and art gallery, housed in a handsome Tudor Revival building. A little further along the High Street (next to the river) is **Eastbridge Hospital**, aka the Hospital of St Thomas the Martyr. Not a hospital as we know it today, but a place of hospitality for pilgrims visiting Becket's shrine for over 800 years, the atmospheric building dates from 1190, with Gothic archways and a 13th-century mural. There's also a small **Roman Museum** containing the remains of a wonderful Roman villa and its beautifully preserved mosaic floors, augmented with clever computer reconstructions and time tunnels. The **Kent Museum of Freemasonry** (half way between the Roman Museum and Eastbridge Hospital) boasts a rare collection of national and international importance, while the **Westgate**, built in 1380 and England's largest surviving medieval gateway, houses an interesting local history museum in its towers and offers spectacular views from its battlements.

One of the city's relatively few parks and gardens, pretty **Westgate Gardens** are well worth a stroll, with the River Stour and Westgate as a backdrop to the beautiful

Westgate Gardens

Marlow Theatre

The Marlowe Theatre is named in honour of local hero Christopher Marlowe (1564-1593), playwright and poet, who hailed from Canterbury. Marlowe was a contemporary of Shakespeare, who was born in the same year.

---

flowerbeds and majestic trees. Along the other branch of the Stour are **Greyfriars** (aka Franciscan) **Gardens**, a haven of peace in the heart of the city (owned by Eastbridge Hospital – see above). It's also the site of **Greyfriars Chapel**, the only remaining building of the first English Franciscan Friary built in 1267. To the south of the city is **Dane John Gardens**, a tranquil historic park containing an AD 1st-century burial mound, located within the city walls and dating back to 1551. Just to the east are the ruins of **Canterbury Castle**, one of three original royal castles of Kent (the others are Rochester and Dover) built soon after the Battle of Hastings in 1066 to mark the route taken by William the Conqueror to London.

Canterbury has a variety of music, comedy and drama venues, including two theatres, the **Marlowe Theatre** (see box) and the **Gulbenkian**, home to a theatre, cinema and café. The cathedral, too, hosts musical and theatrical events – from choral performances and recitals to tea dances – while the Canterbury Festival, which takes place in and around the city in autumn, includes music, art, comedy, circus, theatre, walks, talks and more.

When you've worked up an appetite, you'll find an abundance of restaurants offering a wide choice of cuisines, while foodies will love the **Goods Shed**, a daily farmers' market with an excellent on-site restaurant (see **Food & Drink**). Canterbury also has a plethora of pubs, bars and clubs, thanks in part to its huge student population, many of which are open until the wee hours. Last but not least, if you fancy indulging in a little retail therapy you'll find all the usual household names in town, along with a wide range of independent retailers.

Butchery Lane

Cardiff

Address: Cardiff CF10 3ND (visitcardiff.com)

Getting there: air (Cardiff, 12mi), rail (Cardiff Central, GWR), road (M4)

Highlights: Castle, Llandaff Cathedral, National Museum, Wales Millennium Centre, Cardiff Bay, Bute Park, Victorian shopping arcades

Nearby: Brecon Beacons, Newport, Penarth, Swansea

Sleep

- **Luxury:** St David's Hotel (5*), Havannah St, CF10 5SD (029-2045 4045).

- **Moderate:** The Exchange Hotel (3*), 4-5 Mount Stuart Sq, CF10 5FQ (029-2010 7050).

- **Budget:** Sleeperz Hotel (3*), Station Approach, Saunders Rd, CF10 1RH (029-2047 8747).

The capital of Wales and its largest city, Cardiff (*Caerdydd* in Welsh) is located on the south coast of Wales on the River Taff. It's the most popular visitor destination in Wales and the base of most Welsh cultural institutions and media, and the seat of the National Assembly for Wales. Wales is fiercely proud of its culture, history and language, which have undergone an absorbing and turbulent journey over the past 2,000 years. The area (home to the Silures tribe) was occupied by the Romans in the 1st century AD, but Cardiff remained a relatively obscure town until the early 19th century, when its prominence as a major port – with one of the largest dock systems in the world – for the shipment of coal led to its emergence as a major city. However, it wasn't designated a city until 1905 and only became the capital of Wales in 1955.

No visit to Cardiff would be complete without seeing **Cardiff Castle**, which began life as a Roman fort some 2,000 years ago, since when it has been a Norman castle, Victorian Gothic mansion and Second World War bomb shelter. In the 19th century the Marquess of Bute transformed it into a Victorian fantasy with fabulously opulent interiors. Also worth a visit is **Llandaff Cathedral** located in the ancient 'City of Llandaff' in the north of the city. It dates from 1107, although it has been much altered and extended since, including major restoration after Second World War damage. Cardiff is also home to

Cardiff Bay Panorama

Cardiff Castle

St David's Metropolitan Cathedral, a Roman Catholic church built in 1842.

The **National Museum Cardiff** contains collections of archaeology, botany, fine and applied art, geology and zoology. The museum's art collection is one of Europe's finest and includes 500 years of magnificent paintings, drawings, sculpture, silver and ceramics from Wales and across the world, including one of Europe's best collections of impressionist art. Other interesting museums include beautiful **St Fagans National Museum of History**, an open-air museum located in 100 acres of parkland, the **Cardiff Story Museum** (aka Museum of Cardiff) and **Techniquest** (science museum).

Near the **Senedd** on Cardiff Bay is the **Wales Millennium Centre** – a striking landmark clad in Welsh

Cardiff Castle, Banqueting Hall

In recent decades Cardiff has experienced a renaissance with a number of striking buildings including the **Millennium Stadium** (now the Principality Stadium) opened in 1999 (home of the Welsh national rugby union team and Welsh national football team); the **Wales Millennium Centre** (international arts centre) in 2004; and the **Senedd**, home of the Welsh National Assembly, in 2006 – all visitor attractions in their own right. The rebirth of the city includes Europe's largest waterfront development, **Cardiff Bay** (the former docklands).

slate, bronze-coloured steel, wood and glass – an international arts centre for theatre, musicals, opera, ballet, contemporary dance, hip hop, comedy and art. It houses two theatres and seven resident companies, including the Welsh National Opera. Also nearby is the striking red-brick **Pierhead Building** (1897), one of the city's landmarks with a prominent clock tower, and the picturesque **Norwegian Church**, now an arts centre. Also of note is the internationally acclaimed **Chapter Arts Centre**, which stages performance, art and cinema from around the world, and **St David's Hall**, the national concert hall and conference centre of Wales.

Food & Drink

- **Bully's:** long-established, refined French restaurant (5 Romilly Cres, CF11 9NP, 029-2022 1905, Wed-Fri 5.30-11pm, Sat noon-3pm, 5.30-11pm, Sun noon-4pm, closed Mon-Tue, ££).

- **Café Citta:** family-run Italian restaurant serving delicious traditional dishes and pizzas (4 Church St, CF10 1BG, 029-2022 4040, Tue-Sat noon-11pm, closed Sun-Mon, £).

- **Park House:** elegant restaurant in a 19th century mansion serving British gastro cuisine (20 Park Pl, CF10 3DQ, 029-2022 4343, Tue-Fri 11am-11pm, Sat noon-11pm, closed Sun-Mon, ££-£££).

Known as the City of Arcades for its charming Victorian and Edwardian arcades, Cardiff is one of the UK's best shopping destinations with the vast **St David's Shopping Centre** at its heart. When you've had your fill of retail therapy, the city has an abundance of cafés (try Welsh cakes) and restaurants catering for all tastes and budgets. Cardiff also has a great nightlife, with a surfeit of pubs, bars, clubs and music venues. Check out the pubs along Westgate Street in the city centre.

Cardiff is a green city boasting over 300 parks and gardens. Forming part of the city's 'green lung', **Bute Park** (130 acres – named after the 3rd Marquess of Bute) is an extensive area of landscaped gardens and parkland that once formed the grounds of Cardiff Castle. It's home to a nationally significant arboretum, numerous natural play features, an education centre, three cafés, and an abundance of horticulture and wildlife interest. Opposite Bute Park, across the River Taff (you can take a water taxi along the river to Cardiff Bay), is **Sophia Gardens**, where the cricket ground is home to Glamorgan County Cricket Club.

Millennium Centre & Pierhead Building

Edinburgh

> **Address:** Edinburgh EH1 1YJ (edinburgh.org)
>
> **Getting there:** air (Edinburgh, 8mi), rail (Waverley, Scotrail), road (M8/9, A1/7)
>
> **Highlights:** Castle, Old & New Towns, Holyrood Palace, Golden Mile, St Giles Cathedral, National Museum of Scotland, Scottish National Gallery of Modern Art, Princes Street Gardens, Royal Botanic Garden, Dean Village, Jenners, Edinburgh Fringe
>
> **Nearby:** Forth Bridge, Leith, Linlithgow, Pentland Hills, Portobello Beach

Sleep

- **Luxury:** Waldorf Astoria The Caledonian (5*), Princes St, EH1 2AB (0131-222 8888).
- **Moderate:** Haymarket Hub Hotel (3*), 7 Clifton Ter, EH12 5DR (0131-347 9700).
- **Budget:** KM Central (3*), 5 Richmond Pl, EH8 9ST (0131-651 2117).

One of the UK's (and the world's) great cities, Edinburgh is the capital of Scotland and the seat of the Scottish Parliament. The UK's second most popular tourist destination after London, it enjoys a historic and dramatic setting, where the Old and New Towns are a UNESCO World Heritage Site. The city began life as a fort, captured by the Angles (the early English) in the 7th century and named Eiden's burgh (burgh is an old word for fort). After recapturing the city in the 11th century, the Scots built the castle on Castle Rock in the 12th century and the town grew up around it.

When James VI of Scotland inherited the English throne in 1603 he moved the royal court to London and after the Act of Union in 1707 parliament ceased in Edinburgh. Nevertheless, the city continued to prosper and the construction of the New Town in the 1760s made it one of the most architecturally beautiful cities in the world – dubbed the 'Athens of the North'. Unlike Glasgow, Edinburgh wasn't a manufacturing centre – although there was an important shipbuilding industry at Leith, the city's port – and it lost its status as Scotland's

Edinburgh from Calton Hill

leading city to Glasgow in the 19th century. The city has long primarily been the preserve of professionals and service industries, and is the second-largest financial centre in the UK (after London) and a major tourist centre.

Edinburgh is packed with interesting sights but perhaps the best place to start is **Holyrood Palace**, the Queen's official residence in Scotland and the home of Scottish royalty since the 16th century, where highlights include the 16th-century apartments of Mary, Queen of Scots, and the State Apartments used for official and state entertaining. From the palace,

Edinburgh Castle

> Edinburgh has been the capital of Scotland since 1437 (when it replaced Scone) and has witnessed many a battle between the English and Scots, culminating in the Jacobite rising in 1745.

stroll along the **Golden Mile** – a succession of streets that form the main thoroughfare of the **Old Town** – to **Edinburgh Castle**, which looms over the city. The oldest parts of the castle date from the 12th century, including **St Margaret's Chapel** (the oldest building in Edinburgh), although the castle has been much altered and restored over the centuries.

Other interesting buildings include the churches (Scottish 'kirk') of **St Giles Cathedral** (aka High Kirk of Edinburgh), Magdalen Chapel, Greyfriars Kirk, Canongate Kirk, St Cuthbert's and many more.

Secular building of note include **John Knox's House** (1470), **Gladstone's Land** (17th-century high-tenement house), the Scottish National Gallery (1859), the **Old College** (1827, University of Edinburgh), **Waverley Station** (1846) and the **Scottish Parliament Building** (2004). The latter is one of the city's most controversial buildings, costing £414 million (initial estimates were £10-40 million!), which is in stark contrast to the surrounding traditional architecture of the Old Town.

Edinburgh is blessed with an abundance of green spaces, from extinct volcanoes to hidden gardens and urban parks – you're never far from an open space in this green city. In the centre of town is beautiful **Princes**

Holyrood Palace

Street Gardens (37 acres) below Edinburgh Castle, which separates the Old and New Towns (and where the Scottish National Gallery is located). In summer it's the perfect place to enjoy a picnic and soak up the sun, while in winter it becomes a festive playground with a traditional German Christmas market, fairground rides and an ice-rink. If you're feeling energetic, then climbing **Arthur's Seat** will burn off a few calories; an extinct volcano, it forms an imposing peak in **Holyrood Park** offering panoramic views of the city. A less challenging hike is up **Calton Hill** at the east end of Princes Street, topped with monuments and memorials, while to the south is **Dunbar's Close**, a peaceful haven and hidden gem of a garden to the east of Canongate Kirk.

Also worth a visit is tranquil **Dean Village** occupying a bucolic setting abutting the Water of Leith, with handsome 19th-century industrial buildings and a museum. North of Dean Village is the 70-acre **Royal Botanic Garden**, founded in 1670 as a physic garden to grow medicinal plants and the second-oldest botanic garden in Britain (after Oxford's). Adjoining the botanic garden is lush **Inverleith Park** (54 acres), while south of the city is **The Meadows**, a large area of open grassland with majestic trees.

Food & Drink

• **Dine:** contemporary British brasserie with great value lunch menu (10 Cambridge St, EH1 2ED, 0131-218 1818, Thu-Sun noon-10.30pm, closed Mon-Wed, ££).

• **New Chapter:** award-winning, family-run, modern European restaurant (18 Eyre Pl, EH3 5EP, 0131-556 0006, noon-2,30pm, 5.30-8.30pm, closed Mon-Tue, ££).

• **Valvona & Crolla:** Edinburgh institution and Scotland's oldest deli and wine bar, plus Italian caffe/restaurant (19 Elm Row, EHY 4AA, 0131-556 6066, Mon-Sat 9am-6pm, closed Sun, £-££).

Shopaholics will be pleased to hear that Edinburgh abounds with luxury brands, high street stalwarts and charming boutiques, catering for all tastes, styles and budgets. The main shopping thoroughfare is **Princes Street**, home to flagship stores and an abundance of high street fashion outlets, including iconic 19th-century **Jenners** department store, while at its eastern end (in Leith Street) is John Lewis. Other popular shopping streets include George Street, Multrees Walk, Grassmarket, Victoria Street and the West End 'village' (e.g. William Street). On Saturdays there's a farmers' market (9am-2pm) on Castle Terrace and on Sundays the foodie honeypot that's **Stockbridge Market** (10am-5pm). If shopping centres are more your bag, the city has plenty to choose from, including **Ocean Terminal**

Dean Village

(home to the retired *Royal Yacht Britannia*) in Leith, with over 75 stores, bars and restaurants and a 12-screen cinema – well worth a visit if you're planning a trip to Leith.

When you fancy a break, Edinburgh offers an abundance of eateries, from Michelin-starred gastronomic temples to street food. And after the sun goes down hasten to one of the city's plethora of subterranean clubs, bohemian boozers, live music bars, theatres, comedy clubs, art venues and concerts.

Edinburgh is famous for its festivals, primarily the annual **Edinburgh International Festival** and the famous **Fringe** (both take place over the last three weeks of August). The Fringe is the world's largest annual international arts festival, a spectacular display of drama, music, comedy and street theatre. In winter the city stages the world's biggest New Year's celebration (Hogmanay).

Edinburgh Old Town

Jenners

Museums & Galleries

Edinburgh offers a wealth of museums, including the **National Museum of Scotland**, the **Scottish National Gallery of Modern Art** and the **Scottish National Portrait Gallery** – all of which are must-see attractions. Other favourites include the **Museum of Edinburgh**, the **City Art Centre**, the **Writers' Museum** (dedicated to the lives of Robert Burns, Sir Walter Scott and Robert Louis Stevenson), the **People's Story Museum** (local history), **Dynamic Earth** (science and geology), and the **Camera Obscura & World of Illusions**.

Glasgow

> **Address:** Glasgow G2 1DU (visitscotland.com/destinations-maps/glasgow, peoplemakeglasgow.com)
>
> **Getting there:** air (Glasgow, 8mi), rail (Glasgow Central, Scotrail), road (M8/74/77)
>
> **Highlights:** Cathedral, Kelvingrove Art Gallery & Museum, Riverside Museum, Gallery of Modern Art, Burrell Collection, Glasgow Science Centre, People's Palace, River Clyde, legendary nightlife
>
> **Nearby:** Clydebank, East Kilbride, Greenock, Loch Lomond/Trossachs, Paisley, Stirling

> **Sleep**
>
> • **Luxury:** Kimpton (5*), 11 Blythswood Sq, G2 4AD (0141-248 8888).
>
> • **Moderate:** Grasshoppers Hotel (3*), 87 Union St, G1 3TA (0141-222 2666).
>
> • **Budget:** Point A (3*), 80 Bath St, G2 2EN (0141-352 2650).

Scotland's largest city and the fourth largest in the UK, Glasgow sits astride the River Clyde in the West Central Lowlands, growing from a small riverside settlement to become the largest seaport in Scotland. The gritty, working-class city has long taken a back seat to refined Edinburgh, although in recent decades its regeneration is a classic tale of gentrification, transforming itself from grungy industrial powerhouse to European City of Culture.

In the 18th century Glasgow was a major centre of the Scottish Enlightenment and grew to become one of Britain's main hubs of transatlantic trade. With the onset of the Industrial Revolution, the city expanded rapidly to become one of the world's pre-eminent centres for chemicals, textiles and engineering, particularly shipbuilding, producing many famous vessels, and was dubbed the 'Second City of the British Empire' for much of the Victorian and Edwardian periods.

Glasgow is home to an abundance of beautiful architecture including **Glasgow Cathedral**, aka St Mungo's Cathedral (1136), the city's oldest building, along with a wealth of churches, including two more handsome cathedrals: St Mary's (designed by Sir George Gilbert Scott) and St Andrew's (Roman Catholic). On a hill behind Glasgow Cathedral is the

Clyde Arch Bridge

attractive Victorian **Necropolis**, offering stunning views over the city, while nearby is **Provand's Lordship**, a medieval house (1471) situated next to the unique **St Mungo Museum of Religious Life and Art**. Also worth a visit is Glasgow University, established in 1451 on Glasgow High Street before relocating to Gilmorehill in the West End in the 1870s. Designed by Sir George Gilbert Scott, it encompasses some of the most striking architecture in Glasgow.

There's an abundance of things to see and do in Glasgow, particularly for fans of art and culture, with over 20 world-class museums and art galleries (most offering free entry). They include the imposing red sandstone **Kelvingrove Art Gallery & Museum**, home to one of Europe's great art collections, from ancient Egypt to the 'Glasgow Boys' school of art. In the heart of Glasgow Harbour is the iconic **Riverside Museum**, European Museum of the Year 2013, which traces Glasgow's rich past, from its days as a maritime power to daily life in the early to mid-20th century. The **Gallery of Modern Art**, housed in the former neo-classical townhouse of a prosperous tobacco merchant, is home to the city's extensive modern and contemporary art collection.

Smaller museums include the superb eclectic **Burrell Collection** in Pollok Country Park, the **Hunterian Museum** – Scotland's oldest public museum with an unrivalled collection of anatomical specimens and the largest single holding of Charles Rennie Mackintosh's work – **Scotland Street School Museum**, housed in a former school (designed by Mackintosh), and the **People's Palace**

(Glasgow life) and Winter Gardens (1898) in historic Glasgow Green. More modern attractions include the **Glasgow Tower** and striking **Glasgow Science Centre**

Kelvingrove Art Gallery & Museum

Glasgow Science Centre

– containing three floors of fascinating hands-on exhibits, a planetarium and an IMAX cinema – and the **SEC Armadillo** and **SSE Hydro**, an auditorium and indoor arena respectively.

When you yearn for some fresh air, Glasgow offers acres of green spaces, including **Kelvingrove Park** (1852), **Pollok Country Park** (the city's largest park, home to historic Pollok House), **Glasgow Green**, **Linn Park** (82 acres) and the **Seven Lochs Wetland Park**, Scotland's largest urban nature park. A must-see for garden lovers is the 27-acre Glasgow **Botanic Gardens**, founded in 1817 (in Sauchiehall Street) and now an oasis of calm on the banks of the River Kelvin northwest of the city.

Glasgow is a shopper's paradise catering for all tastes and budgets, from household names to vintage wares, speciality boutiques to exclusive designer clobber. The main shopping area is dubbed Glasgow's 'Style Mile' – taking in Buchanan St, Argyle St, Sauchiehall St and Merchant City – while the West End has quirkier, more bohemian shopping options.

Entertainment-wise, Glasgow can hold its own against most cities, with the best theatres outside London, a pulsating music scene across the whole spectrum, and a burgeoning culinary reputation – it vies with Edinburgh for the title 'foodie capital of Scotland' – while its legendary nightlife includes a plethora of superb pubs, bars, comedy and music clubs.

Inhabitants of the city are referred to formally as 'Glaswegians' or 'Weegies' (often used disparagingly by Edinburghers) and speak a distinct dialect ('Glasgow patter') infamous for being difficult (impossible?) to understand by outsiders.

SEC Armadillo & SSE Hydro

Leeds

Address: Leeds LS1 3AD (visitleeds.co.uk)

Getting there: air (Leeds-Bradford, 8mi), rail (Leeds, LNER), road (M1/M62/M621, A58/A61/A64)

Highlights: industrial heritage, civic buildings (Town Hall, Civic Hall & Corn Exchange), striking modern architecture, Leeds City Museum, Leeds Art Gallery, Henry Moore Institute, Kirkgate Market, Victoria Leeds, theatres & music halls

Nearby: Bradford, **Harrogate**, Ilkley, Kirkstall Abbey, Pontefract, Temple Newsam, **Yorkshire Dales**, Yorkshire Sculpture Park

- **Luxury:** Dakota (4*), 8 Russell St, LS1 5RN (0113-322 6261).

- **Moderate:** Marriot (4*), 4 Trevelyan Sq, Boar Ln, LS1 6ET (0113-236 6366).

- **Budget:** Ibis Leeds Centre (2*), 23 Marlborough St, LS1 4PB (0113-396 9000).

Located on the River Aire in West Yorkshire, Leeds is the cultural, financial and commercial heart of the West Yorkshire urban area, and the unofficial capital of Yorkshire (York is the official capital). It's the perfect place for an inspiring city break; a vibrant, modern city with a rich industrial past on the edge of the magnificent Yorkshire Dales. Today, Leeds is one of the UK's largest legal and financial centres and its third-largest manufacturing centre, encompassing engineering, printing and publishing, food and drink, chemicals and medical technology.

From a small manorial borough and important market town in the Middle Ages, Leeds grew to become a major hub of wool trading and cloth production in the 17th-18th centuries and a powerhouse during the Industrial Revolution. The 127-mile Leeds & Liverpool Canal (1816) – the longest canal in northern England – and the Leeds & Selby Railway (1834) were vital resources

Leeds City Centre

that enabled the city to import raw materials and export finished products to international markets.

Leeds is home to a treasure trove of architecture, particularly grand civic buildings constructed in the city's industrial heyday. These include **Leeds Town Hall** (1858), a magnificent example of Victorian architecture with a splendid interior; beautiful **Leeds Corn Exchange** (1864), one of the city's most iconic landmarks and still a centre for trade and independent boutiques; ornate **Leeds General Infirmary** (1868), designed by Sir Gilbert Scott, which boasts a lively Venetian Gothic-style façade; and Classical/Art Deco **Leeds Civic Hall** in Millennium Square, dating from 1933.

The city has many magnificent industrial buildings, which include **Marshall's Mill** built 1791-2, a former flax spinning mill, now offices; **Armley Mills** on the River Aire/Liverpool & Leeds Canal to the west of the city, once the world's largest woollen mill and now home to the fascinating **Leeds Industrial Museum**; the intriguing **Temple Works** (1840), a former flax mill that took its architectural inspiration from Ancient Egypt; and stunning **St Paul's House** (1878),

Among the city's host of churches are handsome **Leeds Minster**, with magnificent stained-glass windows, built in 1841 by Robert Chantrell on an ancient holy site, and Gothic Revival **Leeds Cathedral** (1904) – one of the finest Roman Catholic cathedrals in England – designed by John Henry Eastwood.

a former warehouse and cloth cutting works, built in a flamboyant Hispano-Moorish style.

Leeds is also home to some notable modern buildings, which include the 230ft **Broadcasting Tower** (2009), a striking, rust-coloured (weathered steel) complex of buildings; the **Roger Stevens Building**, a Brutalist, futuristic 1970 university building, considered a post-modern masterpiece; bold **Central Square**, an impressive glass-fronted office

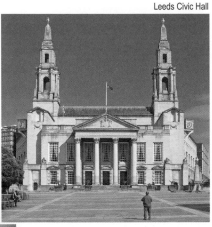

Leeds Civic Hall

development; and stunning **Victoria Leeds**, an imposing shopping and leisure centre with a unique design, combining the 1990 Victoria Quarter (largely based on restored Victorian shopping arcades), and the 2016

Leeds Town Hall

Victoria Gate shopping centre. Sports fans may also wish to pay homage to their sporting heroes at **Elland Road** (Leeds United FC) and **Headingly Cricket Ground**, home of Yorkshire County Cricket Club.

Among the city's many museums are **Leeds City Museum**, housed in a landmark building that's just as impressive inside as it is externally, with a host of intriguing exhibits from ancient Egypt to modern times; imposing **Leeds Art Gallery**, home to one one of the best collections of 20th-century British art in the UK; **Leeds Discovery Centre**, a purpose-built display and storage centre containing over a million objects; the fascinating **Thackray Medical Museum**, housed in the 1861 Leeds Union Workhouse building; and the **Royal Armouries Museum** in Leeds Dock (reached via water taxi from Granary Wharf), one of the UK's best military museums with over 8,500 objects (the dock is a leisure destination in its own right). Other galleries include **The Tetley** (a former brewery founded in 1822, once the largest in the north of England) located in the old Tetley HQ building and now a contemporary art gallery,

Food & Drink

- **Botanist:** Gastropub-style dining and cocktails in a striking 'industrial' interior (67 Boar Ln, LS1 6HW, 0113-205 3240, noon-midnight/2am, £-££).

- **Crafthouse:** Sleek, industrial-look modern restaurant offering seasonal British cuisine (70 Boat Ln, LS1 6HW, 0113-897 0444, Mon 5pm-midnight, Tue-Sat noon-midnight, Sun noon-7pm, ££).

- **The Man Behind the Curtain:** Michelin-starred, artistic fine dining – a culinary tour de force (08-78 Vicar Ln, LS1 7JH, 0113-243 2376, Tue-Sat 6.30-8.30pm, Thu-Sat 12.30-2pm, closed Sun-Mon, £££).

Roger Stevens Building

and the **Henry Moore Institute**, which hosts world-class

Broadcasting Tower

art and sculpture exhibitions. Leeds also has many excellent commercial art galleries and boasts a wealth of street art and murals.

The outskirts of Leeds are home to many beautiful parks and gardens, although there aren't many green spaces in the city centre; one exception is **Park Square**, a lovely Georgian garden square surrounded by classical architecture. Five miles northeast of the city is glorious **Roundhay Park** – 700 acres of rolling parkland with lakes, woodlands, formal gardens, cafés, playgrounds, etc. – home to **Tropical World**, a popular zoo and tropical gardens. Just northwest of the city is **Woodhouse Moor**, a formal park created in 1857 with vast open grassed areas, while a few miles further out is magnificent **Kirkstall Abbey**, the haunting ruins of a 12th-century Cistercian monastery set in a stunning park. A little further afield (6mi) is splendid **Temple Newsam**, a Tudor-Jacobethan house and grounds landscaped by Capability Brown, while 18 miles to the south is the stunning **Yorkshire Sculpture Park**, home to a spectacular collection of sculptures by renowned artists such as Henry Moore and Barbara Hepworth.

If you fancy splashing the cash few cities can match Leeds, which is a shopper's paradise with an array of beautiful Victorian arcades and some of the country's best modern shopping

Victoria Gate

centres. Highlights include **Victoria Leeds** (see page 46), with the largest glass roof in the UK; **Trinity Leeds** with over 120 stores, restaurants, street food and a cinema; and

Victorian Arcade

Kirkgate Market

The largest covered market in Europe (and the birthplace of Marks & Spencer), Kirkgate has hundreds of traditional stalls selling everything from fresh fruit and veg to tea and coffee, exotic spices to award-winning pies.

Leeds Corn Exchange, which houses independent boutiques.

A mecca for foodies, Leeds offer a smorgasbord of creative restaurants, from fine dining gastronomic temples to fast food and everything in between, including a host of ethnic eateries (including some of the best Indian cuisine in the UK). After you've wined and dined, Leeds offers a cornucopia of entertainment and a raucous nightlife, including a host of world-class theatres (Leeds Grand Theatre is home to Opera North and the Northern Ballet) and Victorian music halls, live music venues, comedy clubs, a casino, a host of lively cocktail bars and pubs (visit Briggate's cobbled lanes for historic pubs), and enough night/dance clubs to more than satisfy the city's huge student population. Leeds also hosts many festivals and celebrations throughout the year, including Leeds Indie Food and Live at Leeds (both May), Leeds Pride and Leeds (music) Festival (both August), and the Leeds International Beer Festival (September).

Liverpool

Address: Liverpool L2 3SW (visitliverpool.com)

Getting there: air (Liverpool, 8mi), rail (Liverpool Lime Street, Northern), road (M62/M53)

Highlights: Pier Head & 'Three Graces', Royal Albert Dock, waterfront/River Mersey, Town Hall, cathedrals, Maritime Museum, Tate Liverpool, Walker Art Gallery, Museum of Liverpool, Beatles Trail, industrial heritage, Stanley Park, nightlife

Nearby: Birkenhead, Bootle, **Chester**, Ellesmere Port, North Wales, Port Sunlight, Southport

- **Luxury:** Hope Street Hotel (4*), 40 Hope St, L1 9DA (0151-709 3000).
- **Moderate:** Aloft (3*), 1 N John St, L2 5QW (0151-294 3970).
- **Budget:** The Z Hotel (3*), 2 N John St, L2 4SA (0151-556 1770).

The fifth largest city in Britain, Liverpool sits on the Mersey estuary in Lancashire in the northwest of England. Granted a royal charter in 1207 by King John, it grew slowly during the Middle Ages until the 18th century, when its port expanded rapidly with the decline of Chester. Its growth as a major port was paralleled by the expansion of the city during the Industrial Revolution, and by the late 18th century Liverpool was a wealthy and influential city, and one of the most important ports in the British Empire.

Today, Liverpool is famous for its magnificent architecture (it has over 2,500 listed buildings!) and sculpture (second only to Westminster, London), and has been declared England's finest Victorian city by English Heritage. Several areas – known as **Liverpool Maritime Mercantile City** – were granted UNESCO World Heritage Status in 2004 (which it lost in 2021), including Albert Dock, Castle Street, Duke Street/Ropewalks, the Pier Head, Stanley Dock and William Brown Street. Like many of Britain's former industrial powerhouses, Liverpool has reinvented itself as a city of culture and tourism – home to the second highest number of art galleries and national museums in the UK (after London).

Pier Head & the 'Three Graces'

The only place to start a visit to Liverpool is its historic docklands, where **Pier Head** is home to a renowned trio of buildings – the **Royal Liver Building** (pronounced Lie-ver), the **Cunard Building** and the **Port of Liverpool Building** – collectively referred to as the 'Three Graces'. The buildings are testament to the wealth of the city during the 19th and early 20th centuries (when they were built), the most potent symbol of Maritime Liverpool and one of the world's most impressive waterfronts.

Natives and residents of the city of Liverpool are referred to formally as Liverpudlians, but more often as Scousers, a reference to 'scouse', a form of stew. The word 'scouse' has become synonymous with the Liverpool accent and dialect.

The best-known dock in Liverpool is **Royal Albert Dock**, constructed in 1846 and comprising the largest single collection of Grade I listed buildings in Britain. Today it's home to restaurants, bars, shops and hotels, along with the **Merseyside Maritime Museum**, the **International Slavery Museum**, **Tate Liverpool** and

Beatles Statue, Pier Head

The Beatles Story. Among Liverpool's many renowned museums and galleries are the **World Museum** (covering archaeology, ethnology, natural and physical sciences, and more) and the **Walker Art Gallery** – one of the UK's largest art collections, especially strong in pre-Raphaelite paintings – which are located in the Cultural Quarter on William Brown Street along with the **Central Library** and **Picton Reading Room**. Other highlights include the splendid **Museum of Liverpool** just north of Albert Dock, **Sudley House** (1824) museum and art gallery, and the **Lady Lever Art Gallery** in Port Sunlight. The National Trust has preserved the childhood homes of **John Lennon** (251 Menlove Avenue) and **Paul McCartney** (20 Forthlin Road), which you can visit.

Other buildings worth a visit include Anglican **Liverpool Cathedral** – the largest cathedral in Britain – designed by (Sir) Giles Gilbert Scott and built between 1904 and 1978, and the striking Roman Catholic **Metropolitan Cathedral** of Liverpool, designed by Frederick Gibberd and completed in 1967. Imposing **St George's Hall** (1854), opposite Lime Street station,

Waterfront at sunset

was described by architectural historian Nikolaus Pevsner as 'one of the best Neo-Grecian buildings in the world', while Liverpool's magnificent **Town Hall** is one of the UK's finest surviving 18th-century Georgian town halls. Also of note are the **India Building** (1924-1932), the **Victoria Building** (University of Liverpool, 1892), Stanley Dock Tobacco Warehouse (see box on page 52) and **Speke Hall** (1530-98), a Tudor manor house.

Liverpool is a surprisingly green city with a host of parks and gardens, including **Stanley Park**, which divides Everton and Liverpool soccer grounds (both worth a visit), **St James Mount & Gardens** – peaceful cemetery gardens next to Liverpool Cathedral – **Newsham Park** (121 acres) and gardens opened in 1868, **Wavertree Botanic Gardens** (dating from the 1830s), expansive **Sefton Park** (235 acres) and **Everton Park** (created in the '80s), to name just a few. If shopping is your thing, then Liverpool won't disappoint, with a plethora of shopping centres, such as vast **Liverpool ONE** on the waterfront with over 170 stores.

When you fancy a bite to eat, Liverpool offers a wide range of excellent restaurants, enough to satisfy the most passionate foodie, from tasty street food in the Baltic Market to Michelin-standard

Food & Drink

• **The Art School:** fine dining British restaurant in a large light-filled room (1 Sugnall St, L7 7EB, 0151-230 8600, Tue-Sat noon-2.15pm, 5-9.15pm, Sun noon-4pm, closed Mon, ££-£££).

• **Bacaro:** popular Italian restaurant offering sharing plates and Campari bar (47 Castle St, L2 9UB, 0151-665 0047, noon-10.30pm, £).

• **Panoramic 34:** superb, modern European cuisine with panoramic views (West Tower, Brook St, L3 9PJ, 0151-236 5534, 11am-11pm, closed Mon, £££).

Liverpool Metropolitan Cathedral

fine dining. The city's celebrated nightlife is second to none and the compact city centre is home to a multitude of theatres and concert halls, not to mention a host of bars, pubs and clubs, including the famous **Cavern Club** ('birthplace' of the Beatles).

Finally, before heading home, you should take a ferry ride across the River Mersey to Birkenhead – worth it just for the magnificent view of the Three Graces from the river – where you can visit the

Liverpool Cathedral

Spaceport and **U-boat Story**. Also worth a visit is **Port Sunlight**, a model village in the Wirral six miles south of Liverpool on the west bank of the River Mersey, built by the Lever Brothers for workers in its soap factory.

Port Sunlight

Stanley Dock

North of the city centre, Stanley Dock is home to the massive **Stanley Dock Tobacco Warehouse**, which at the time of its construction in 1901 was the world's largest building (it remains the world's largest brick-built building).

Victoria Building
(Liverpool University)

Speke Hall

London

Address: London SW1A 1AA (visitlondon.com)

Getting there: air (Heathrow, Gatwick, London City, etc.), rail (King's Cross/St Pancras, Liverpool St, Marylebone, Paddington, Victoria, etc.), road (M1/2/3/4)

Highlights: Westminster Abbey, St Paul's Cathedral, Palace of Westminster, Tower of London, Buckingham Palace, St James's Palace, British Museum, V&A Museum, National Gallery, Tate Modern, royal parks, markets, theatres

Nearby: Chilterns, **St Albans**, **Windsor**

- **Luxury:** Goring Hotel (5*), 15 Beeston Pl, SW1W 0JW (020-7396 9000).

- **Moderate:** The Colonnade (4*), 2 Warrington Cres, W9 1ER (020-7286 1052).

- **Budget:** Church Street Hotel (3*), 29-33 Camberwell Church St, SE5 8TR (020-7703 5984).

One of the oldest settlements in the Western world, London's history stretches back to the Bronze Age, through Roman rule and the Norman Conquest, the machinations of the Middle Ages and the inventiveness of the Industrial Revolution, to the Swinging Sixties and the new Millennium. The largest city in Europe, Greater London extends to over 610mi² (1,580km²) with a population of more than eight million. It's Britain's seat of government, the home of the Royal Family, the UK's commercial, cultural and sporting centre, Europe's leading financial market, the 'capital' of the English-speaking world, and a world leader in architecture, art, fashion, food, music, publishing, film and television (and more). To add to the city's diverse population – it's one of the world's most cosmopolitan cities – London welcomes over 30 million visitors a year.

Whether your idea of a good time is a quiet stroll around an art gallery or a frenzied dance at a deafening

City of London from Tower Bridge

Kids' London

If you have kids in tow, London offers a profusion of attractions, from **London Zoo** – the world's oldest scientific zoo opened in 1828 – to the **London Aquarium**, child-friendly museums (such as the Natural History and Science Museums), a surfeit of parks with children's playgrounds and a number of dedicated children's theatres – to name just a few.

British Museum

nightspot, London is one of the best places in the world to indulge yourself. It doesn't matter whether you're 19 or 90, a drinker or a thinker, gay or straight, single or a mother of four, there's something for you – in fact you'll never be short of things to do in London. The variety of leisure opportunities is vast, with the city offering more cultural activities than any other city in the world, including over 1,500 events a week!

Among the city's abundance of architectural gems are the **Palace of Westminster**, **Westminster Abbey**, **Buckingham Palace**, **St James's Palace**, the **Tower of London**, **St Paul's Cathedral**, the **Old Royal Naval College**, **St Pancras Renaissance Hotel**, **Mansion House**, the **Royal Exchange**, **Royal Albert Hall**, the **London Eye, Tower Bridge** and most of the city's national museums (mentioned below). More modern landmarks include the **Lloyd's Building**, the **Gherkin** (30 St Mary Axe), the **Shard**, **City Hall** and **20 Fenchurch Street**, aka the 'Walkie-Talkie' due to its shape. London is also home to an abundance of beautiful churches, many – including magnificent St Paul's Cathedral – designed by England's most celebrated architect, Sir Christopher Wren (1632-1723), and an abundance of sculptures, memorials and monuments.

London is world-famous for the number and quality of its museums and art galleries, boasting some of the world's finest collections – most of which offer free entrance! The greatest concentration of museums is in South Kensington, where you can easily spend several days exploring the delights of the **Natural History Museum**, the

Palace of Westminster

The Gherkin

Science Museum and the magnificent **Victoria & Albert Museum**, while the vast **British Museum** in Bloomsbury could keep you occupied for a week on its own! The world's first public museum, its permanent collection of over eight million works is among the largest and most comprehensive in the world. If art is more your thing, London boasts the **National Gallery** and the **National Portrait Gallery** in Trafalgar Square, while modern art fans are spoilt for choice with **Tate Britain** and **Tate Modern** on the River Thames, and the avant-garde **Saatchi Gallery** in Sloane Square. Other collections worth a visit include the **Imperial War Museum**, the **National Maritime Museum**, the **Museum of London**, the **Wallace Collection**, the

Food & Drink

• **Dinner by Heston Blumenthal:** elegant, contemporary dining in opulent hotel (Mandarin Oriental Hotel, 66 Knightsbridge, SW1X 7LA, 020-7201 3833, noon-2/2.30pm, 6-9/9.30pm, £££).

• **Randall & Aubin:** seafood, oysters and modern British menu (14, 16 Brewer St, W1F 0SG, 020-7287 4447, noon-11pm/midnight, Sun noon-11pm, ££).

• **Smith & Wollensky:** high end restaurant specialising in American steaks and wines (The Adelphi, 1-11 John Adam St, WC2N 6HT, Mon 5-11.30pm, Tue-Thu noon-11.30pm, Fri-Sat noon-12.30am, Sun noon-10.30pm, ££-£££).

Courtauld Institute, **Hayward Gallery**, **Queen's Gallery**, **Royal Academy of Arts** and the **Dulwich Picture Gallery** (and many more).

Tower of London

Buckingham Palace

St Paul's Cathedral

Few cities in the world are better endowed with public parks, gardens and open spaces than London, where almost 30 per cent of the city is 'green'. The glorious Royal Parks of **Hyde Park**, **Kensington Gardens**, **Green Park** and **St James's Park** form an extensive green swathe across central London, while a bit further north is magnificent **Regent's Park** (home to London Zoo) and to the west (in Kensington) lovely **Holland Park**. All London's major parks contain gardens, but **Queen Mary's Gardens** (tucked away in the Inner Circle of Regent's Park) are worthy of special mention, home to the city's largest formal rose garden with over 400 different varieties and some 30,000 plants.

London is renowned for the quality, quantity and variety of its **Theatres**, which are widely regarded as the best in the world. The city boasts over 150 theatres (50 in the West End alone) producing up to 25 new productions every week, including modern drama, classical plays, comedies, modern and traditional musicals, revue and variety shows, and pantomime and other children's entertainment. There's also a wide variety of opera and operetta, ballet and contemporary dance. Film-lovers are also spoilt for choice, not only mainstream cinema (centred on Leicester Square) but also a thriving 'fringe' or 'arthouse' cinema scene. Don't forget to allow time for some retail therapy, as London is one of the world's great shopping meccas, particularly for fashion, art and antiques – not forgetting its world famous markets such as Borough (for food) and Portobello (for antiques).

There has been a revolution in London's restaurant scene in the last few decades, and the capital now boasts a plethora of restaurants and cafés to rival those of Paris, New York and Hong Kong – and an infinitely wider choice of cuisines. They include everything from Michelin-star culinary temples (almost 70 at the last count!) to some of the world's tastiest street food and an abundance of ethnic restaurants (representing over 100 countries), including some of the best Chinese, Indian and Japanese cuisine outside Asia. The city also has countless superb pubs and bars, including a burgeoning number of gastropubs offering classy food and fine wines.

When it comes to nightlife and musical entertainment, London has few rivals – you can enjoy just about every musical genre imaginable somewhere in the capital – which is one of the leading cities in the world for classical music with no fewer than five

London Eye

major orchestras. The city has a profusion of rock and pop music venues (such as the O2), complemented by hundreds of smaller locales such as pubs, clubs and halls, where you can enjoy everything from jazz and blues to reggae and rap, heavy metal and house to garage and swing/hip-hop. London also hosts an abundance of festivals, such as the famous **Notting Hill Carnival** in August (see thelondonnottinghillcarnival. com).

Kensington Gardens

River Bus

For a great day out and an alternative view of the city, hop on a Thames Clipper river bus from central London to historic Greenwich, taking in many of the city's most famous sights along the way, culminating in a visit to the **National Maritime Museum**, the **Old Royal Naval College** (below, designed by Sir Christopher Wren), **Greenwich Park** and the **Royal Observatory**.

Not surprisingly, it isn't possible to enjoy all London has to offer in a few days – or even a week – so it's advisable to do some research before visiting and decide what you really (really) want to see and do.

Old Royal Naval College, Greenwich

Manchester

Address: Manchester M2 5DB (visitmanchester.com)

Getting there: air (Manchester, 8mi), rail (Manchester Piccadilly, Northern), road (M6/60/62/56)

Highlights: Cathedral, Town Hall, Corn Exchange, Chetham's Library, Manchester Museum, Manchester Art Gallery, Whitworth Art Gallery, The Lowry, National Football Museum, Fletcher Moss, Trafford Centre, vibrant nightlife

Nearby: Altrincham, **Chester**, Bolton, **Peak District**, Stockport, Wilmslow

Sleep

- **Luxury:** Hotel Gotham (5*), 100 King St, M2 4WU (0161-413 0000).

- **Moderate:** Midland Hotel (4*), 16 Peter St, M60 2DS (0161-236 3333).

- **Budget:** Ibis Budget Manchester Centre (2*), 2 Pollard St, M4 7DB (0161-272 2020).

The third largest city in Britain and one of the UK's most liveable cities, Manchester in the northwest of England sits on the River Irwell in Lancashire, bordered by the Cheshire Plain to the south, the Pennines to the north and east, and an arc of towns with which it forms an almost seamless conurbation (Note: Salford City is part of Greater Manchester).

The city's recoded history began with a Roman fort (*Mamucium/Mancunium*) in around AD79. Throughout the Middle Ages Manchester was a manorial township and became an important centre for the manufacture of woollens and linens in the 16th century, which around the turn of the 19th century led to a booming textile industry during the Industrial Revolution, when Manchester became the world's first industrial city – dubbed 'Cottonopolis' – achieving city status in 1853. With the opening of the Manchester Ship Canal in 1894, which created the Port of Manchester, the city had a direct link to the Irish Sea 36 miles to the west. The canal was built to circumvent the extortionate cost of using Liverpool docks (for imports/exports), but no sooner was it completed than Liverpool docks slashed their fees in an effort to bankrupt the canal, which caused a rift that remains to this day.

Salford Quays

Manchester's fortunes declined with de-industrialisation after the Second World War, but the city has long since been regenerated – with the UK's most extensive tram/light rail network – and it's now one of the country's most vibrant, successful and fastest growing cities – and the third most popular among visitors after London and Edinburgh.

Manchester has an abundance of architectural masterpieces, including **Chetham's Library** (1653) – housed in a beautiful sandstone building dating from 1421, built to accommodate the priests of Manchester's Collegiate Church – and **Manchester Cathedral**, a former parish church rebuilt in Perpendicular Gothic style after the foundation of the collegiate body in 1421, but much enlarged, altered and restored since. It was raised to a cathedral in 1847. Other gems include the Greek Revival **Portico Library** (1806), the **Free Trade Hall** (1856), built to commemorate the repeal of the corn laws in 1846; the splendid Neo-Gothic **Manchester Town Hall** (1868); the grand **Palace Theatre** (1891), which originally had a capacity of 3,675; the **Corn Exchange** (1897-1903), bombed by the IRA in 1996; the magnificent Victorian Gothic **John Rylands Library** (1899); the imposing **Midland Hotel** – built in 1903 by the Midland Railway – the **Royal Exchange** (1921) and the **Central Library** (1934), along with all the city's major museums (see below). Modern landmarks include the **Beetham Tower**, the **CIS Tower**, the **Urbis Building** (National Football Museum) and **Bridgewater Hall**, to name just a few.

Manchester Corn Exchange

The city's treasure trove of museums and galleries includes Neo-Gothic **Manchester Museum** – archaeology, anthropology and natural history – owned by Manchester University, and the **Manchester Art Gallery**, partly designed by Sir Charles Barry, which houses many works of international importance. The city is also home to the **Whitworth Art Gallery** – with significant collections

Manchester Town Hall

Food & Drink

- **Adam Read at The French:** Acclaimed modern British cuisine in the historic dining room of the Midland Hotel (16 Peter St, M60 2DS, 0161-235 4780, see website for opening times, £££).

- **Kala:** smart bistro from celebrated chef Gary Usher (55 King St, M2 4LQ, 0161-839 3030, Wed-Sat noon-2.30pm, 5-8.30/9.30pm, Sun noon-5pm, closed Mon-Tue, ££).

- **MyLahore:** bustling modern café/diner with a globally inspired British-Asian menu (14-18 Wilmslow Rd, M14 5TQ, 0161-248 8887, Mon-Thu noon-midnight, Fri 1am, Sat-Sun 11am-1am, midnight Sun, £).

the largest collection of Lowry's works. Other major museums include the **Science & Industry Museum** – dedicated to the development of science, technology and industry, and the city's achievements in these fields – the **People's History Museum**, which tells the story of the history of democracy in Britain and people's lives over the last 200 years, and the **Imperial War Museum North** (aka IWM North) at Salford Quays, one of five UK branches of the IWM. If industrial heritage is your thing, don't neglect to visit **Ancoats**, a cradle of the Industrial Revolution that's now a conservation area.

Manchester isn't well endowed with city parks and gardens, although Greater Manchester and the surrounding area is home to dozens of green spaces. Exceptions in the city centre include **St John's Gardens** (on an old church site) and tranquil **Sackville Gardens** – home to a striking Alan Turing statue – alongside the Rochdale Canal, while in Salford there's **RHS Bridgewater**, a stunning new RHS garden opened in 2020. Six miles north of the city centre is 600-acre

of British watercolours, drawings, prints, modern art and sculpture – and **The Lowry**, named after Manchester's most famous artist, LS Lowry, a waterside cultural venue (in Salford) containing

Chetham's Library

Fletcher Moss

Footie Heaven

A must-see for footie fans is the striking **National Football Museum** (2001), which holds important collections of football memorabilia. You may also wish to tour the **Etihad Stadium** (Manchester City) or **Old Trafford**, Manchester United's 'Theatre of Dreams' – even better when there's a match on!

Heaton Park, the largest park in Greater Manchester, while six miles to the south (in Didsbury) is beautiful **Fletcher Moss** (founded 1917), part botanical garden and part wildlife habitat.

Manchester has a thriving restaurant scene and is particularly noted for its wealth of ethnic restaurants (try the famous Curry Mile along Wilmslow Road in South Manchester). The city is renowned for its dynamic nightlife and abounds with lively pubs, posh cocktail bars and cool clubs, where you can dance the night away (Canal Street is the gay centre). For something a little more sedate, the city has many excellent theatres where you can enjoy the latest shows, plays and films, along with a wide variety of music, dance, concerts and cultural events.

If you fancy splashing the cash, then Manchester has some of the country's largest shopping centres, including the **Arndale Shopping Centre** – home to over 200 stores – which is linked to Selfridges and other major stores via a bridge to Exchange Square, while the nearby charming Northern Quarter is home to quirky independent shops. Further out is the Lowry Outlet mall on Salford Quays and the **Trafford Centre** (5mi southwest of the centre), the third largest shopping mall in the UK with over 300 stores.

National Football Museum

Etihad Stadium

Old Trafford 'Theatre of Dreams'

Newcastle

Address: Newcastle NE1 8SF
(newcastlegateshead.com)

Getting there: air (Newcastle, 8mi), rail
(Newcastle, LNER/Northern), road (A1, A167)

Highlights: Castle, Cathedral, Guildhall, Theatre
Royal, Quayside, Tyne bridges, Baltic Center for
Contemporary Art, Great North Museum, Laing Art
Gallery, Jesmond Dene, legendary nightlife

Nearby: Durham, Gateshead, North Pennines,
Northumberland National Park, Tynemouth

Sleep

- **Luxury:** The Vermont Hotel (4*), Castle Garth,
NE1 1RQ (0191-233 1010).

- **Moderate:** Motel One Newcastle (3*), 15-25 High
Bridge, NE1 1EW (0191-211 1090).

- **Budget:** Royal Station Hotel (3*), Neville St, NE1
5DH (0191-232 0781).

The most populous city in Northeast England,
Newcastle-upon-Tyne began life as a Roman fort
(*Pons Aelius*) defending the eastern end of Hadrian's
Wall. Situated on the north bank of the River Tyne, it
forms a huge conurbation with Gateshead south of the
river, to which it's connected by seven bridges. The
city is named after the castle built in 1080 by Robert
Curthose, the eldest son of William the Conqueror. It
was an important centre for the wool trade in the 14th
century and later became a major coal mining area,
while the port developed in the 16th century and, along
with the shipyards lower down the Tyne, was among the
world's largest shipbuilding centres. Today, little remains
of Newcastle's industrial heritage and its economy is
based largely on the services sector, digital technology,
financial services and tourism.

Among the city's most famous landmarks is
Newcastle Castle, begun in 1080 and completed in
1172, highlights of which include a late Norman Chapel
and the King's Chamber. Nearby is the **Black Gate**,
built in 1247-50, the last of the castle's defences. The
Cathedral Church of St Nicholas was built in the 14th
century in Perpendicular style with a striking 15th-

Newcastle Panorama

Black Gate looking towards St Nicholas

Food&Drink

- **Blackfriars:** British cuisine in former friary dating from 1239 (Friars St, NE1 4XN, 0191-261 5945, Mon-Fri noon-2.30pm, 5.30-9.45pm, Sat 9.30am-9.45pm, Sun 9.30am-4pm, £-££).

- **The Broad Chare:** comfortable Quayside pub serving tasty pub grub (25 Broad Clare, NE1 3DQ, 0191-211 2144, noon-11pm, Sun 10pm, £).

- **Peace & Loaf:** handsome bare-brick restaurant serving acclaimed modern British cuisine (217 Jesmond St, NW2 1LA, 0191-281 5222, Wed-Sat 10.30am-9pm, closed Sun-Tue, ££-£££).

century lantern spire, and was raised to cathedral status in 1882. Newcastle is also home to the Roman Catholic **Cathedral Church of St Mary**, designed by Augustus Pugin in 1844. Other historic buildings worth a look include the **Guildhall** (1655), **Bessie Surtees House** – two 16th/17th-century merchants' houses with a restored Jacobean façade **Trinity House** (1721), the **Assembly Rooms** (1766), the **Custom House** (1766) and the splendid **Theatre Royal** (1837). Footie fans may also like to visit **St James' Park**, home of Newcastle United FC. Also worth a mention is the splendid modern **Civic Centre** (1968), which is adorned with some striking modern sculptures.

Since the Millennium, the Newcastle/Gateshead quays have been transformed into a futuristic and arty landscape, where the iconic **Tyne, Swing and High Level Bridges**, along with the striking **Gateshead Millennium Bridge** (2001) – a unique pedestrian 'drawbridge' – are city landmarks. Take a stroll along the riverside and cross the Millennium Bridge to the **Baltic Centre for Contemporary Art**, housed in a converted

flour mill. Newcastle is also home to the **Discovery Museum** (local history), the **Great North Museum: Hancock** (natural history), the **Life Science Centre** (with a planetarium), the **Laing Art Gallery**, the **Hatton Gallery** (Newcastle University), the **Biscuit Factory** (commercial gallery) and **Seven Stories**, the National Centre for Children's Books.

Theatre Royal

River Tyne & Tyne Bridge

Although it isn't noted for its parks and gardens, Newcastle is home to **Exhibition Park** and the vast **Town Moor** and adjacent **Nuns Moor**. However, the star turn is **Jesmond Dene** in the northeast of the city, a charming city park that's a haven of peace and tranquillity. It comprises a narrow, wooded valley that follows the River Ouseburn between South Gosforth and Jesmond Vale, providing an important wildlife corridor with a mix of native and exotic trees.

If you fancy a bit of retail therapy, then head for Eldon Square Shopping Centre, where you'll find John Lewis and other high street names, Northumberland Street (Fenwick's flagship store), Granger Market (1835) and Central Arcade (1906), while on Sunday there's the Quayside Market. After you've done the sights and shopped until you've dropped, you'll find Newcastle is a surprising foodie mecca crammed with great restaurants. And when the sun goes down the city's legendary nightlife offers an abundance of entertainment options, from pubs, bars and clubs to theatre and cinema, stand-up comedy to live music to suit all tastes and ages.

Angel of the North

A striking contemporary steel sculpture (1998) by Anthony Gormley, the Angel is located in Gateshead, six miles south of Newcastle (at Low Eighton, NE9 7TY) overlooking the A1 and A167 roads. The huge sculpture, measuring 66ft high with a wingspan of 177ft, is a sight to behold and well worth making the short trip from the city.

Oxford

> **Address:** Oxford OX1 1BX (oxfordcity.co.uk)
>
> **Getting there:** air (Oxford, 8mi), rail (Oxford, Chiltern/GWR), road (M40/A40, A34/A420)
>
> **Highlights:** university colleges, Christ Church Cathedral & Picture Gallery, Ashmolean Museum, Pitt Rivers Museum, Bodleian Library, Museum of Oxford, Modern Art Oxford, University Parks, Botanic Garden, theatres, historic pubs
>
> **Nearby:** Abingdon, Bicester, Blenheim Palace, Chilterns, **Cotswolds**

Sleep

- **Luxury:** Randolph (5*), Beaumont St, OX1 2LN (0344-879 9132).
- **Moderate:** The Royal Oxford (3*), Park End St, OX1 1HR (01865-248432).
- **Budget:** George Oxford Hotel (3*), 29 George St, OX1 2AY (01865-727400).

Famous for its world-famous university and forest of 'dreaming' spires, Oxford is the county town of Oxfordshire on the edge of the Cotswolds. Located 51 miles west of London on the River Thames (known locally as the River Isis) and its tributary the River Cherwell, it's a grand cosmopolitan city, steeped in history, privilege and prestige. First settled in Saxon times, it began life as a river crossing around AD900. Today, history and superb architecture – every period of English architecture is represented, from the late Saxon period to the 20th century – greet you around every corner. Oxford has more of a city feel than its academic rival Cambridge (see page 27), but its honey-coloured colleges and buildings are just as beautiful, and its superb museums are second only to London's.

Established in the 12th century, **Oxford University** (ox.ac.uk) is the oldest university in the English-speaking world, and one of the most prestigious, comprising 38 independent colleges scattered throughout the city. Most colleges open their doors to visitors – usually the college quad, gardens and chapel – and many are free to visit (see box on page 66). Some colleges also open their dining hall to visitors, such as **Wadham College** and **Christ Church**, whose grand hall was the setting for Hogwarts' Great Hall in the *Harry Potter* films.

Oxford Panorama

College Visitor Information & Fees

For college opening times and fees (if applicable), see ox.ac.uk/visitors/visiting-oxford/visiting-the-colleges?wssl=1.

Christ Church is also home to the city's spectacular **Cathedral** and incorporates **Tom Tower**, designed by Sir Christopher Wren. A tour of some of the hallowed university colleges is a must, the most popular of which include **Christ Church**, **Trinity**, **Exeter**, **All Souls**, **Magdalen** and **New College**.

Other iconic buildings include the **Bodleian Library** (see below), the **Radcliffe Camera** – camera meaning 'room' in Latin and now a reading room for the Bodleian Library – and the 15th-century **Divinity School**. Then there's the **Bridge of Sighs**, aka Hertford Bridge (modelled on the one in Venice), which joins two parts of Hertford College over New College Lane; the **Sheldonian Theatre** (Wren's first major design); the **University Church of St Mary the Virgin** with a 13th-

century Gothic tower; **Carfax Tower**, which is all that remains of 12th-century St Martin's Church; **Oxford Castle & Prison**, built in Norman times; and beautiful **Oxford Town Hall**, a Jacobethan gem from 1897.

Oxford boasts more than its fair share of world-class museums, most of which are university departments. The first stop has to be the celebrated **Ashmolean Museum**. Britain's oldest public museum, established in 1683, it's home to an amazingly diverse collection of artwork and objects from around the world – everything from exquisite drawings by Renaissance master Raphael to modern Chinese paintings. Another must-see is quirky **Pitt Rivers Museum**, home to the university's archaeological and anthropological collections of over

Oriel College

All Souls College

Bridge of Sighs

600,000 objects, photographs and manuscripts from all periods of human existence. The magnificent **Bodleian Library**, founded in the 1300s, contains more than 12 million items.

Christ Church Picture Gallery houses a wonderful collection of Old Master paintings and drawings, including treasures by Filippino Lippi, Veronese, Anthony van Dyck, Leonardo, Dürer and Rubens. Other important collections include the Gothic Revival **Museum of Natural History**, the **History of Science Museum**, the **Museum of Oxford**, and the **Bate Collection** of musical instruments in the university's Faculty of Music, all of which offer free entrance. Oxford also boasts a thriving contemporary art scene, with many commercial art galleries.

The city is blessed with an abundance of green spaces, including **University Parks** (70 acres) in the heart of the city with a stunning collection of trees and

Food & Drink

• **The Bear Inn:** one of the city's oldest pubs (17th-century) serving traditional pub grub (6 Alfred St, OX1 4EH, 01865-728164, noon-10.30/11pm, Sun 10pm, £).

• **Gee's Restaurant & Bar:** Mediterranean grills and sharing plates in elegant glass conservatory (61A Banbury Rd, OX2 6PE, 01865-553540, Mon-Fri 10am-10.30pm, Sat-Sun 9am-10.30pm, £-££).

• **The Oxford Kitchen:** stylish, contemporary fine dining (with a Michelin star) offering creative cuisine and tasting menus (215 Banbury Rd, OX2 7HQ, 01865-511149, Tue-Sat noon-2.30pm, 6-9.30pm, closed Sun-Mon, ££-£££).

plants and a huge variety of walks. Oxford is famous for its beautiful **Meadows**, which include the vast Port Meadow to the northwest bordering the River Thames, the Water Meadow, the Angel & Greyhound Meadow, Christ Church Meadow and more. The university's **Botanic Garden** – instituted in 1621 – is the UK's oldest and a haven of tranquillity, containing exquisite plants from around the world. Then there's the splendid college gardens, most of which are open to the public, and a host of

Radcliffe Camera

For cutting-edge art visit **Modern Art Oxford**, one of the UK's most exciting contemporary art spaces featuring a changing programme of exhibitions and installations (mostly free).

Port Meadow

walks along the city's waterways. Just to the east of St Clement's Church is **Headington Hill Park** and **South Park** (50 acres), the city's largest parks which host open-air concerts and circuses in summer.

Oxford has an enviable roll call of world-class venues for dance, drama and music, with around a dozen theatres and cinemas dotted around the city. The city has a vibrant music scene, a vast choice of lively bars and clubs, a profusion of irresistible historic pubs, and a huge range of superb restaurants and eateries – you really are spoilt for choice. If shopping is your bag, then Oxford is a nirvana, with a multitude of independent shops and boutiques and a wonderful covered market dating back to 1774.

Botanic Garden

River Cherwell

Stratford-upon-Avon

Address: Stratford-upon-Avon CV37 6EF
(visitstratforduponavon.co.uk)

Getting there: air (Birmingham, 26mi), rail
(Stratford, West Midlands/Chiltern), road (M40,
A46/A429)

Highlights: Elizabethan buildings, Shakespeare's
birthplace and grave, Holy Trinity Church, Anne
Hathaway's Cottage, Royal Shakespeare Theatre,
River Avon, Bancroft Gardens, historic pubs

Nearby: **Cotswolds**, **Coventry**, Royal Leamington
Spa, Warwick, **Worcester**

Sleep

• **Luxury:** The Arden (4*), 58-59 Rother St, CV37
6LT (01789-298682).

• **Moderate:** DoubleTree (4*), Arden St, CV37 6QQ
(01789-271000).

• **Budget:** New Inn Hotel (2*), Clifford Chambers,
CV37 8HR (01789-293402).

A market town in the county of Warwickshire,
Stratford-upon-Avon is 91 miles northwest of London
and 22 miles southeast of Birmingham. It owes its fame
and popularity as a tourist destination – it's inundated
with some three million visitors annually (visit out of
season to avoid the crowds) – to its status as the
birthplace and gravesite of playwright and poet
William Shakespeare (1564-1616).

Founded by Anglo-Saxons in the
8th century AD, Stratford was still a
village when Lord of the Manor, John
of Coutances, set out his plans to
develop it into a town in 1196, when
a charter to hold a weekly market
was granted by Richard I. The town
prospered during the Middle Ages
and was an important trading centre,
particularly after **Clopton Bridge**
was constructed in 1480. Its proximity to the major
wool-producing region of the Cotswolds led to Stratford
becoming one of the main centres for the processing,
marketing and distribution of sheep and wool (it was also
a centre for tanning during the 15th-17th centuries).

Today, Stratford is synonymous with William
Shakespeare – who would still recognise much of the
town today – whose birthplace and grave are major
pilgrimage sites and the **Royal Shakespeare Theatre**

Shakespeare's Birthplace

Royal Shakespeare Theatre

(see box opposite) is dedicated to the playwright.
Shakespeare's Birthplace, a restored 16th-century
half-timbered house in Henley Street, is now a small
museum, while his last resting place is the 15th-century
chancel of beautiful **Holy Trinity Church**, Stratford's
oldest building dating from the 13th-century. Other
buildings associated with Shakespeare include 16th-
century **Mary Arden's Farm** (4mi), where his mother

Town Centre

Food & Drink

- **Lambs Restaurant:** charming British restaurant
in a historic 16th-century house (12 Sheep St, CV37
6EF, 01789-292554, Mon 5-9pm, Tue-Sun noon-
2pm, 5/6-9pm, £-££).

- **Loxley's:** cosy restaurant serving everything from
breakfast to dinner and Sunday roasts (3 Sheep St,
CV37 6EF, 01789-292128, Mon-Thu 11.30am-11pm,
Fri-Sun 9.30am-10.30/11pm, £-££).

- **The Scullery:** popular, family-run restaurant
serving classic British cuisine (33 Greenhill St, CV37
6LE, 01789-205700, Tue-Sat 5-11pm, Fri-Sat noon-
2pm, Sun 5-8pm, closed Mon, £-££).

grew up; **Anne Hathaway's Cottage** (the family home of
his wife to the west of the town centre); **Shakespeare's
New Place**, the site of Shakespeare's family home
where he lived for 19 years (the house no longer exists);
and **Hall's Croft**, the home of Shakespeare's daughter
Susanna and her husband, physician John Hall. You can
buy a 'full story' ticket for all five venues managed by the
Shakespeare Birthplace Trust (Shakespeare's Birthplace
plus the aforementioned four), which is advisable as
the cost of visiting them separately is prohibitively
expensive.

Take some time to explore the old town, where the
abundance of half-timbered façades are a delight.
Important buildings here include **Harvard House** in
the High Street, built in 1596 by Thomas Rogers,

grandfather of the benefactor of Harvard University (USA); **Nash's House** (1600) in Chapel Street – now a museum – located next to the ruins and gardens of Shakespeare's former home (New Place); the 13th-century Perpendicular **Guild Chapel of the Holy Cross** – which passed into the control of the town corporation in 1553 when the Guild was suppressed by Edward VI – and Shakespeare's **Schoolroom & Guildhall**. The Guild's school was re-founded as **King Edward VI** school in 1553 when Stratford was created a borough. If you're a museum fan, then you'll love the **Mechanical Art & Design (MAD) Museum**, where you can see and interact with mind-boggling mechanical creations, while **Tudor World** is an interactive attraction in a beamed period building that brings the 16th century to life.

Royal Shakespeare Theatre

A visit to Stratford is incomplete without seeing a performance of one of Shakespeare's works at the **Royal Shakespeare Theatre** (1932) or the smaller **Swan Theatre** (1986) built alongside. Designed by Elisabeth Scott (with Art Deco features), the RST has a proscenium-arch stage and a seating capacity of 1,400. Try to book well in advance.

If gardens are your fancy, then Anne Hathaway's Cottage, Hall's Croft and New Place all have beautiful gardens, while **Bancroft Gardens** beside the Royal Shakespeare Theatre are a nice place to chill out, too. There are also lovely walks along the River Avon – you can walk from the bridge to Holy Trinity Church – and the tranquil Stratford-upon-Avon Canal (built 1792-1816), which you can also explore by boat. Across Clopton Bridge on the south bank of the Avon is delightful

Stratford Butterfly Farm, the UK's largest tropical butterfly attraction with splashing waterfalls and fish-filled pools.

If you have time for some shopping, Stratford has some interesting antiques shops and galleries along with an abundance of other independent shops. When you're peckish, you'll find Stratford is a foodie hotspot with many fine restaurants and historic pubs (the **Dirty Duck** was allegedly Shakespeare's local), while the rest of the town's nightlife consists mainly of its myriad theatres, a cinema and a few nightclubs.

Holy Trinity Church

Winchester

> **Address:** Winchester SO23 9LJ (visitwinchester. co.uk)
>
> **Getting there:** air (Southampton, 11mi), rail (Winchester, SWR), road (M3, A31/A34)
>
> **Highlights:** Cathedral, Great Hall, Deanery, Cheyney Court, Pilgrim's Hall, City Mill, Guildhall, Hospital of St Cross, City Museum, Military Quarter Museums, Theatre Royal, Abbey Gardens, market
>
> **Nearby:** Chawton, **New Forest**, Southampton, South Downs

Located on the edge of the South Downs National Park straddling the River Itchen, 60 miles southwest of London, Winchester is one of Britain's most historic cities. It developed from the Roman town of *Venta Belgarum*, which was formerly a Celtic fortified town. Winchester reached its zenith in the 9th century AD under Alfred the Great (c 847-899) – King of the Anglo-Saxons (his statue is at the eastern end of The Broadway) – who made it his capital, and its prominence continued under the Normans, who built its magnificent cathedral.

Winchester Cathedral (free on Sundays) is one of the largest in Europe, with the greatest overall length of any Gothic cathedral. It's also an outstanding example of all the main phases of English church architecture

from the 11th century to the early 16th century, when much of today's building was completed. Work began on the cathedral in 1079 and it was consecrated in 1093, although there have been many changes, additions and restorations over the ensuing centuries. Among the cathedral's many treasures are the Norman crypt, medieval carvings, 12th-century wall paintings, magnificent 15th-century stone altar screen and the 17th-century Morley Library, which houses the beautiful illuminated Winchester Bible (1160-1175).

Winchester Cathedral & Altar Screen (above)

Hospital of St Cross

Sleep

- **Luxury:** Hotel du Vin & Bistro (4*), Southgate St, SO23 9EF (01962-896329).
- **Moderate:** Wykeham Arms (3*), 75 Kingsgate St, SO23 9PE (01962-853834).
- **Budget:** Marwell Hotel (3*), Thompson's Ln, Colden Common, SO21 1JY (01962-777681).

Cathedral Close contains a number of historic buildings from the time when the cathedral was also a priory, including the 13th-century **Deanery**, 15th-century timber-framed **Cheyney Court**, and **Pilgrim's Hall**, the earliest hammer-beamed building still standing in England, built to accommodate pilgrims to Saint Swithun's shrine. Near the western end of the High Street is the imposing **Great Hall**, the only remaining part of Winchester Castle. The castle was built in 1067 and for over 100 years was the seat of government of the Norman kings. The hall is one of the finest surviving aisled halls of the 13th century (built 1222-1235) containing the iconic symbol of medieval mythology, **King Arthur's Round Table**, originally constructed in the 13th century and repainted in its present form for Henry VIII.

Other notable buildings and structures in Winchester include 15th-century **Butter Cross** on the High Street; **Hyde Abbey Gatehouse**, the sole remains of 12th-century Benedictine Hyde Abbey and nearby Norman **St Bartholomew's Church**; the ruins of **Wolvesey Castle**, the bishop's palace during medieval times; and 13th-century **St Swithun-upon-Kingsgate Church**, located above one of the (restored) city gates. Close to Abbey gardens is **Winchester City Mill** (National Trust), a working 18th-century corn mill with a 1,000-year history, and the imposing Victorian **Guildhall** completed in 1873, while a mile south of the city is the serene **Hospital of St Cross** dating from 1132, one of England's oldest continuing almshouses (still home to 25 'brothers').

Winchester has a number of museums, including **Winchester City Museum**, which tells the story of England's ancient capital, from its origins as an Iron Age

Abbey Mill

King Canute and William II were buried in Winchester Cathedral, Henry III was baptised there, and it's where Mary Tudor married Philip of Spain. It's also the last resting place of novelist Jane Austen (1775-1817) – she lived nearby at Chawton from 1809 and died in Winchester – who has a memorial in the north aisle of the nave.

Great Hall & Round Table

trading centre to Anglo-Saxon glory, the last journey of Jane Austen to the hunt for King Alfred's remains. The **Military Quarter**, the site of 18th-century **Peninsula Barracks**, is home to Winchester's six **Military Museums** which are located within yards of each other. They are **HorsePower** (the Regimental Museum of The King's Royal Hussars), the **Royal Hampshire Regiment Museum**, the **Royal Green Jackets Museum**, the **Rifles Museum**, the **Gurkha Museum**, and the **Guardroom Museum** (the Museum of the Adjutant-General's Corps). The **Westgate Museum** is housed in the last remaining 12th-century gate into the city, which was used as a debtor's prison for 150 years.

Winchester offers an abundance of entertainment options, including

three theatres: the Theatre Royal, the Chesil Theatre and the Discovery Centre theatre. The **Theatre Royal** is the city's flagship venue, presenting drama, dance, children's theatre, comedy, music and pantomime in a beautiful Edwardian-style auditorium. The intimate **Chesil Theatre** occupies St Peter's Church (near the river), parts of which date from the 12th century, and is home to the amateur Winchester Dramatic Society. The **Winchester Discovery Centre** is a world-class venue for creativity, learning and culture, and houses the main library, public galleries and a 180-seat theatre that stages gigs, concerts, talks, shows and exhibitions.

Winchester is surrounded by green spaces, notably the **South Downs National Park**, although the city itself

Cheyney Court & King's Gate

Winchester College Chapel

Winchester College

One of the UK's most illustrious public schools, Winchester College is one of the oldest continuously running schools in the country, founded in 1382 by William of Wykeham, Bishop of Winchester (1366-1404). You can take a guided tour of the school buildings and the **Treasury Museum**, a 14th-century stable block housing the College's treasures.

has relatively few parks and gardens. One exception is beautiful **Abbey (Mill) Gardens**, part of the site of St Mary's Abbey, once one of the largest religious houses in England. The gardens encompass the Mayor of Winchester's official residence (Abbey House) and the original **Abbey Mill**. To the north of the city is **Winnall Moors Nature Reserve**, which is criss-crossed by the River Itchen and includes a wide range of habitats.

Winchester has a surfeit of excellent restaurants, cafés and pubs, catering for all tastes and budgets, while if you fancy doing some shopping then **Winchester Market** (Wed-Sat) is a must, not to mention the city's profusion of independent boutiques and high street outlets. Small it may be, but after dark Winchester offers enough pubs, bars, clubs, cinemas, theatres and music venues to cater for the most discerning visitor.

Food & Drink

- **Chesil Rectory:** classic modern British food in a magnificent 600-year-old building (1 Chesil St, SO23 0HU, 01962-851555, Wed-Sat noon-2.20pm, 6 9.30/10pm, Sun noon-3pm, 6-9pm, closed Mon-Tue, ££).

- **The Dispensary Kitchen:** charming coffee shop/café near the cathedral (5-6 The Square, SO23 9ES, Thu-Sun noon-8pm, closed Mon-Wed, £).

- **The Wykeham Arms:** Fuller's pub (with rooms) in a gorgeous 18th-century building, offering seasonal food (75 Kingsgate, SO23 9PE, 01962-853834, noon-11pm, Sun 10pm, £-££).

Windsor

Address: Windsor SL4 1QF (windsor.gov.uk)

Getting there: air (Heathrow, 12mi), rail (Windsor & Eton Central/Riverside, GWR, SWR), road (M4, A308/332/355)

Highlights: Castle, Guildhall, Windsor & Royal Borough Museum, Eton College & village, River Thames, Home Park, Theatre Royal

Nearby: Colne Valley, Cookham, Eton, Legoland

Sleep

- **Luxury:** Sir Christopher Wren Hotel & Spa (4*), Thames St, SL4 1PX (01753-442400).

- **Moderate:** Royal Adelaide Hotel (4*), 46 King's Rd, SL4 2AG (01753-863916).

- **Budget:** Goswell House Hotel (3*), 134 Goswell Hill, SL4 1DS (01753-444444).

A historic market town on the River Thames in Berkshire, 22 miles west of London, Windsor is world-famous as the site of majestic Windsor Castle, one of the official residences of the British royal family. The river forms the boundary with neighbouring Eton, with its world-famous public school. Three miles southeast of Windsor is the village of Old Windsor – once the site of an important Anglo-Saxon palace – which predates Windsor by some 300 years.

St George's Chapel

The early history of Windsor is unknown, but it was believed to have been settled before 1070, when William the Conqueror constructed the first timber motte and bailey castle (the stone walls weren't built until

Windsor Castle

1173-79). Today, magnificent **Windsor Castle** (see box) dominates the skyline for miles around; covering 13 acres, it's the largest and oldest occupied castle in the world, extensively remodelled and enlarged over the centuries. Today's castle is, in essence, a Georgian and Victorian design based on a medieval structure, with Gothic features reinvented in a modern style.

Home Park

Windsor Castle Tours

Public tours take in the castle precincts, the Round Tower, St George's Chapel, the State Apartments (with opulent furnishings and paintings from the royal art collection) and Queen Mary's famous Dolls' House (see rct.uk/visit/windsor-castle for info).

Other buildings of note include the parish **Church of St John the Baptist** in the High Street, dating from 1822. In the west gallery is a notable painting of *The Last Supper* by German artist Francis de Cleyn, court painter to James I. Nearby is **Windsor Guildhall,** designed by Sir Thomas Fitch in 1687 and completed by Sir Christopher Wren. It's home to the **Windsor & Royal Borough Museum** on the ground floor, which tells the history of the town and its people. Windsor contains a host of handsome listed buildings dating from the 16th-19th centuries, including the **Theatre Royal**, along with hotels, pubs, shops and private dwellings. The 17th-century **Crooked House of Windsor** (1687), on the High Street next to Queen Charlotte Street, is located in the shortest street in Britain (just 51ft in length). Half a mile south of Windsor Castle (in Home Park) is grand **Frogmore House**, built in 1680-4 by Charles II and subsequently occupied by a succession of royal residents (nearby **Frogmore Cottage** is the UK base of the Duke & Duchess of Sussex). The opulent gardens (restricted opening) were laid out in the 1790s and contain the **Royal Mausoleum**, the burial site of Queen Victoria and Prince Albert.

Across the river, historic **Eton** is a pretty little town, quieter than Windsor and well worth a visit. It's dominated by the world-famous public school, **Eton College**, founded by Henry VI in 1440 to provide free education to 70 poor boys who would go on to study at King's College, Cambridge, which Henry founded in 1441. Today, it's an independent boarding school and

Eton College

Queen's Drawing Room, Windsor Castle

![Queen's Drawing Room, Windsor Castle]

sixth form for boys and the most prestigious private school in the world, where some 20 British Prime Ministers and generations of royalty and aristocracy (British and foreign) have been educated.

When it comes to green spaces, Windsor has glorious **Home Park** on its doorstep, a 655-acre royal park on the eastern side of Windsor Castle administered by the Crown Estate. The park – which is divided from the main Windsor Great Park (4,800 acres) by Albert Road (A308) – was part of the private grounds of Windsor Castle until 1851, when Queen Victoria decreed that it be used for public recreation. Along with beautiful open parkland, gardens and avenues of fine trees, the park contains farmland, a golf course, playing fields and sports facilities. Other smaller parks in Windsor include attractive **Alexandra Gardens** alongside the river, which hosts an ice rink in winter; **Bachelor's Acre**, a charming small park with a water feature; and **The Brocas**, an expansive meadow in Eton affording great views of the castle.

Eton College has three interesting museums (Sun 2.30-5pm) – the **Museum of Eton Life,** the **Natural History Museum** and **Eton Museum of Antiquities** – while Eton Wick is home to the **History on Wheels**

Museum. Entertainment in Windsor includes the **Old Court**, a vibrant arts centre hosting an eclectic mix of live music, drama, comedy and film, while the **Old Ticket Hall** is Windsor's best live music venue. If drama is your thing, the intimate Edwardian **Theatre Royal** offers a wide-ranging repertoire, from classics and pantomime to first-run drama productions.

When you need to refuel, Windsor offers an abundance of eating and drinking establishments, from fast food to fine dining, gastro pubs to ritzy bars. Shoppers are well catered for, too, with independent shops, arcades – such as historic **Windsor Royal Station**, located in a former Victorian railway station – and popular street food and farmers' markets.

Food & Drink

• **Browns Windsor:** bar and brasserie with lovely views, serving tasty British food (The Promenade, SL4 1QX, 01753-831976, Mon-Thu noon-11pm, Fri-Sat 10am-midnight, Sun 10am-9.30pm, £-££).

• **Cinnamon Café:** intimate café with great coffee, cakes and savoury dishes (Goswell Hill, SL4 1PJ, 01753-857879, 7.30/8am-5.30pm, £).

• **The Duchess of Cambridge:** welcoming Victorian pub serving creative British grub and award-winning ales (3-4 Thames St, SL4 1PL, 01753-864405, Mon-Thu noon-11pm, Fri-Sat noon-midnight, Sun noon-10.30pm, £).

York

> **Address:** York YO1 6GA (visityork.org)
>
> **Getting there:** air (Leeds-Bradford, 30mi), rail (York, LNE), road (A19/59/64/166)
>
> **Highlights:** York Minster, medieval City Walls, Minster Library, Merchant Adventurers' Hall, Guildhall, Jorvik Viking Centre, Yorkshire Museum, York Art Gallery, York's Chocolate Story, National Railway Museum, River Ouse, Shambles, nightlife
>
> **Nearby:** Castle Howard, **Harrogate**, Howardian Hills, Malton, North York Moors, Selby, Wetherby, York Racecourse, Yorkshire Air Museum

- **Luxury:** Grays Court (5*), Chapter House St, YO1 7JH (01904-612613).

- **Moderate:** Middletons York (3*), Cromwell Rd, YO1 6DS (01904-611570).

- **Budget:** Bar Convent Guest House (3*), 17 Blossom St, YO24 1AQ (01904-643238).

The county town of Yorkshire, majestic York is located on the River Ouse in North Yorkshire and is one of the UK's most attractive and popular cities, famous for its landmark historical buildings and monuments Founded by the Romans as *Eboracum* in AD71, York was the capital of the Roman province of Britannia Inferior. In the Middle Ages it was a major wool trading centre and has been the northern ecclesiastical province of the Church of England since the Reformation (the Archbishop of York is second in rank to the Archbishop of Canterbury). In the 19th century the city became a major railway hub and a confectionery manufacturing centre, although today its economy is based mainly on service industries and it's a major tourist centre.

York Minster & Rood Screen

York Guildhall

Among York's many claims to fame are its medieval (mostly 13th-14th-century) **City Walls**, aka Bar Walls – the longest (around 2 miles) intact walls of any English city – parts of which date from the city's Roman period. You can walk around the walls (8am-dusk), which offer superb views over the city and surrounding countryside, incorporating four main bars or fortified gateways, two smaller gateways with more modern stonework and one postern, along with frequent intermediate towers, windows, arrow-slits, gun ports, sculptures and masons' marks.

York is dominated by magnificent Gothic **York Minster**, officially the Cathedral and Metropolitical Church of Saint Peter in York, the second-largest Gothic cathedral in Northern Europe and one of the most beautiful in the world. The site of a church since at least 627, the present Norman building was begun in around 1230 and completed in 1472. In 1984 the cathedral suffered a serious fire in its south transept, which was repaired and restored by 1988. Outside the Minster is a **Statue of the Roman Emperor Constantine**, who died in York in AD306, while nearby is a **Roman Column** – excavated from beneath York Minster in 1969 – from the Roman headquarters building constructed around AD100. Close by – in York Museum Gardens – are the ruins of Benedictine **St Mary's Abbey**, established in 1088 and dissolved in 1530. The city is also home to an abundance of ancient churches dating from the 12th to 18th centuries.

Tucked behind York Minster is the **Treasurer's House** (National Trust), parts of which date from the original house built in 1091, although it has been much altered over the centuries and was almost entirely rebuilt in the early 17th century. Nearby **Grays Court** (1080) is possibly the oldest occupied house in Britain – now a five-star hotel and restaurant – commissioned by the first Norman Archbishop of York as the official residence of the Treasurer of York Minster. Also nearby is **Minster Library** – the largest cathedral library in the

Ruins of St Mary's Abbey

National Railway Museum

Appropriately located close to the railway station, the NRM tells the story of rail transport in Britain and its impact on society. It's the world's largest railway museum, home to the national collection of historic railway engines, including the *Mallard* (pictured) – the world speed record holder for steam locomotives (126mph) – and the only Japanese bullet train outside Japan.

York is home to a number of outstanding museums, including the **Yorkshire Museum** (1830), which traces the county's history from the Jurassic period to modern times; it overlooks pretty **Museum Gardens**, a lovely place to rest on a summer's day. Nearby is **York Art Gallery**, which houses a collection of paintings from the 14th century to the present day. Further south is **York Castle Museum**, which sits on the site of York Castle built by the Normans in 1068, and is housed in the city's imposing former debtors' (built 1701–05) and female prisons (1780–85). Close by is **Clifford's Tower**, the ruined keep of the original Norman castle. Also worth a visit is the **Jorvik Viking Centre** – which tells the story of Viking life in the city (the Vikings captured York/*Jórvík* in 866 and held it until 954) and also stages the Jorvik Viking Festival in February – and **York's Chocolate Story**, which explores the history of chocolate making in the city, including Craven's, Terry's (closed in 2005) and Rowntree's (now owned by Nestlé).

UK with over 120,000 volumes of early English printed books and manuscripts – housed in the private chapel of Archbishop Walter Gray built in 1230.

Other medieval gems include the **Merchant Adventurers' Hall** (1357), a charming medieval guildhall (set in beautiful gardens), which now functions as a museum, café and wedding venue; the Company of Merchant Adventurers received its royal charter in 1407 and helped make York the city it is today. **Barley Hall** is a reconstructed medieval townhouse built around 1360 by the monks of Nostell Priory near Wakefield, while **York Guildhall** (1459) was constructed as a meeting place for the city's guilds. Also worth a visit are the 18th-century Palladian **York Assembly Rooms**, originally a venue for upper class social gatherings (now home to a restaurant).

York and its surrounds are home to an abundance of green spaces, including the **Museum Gardens** (mentioned above), the lovely oasis of **Dean's Park** on the north side of York Minster and **Rowntree Park** (20 acres) alongside the River Ouse south of the city –

York Castle Museum

Food & Drink

- **The Rattle Owl:** New York loft meets 17th-century listed building, with creative British menu (104 Micklegate, YO1 6JX, 01904-658658, Wed-Fri 6-9.30pm, Sat noon-2pm, 6-9.30pm, Sun noon-6.30pm, closed Mon-Tue, ££).

- **Skosh:** superb contemporary British cooking with international influences (98 Micklegate, YO1 6JX, 01904-634849, Wed-Thu noon-1pm, 4.30-8pm, Fri-Sat noon-8pm, Sun noon-3.30pm, closed Mon-Tue, £-££).

- **The Star Inn The City:** contemporary restaurant with riverside terrace and all-day modern British menu (Museum St, YO1 7DR, 01904-619208, Mon-Thu 11.30am-10pm, Fri-Sun 9.30am-10/11pm, ££).

market, to the **Coppergate Centre**. The city boasts a profusion of designer stores and independent boutiques, along with all the major high street names. For fashion fans there's **McArthurGlen's York Designer Outlet** (just south of the city), offering over 120 leading designer brands at discount prices.

After you've done the sights and shopped 'til you drop, York offers a veritable feast of superb restaurants, bars and pubs, and a vibrant nightlife to match the UK's best. The city's entertainment includes a number of excellent historic theatres (opera, ballet, plays, musicals, etc.) – including the York Theatre Royal, Grand Opera House and York Barbican – cinemas, comedy, nightclubs and music venues.

created in memory of Rowntree employees who died in the Great War. **Goddards House and Garden** (National Trust) near York Racecourse is a handsome Arts & Crafts house built in 1927 (by a member of the Terry's chocolate-manufacturing family) with lovely gardens, while a little further south is **Middlethorpe Hall Gardens** (20 acres), a plantsman's garden full of unusual and interesting treasures scattered throughout a maze of small gardens. York also offers miles of lovely walks along the **River Ouse** – boat trips are available – not forgetting the two-mile circuit of the **City Walls**.

If you have any energy left for some retail therapy, York offers a unique shopping experience, from the **Shambles** (see box opposite), also the site of a daily

Rowntree Park

The Shambles

The Shambles

One of Europe's most visited streets, the Shambles encapsulates the city's quaint historic atmosphere beautifully. The overhanging timber-framed buildings – some dating from the 14th century – connect and enclose a narrow, cobbled alleyway lined with shops.

Gray's Court Hotel & York Minster

Ely Cathedral (see page 101)

2.

Architectural Treasures

This chapter features many of the UK's most architecturally irresistible cities and towns, most of which owe their inclusion to their splendid medieval cathedrals and castles, but are also home to an abundance of other outstanding buildings, both ancient and modern. From the Romans to the Normans, Tudors to the Georgians and Victorians – all left an indelible mark on our cities. Entries include beautiful world-famous cities such as Chester, Durham, Lincoln, Salisbury and Worcester, alongside lesser-known gems like Beverley, Chichester, Ely, Lichfield, Ripon and Southwell. All engender a sense of wonder at the magnificent edifices our ancestors managed to construct using only primitive tools, which have miraculously survived the ravages of time, the Reformation, the English Civil War and Nazi bombs.

Beverley

Sleep

Address: Beverley HU17 9BL
(visithullandeastyorkshire.com)

Getting there: air (Humberside, 18mi),
rail (Beverley, Northern/Hull Trains), road
(A164/1035/1079)

Highlights: Minster, Georgian Quarter, Guildhall,
Treasure House Museum & Art Gallery, racecourse,
Beverley Beck, Westwood, markets, historic pubs

Nearby: Bempton Cliffs Seabird Reserve,
Bridlington, Flamborough, **Hull**, Sewerby Hall,
Yorkshire Wolds

- **Luxury:** King's Head (3*), 37-38 Saturday Market,
HU17 9AG (01482-868103).

- **Moderate:** Best Western Lairgate (3*), 30-34
Lairgate, HU17 8EP (0333-003 4184).

- **Budget:** Premier Inn (3*), Flemingate, HU17 0NR
(0871-527 9490).

The county town of the East Riding of Yorkshire on the
River Hull, Beverley is a historic market town
regarded as one of the best places to live in the
UK. A major tourist centre, it's noted for its exquisite
13th-century Minster, lively Saturday market,
thriving music scene, racecourse and unspoilt
medieval skyline.

Originally known as *Inderawuda*, the town was
founded around AD700 by St John of Beverley during
the time of the Anglian Kingdom of Northumbria. It
gained religious prominence under the House of Wessex
(519-1125) and was an important trading centre in the
12th century under
the Normans. A
place of pilgrimage
throughout the
Middle Ages, it
became a significant
wool-trading town
and by the late 14th
century was one
of the largest and
richest towns in
England. After the
Reformation the town
declined due to its
loss of status as a
centre of pilgrimage.

Beverley Minster

Guildhall

The main attraction is beautiful **Beverley Minster**, a Perpendicular-Gothic parish church with the grandeur of a cathedral (it's longer than many English cathedrals), begun in 1220 and completed some four centuries later. One of the UK's most awe-inspiring churches, the west front was said to be the model for Westminster Abbey. Internally the Minster has many outstanding features, including exceptional stone carvings of medieval musical instruments, almost 70 medieval misericords, superb stained glass and an intricately carved organ screen designed by Sir George Gilbert Scott.

St Mary's (see box on page 88) is located in the **Georgian Quarter**, where you'll find many of the town's listed buildings, including **Beverley North Bar**, a 15th-century gate that acted as a toll gate. Other buildings of note are the 15th-century **Guildhall** on Register Square (home of **Beverley Community Museum**), with a stunning Georgian courtroom featuring plaster stuccowork by Giuseppe Cortese; **Beverley Friary**, believed to be part of a 13th-century Dominican friary (now a youth hostel); **The Hall**, an 18th-century merchant's house on Lairgate; handsome Georgian

Food & Drink

- **Ogino Japanese Restaurant:** classy spot serving contemporary fusion, sushi and Japanese cuisine (Beaver House, HU17 0AA, 01482-679500, Tue-Thu 6-10pm, Fri 5.30-10.30pm, Sat-Sun noon-3pm, 5.30-10.30pm, closed Mon, £).

- **Potting Shed:** popular pub with terrace serving homemade pub classics (Flemingate, HU17 0NU, 01482-870942, noon-midnight, 1am Fri-Sat, £).

- **Westwood:** superb fine dining British restaurant in a Georgian courthouse (New Walk, HU17 7AE, 01482-881999, Wed-Sat noon-2pm, 6-9.30pm, Sun noon-3pm, closed Mon-Tue, ££).

Norwood House, formerly part of Beverley High School; and the town's impressive **Market Cross** (1714). If museums are your fancy, Beverley is home to the **Treasure House Museum**, a cultural centre housing a local history museum and **Beverley Art Gallery**; the top floor has an elevated sightseeing platform offering panoramic views of Beverley Minster and the town.

Treasure House Museum

When you want to stretch your legs, just a short distance west of the town centre is expansive **Beverley Westwood**, a large area of rolling pastureland offering spectacular views of the town and countryside; it also encompasses 300-year-old **Beverley Racecourse** (Apr-Sep – a great day out) and a golf course. The Westwood offers an infinite number of walks or you can head east from the town centre to **Beverley Beck** and along the banks of Beverley's historic waterway to the River Hull (0.8mi), while in town the **Coronation Garden** is a peaceful spot to relax.

A short distance from the centre is Flemingate, one of East Yorkshire's largest shopping destinations with big name stores and an impressive range of independent shops. The town also hosts two markets (Wed and Sat) in the two main squares at either end of the pedestrianised shopping streets of Butcher Row and Toll Gavel (the larger Saturday market's charter dates back to the Middle Ages). In recent years Beverley has earned a reputation as a foodie hotspot, with a number of excellent restaurants, cafés and gastropubs. The town also offers a host of historic pubs – the White Horse Inn (aka Nellies) is one of the oldest, dating from 1666 – and some excellent bars and clubs, a theatre and a cinema.

St Mary's Church

Located just inside the medieval town gate of North Bar Within, St Mary's is one of the great parish churches of England. Founded in 1120, the west front of the church is said to have influenced the architecture of Kings College Chapel (Cambridge), while inside is a carving of a rabbit – said to have inspired the March Hare in Lewis Carroll's *Alice in Wonderland* – and a beautiful ceiling depicting English kings painted in 1446.

Beverley North Bar (centre)

Bury St Edmunds

Address: Bury St Edmunds IP33 1UZ (visit-burystedmunds.co.uk)

Getting there: air (Stansted, 40mi), rail (Bury St Edmunds, Greater Anglia), road (A14, A134/A143)

Highlights: Abbey ruins & Gardens, Cathedral, St Mary's Church, Guildhall, Moyse's Hall Museum, Theatre Royal, Greene King brewery, historic pubs, markets (Wed & Sat)

Nearby: Cambridge, Ely, Ickworth House, Lavenham, Newmarket, Thetford

Sleep

- **Luxury:** The Northgate (5*), Northgate St, IP3 1HP (01284-339604).
- **Moderate:** The Angel (4*), 3 Angel Hill, IP33 1LT (01284-714000).
- **Budget:** Premier Inn (3*), New Shire Hall, The Churchyard, Raingate St IP33 1RX (0333-321 9354).

A delightful market town on the Rivers Lark and Linnet in Suffolk with a turbulent, bloody history, Bury St Edmunds is often referred to as the 'jewel in Suffolk's crown' due to its wealth of superb architecture, including its fine cathedral, cobbled medieval streets, elegant Georgian squares, Britain's last remaining Regency theatre and much more.

Bury was one of the royal boroughs of the Saxons – who founded a monastery here around AD633 – the burial place of King Edmund in AD903 (slain by the Danes) and a site of pilgrimage. The modern town (originally called *Beodericsworth*) was built on a grid pattern by Norman Abbot Baldwin around 1080. In the Middle Ages, Bury developed into a flourishing cloth-making town and had a thriving woollen trade by the 14th century, although it declined in the 17th century. Today, it's known for brewing (Greene King brewery – tours available) and its sugar-processing (British Sugar) factory, and is a major cultural and tourist centre for West Suffolk.

First stop must be magnificent 11th-century **St Edmundsbury Cathedral** (Suffolk's only cathedral), which stands among the ruins of the 11th-Century Abbey of St Edmund – once one of the wealthiest Benedictine monasteries in medieval Europe – set in stunning Abbey Gardens. The church was rebuilt in the 12th and 16th centuries as a parish church and was elevated to cathedral status in 1914. The **Guildhall** is believed to date from the 12th century, the oldest surviving civic building in the country; the iconic grand **Athenaeum**

St Edmundsbury Cathedral

was built in the early 18th century as the 'Assembly Rooms', while the **Theatre Royal** (1819, National Trust) is the country's only surviving Regency theatre (guided tours).

Among the town's many historic buildings is **St Mary's Church**, parts of which date from the 13th century, where Mary Tudor, briefly Queen consort of France, and sister of Henry VIII, was re-buried, having been moved from the Abbey after the Dissolution.

Among the town's attractions are fascinating **Moyse's Hall Museum** (1899), located in a landmark 12th-century building, which charts the town's early history (including witchcraft and a murderer whose skin was used to bind a book after he was hanged), and the **Suffolk Regiment Museum** (1935) housed in the regiment's former armoury.

Bury St Edmunds boasts a number of lovely green spaces, including beautiful 14-acre **Abbey Gardens** which surround the ruins – including the magnificent 14th-century **Abbey Gate** (complete with portcullis) and the 12th-century **Norman Tower** – of the former Benedictine abbey. Further afield are Nowton Park, West

Food & Drink

• **1921 Angel Hill:** creative, British fine dining and local produce (19-21 Angel Hill, IP33 1UZ, 01284-704870, Tue-Sat noon-2.30pm, 6-9.30pm, closed Sun-Mon, ££).

• **Maison Bleue:** stylish upmarket restaurant serving modern French cuisine (30-31 Churchgate St, IP33 1RG, 01284-760623, Tue-Sat 10am-6pm, closed Sun-Mon, ££).

• **The One Bull:** rustic-chic pub with own-brew beer and modern British menu (25 Angel Hill, IP33 1UZ, 01284-848220, Mon-Thu noon-11pm, Fri-Sat until midnight, Sun 10pm, £-££).

Stow Country Park (with a reconstructed Anglo-Saxon village) and Ickworth House & Park, while there are some delightful walks along the rivers Lark and Linnet, too.

If you fancy a spot of retail therapy, Bury offers an abundance of independent boutiques, leading high street names and a twice-weekly market (Wed & Sat), while foodies will delight in the town's treasure trove of award-winning restaurants and cafés. Bury also has many historic pubs (including the Nutshell, officially the smallest pub in Britain – coach parties not welcome!), lively bars and clubs, music venues, cinemas and the Theatre Royal. It's also the perfect base for exploring the delightful towns and villages of Suffolk and neighbouring Cambridgeshire, including Lavenham, Newmarket and Thetford.

St Mary's Church

Chester

i

Address: Chester CH1 2HQ (visitcheshire.com)

Getting there: air (Liverpool, 25mi), rail (Chester, Northern/Merseyrail), road (M56/A41)

Highlights: Cathedral, Castle, City Walls, the Rows, Roman remains, Zoo, Racecourse, Dewa Roman Experience, Grosvenor Museum & Park

Nearby: Ellesmere Port, **Liverpool**, **Manchester**, North Wales, Wrexham

Sleep

• **Luxury:** The Chester Grosvenor (5*), Eastgate, CH1 1LT (01244-324024).

• **Moderate:** Mill Hotel & Spa (3*), Milton St, CH1 3NF (01244-350035).

• **Budget:** Townhouse Hotel (3*), 49-51 Lower Bridge St, CH1 1RS (01244-567300).

The county town of Cheshire located on the River Dee, delightful Chester was founded as a fort (*Deva Victrix*) by the Romans in AD79, who also built the city walls. The town was one of the last to fall to the Normans, who built Chester Castle in 1070. By the Middle Ages, Chester was a wealthy trading port, granted city status in 1541, although the harbour silted up over the centuries and by Georgian times the port was virtually gone. The Industrial Revolution brought railways, new roads which saw expansion canals and to the city, substantial and development during the Victorian period.

The first call has to be majestic **Chester Cathedral**, originally a Saxon Minster rebuilt as a Benedictine Abbey in 1092. The original church was built in Romanesque or Norman style, but was rebuilt from around 1250 in

Chester Cathedral & Baby Jesus Window

Gothic style, a process which took around 275 years! The cathedral has been constantly modified over the centuries – including an extensive restoration by George Gilbert Scott in the 19th century – and all the major styles of English medieval architecture, from Norman to Perpendicular, are represented. It includes the former (Benedictine) monastic buildings to the north. The city also has a number of ancient churches, including **St John the Baptist's Church** in Vicar's Lane, dating from the 11th century.

High on the list of Chester's visitor attractions is **Chester Castle**, founded by William the Conqueror in 1070. The 12th-century **Agricola Tower** was the first stone gateway to Chester Castle, while on the first floor is the chapel of St Mary de Castro containing some fine wall paintings from around 1240. From the castle you can climb the nearby steps to the Roman **City Walls**, which extend for around two miles and offer a superb elevated view of the city. Chester also has the remains of a **Roman Amphitheatre**, the largest ever discovered in Britain, while nearby are the **Roman Gardens** where building fragments from the Roman fort are displayed. Later landmarks include the magnificent Gothic-style

Food & Drink

• **Marmalade:** intimate licensed café serving breakfast and lunch (67 Northgate St, CH1 2HQ, 01244-314565, Mon-Fri 9am-4pm, Sat 9am-5pm, Sun 10am-4pm, £).

• **Old Harkers Arms:** red-brick hostelry serving innovative international cuisine (1 Russell St, CH3 5AL, 01244-344525, Mon-Sat 10.30am-11pm, Sun 10.30pm, £).

• **Upstairs at the Grill:** smart, Manhattan-style steakhouse and cocktail bar (70 Watergate St, CH1 2LA, 01244-344883, Mon-Thu noon-3pm, 5-10.30pm, Fri-Sun noon-10.30pm, Sun 9.30pm, ££).

Town Hall opened in 1869 and the **Eastgate Clock**, erected in honour of Queen Victoria's Diamond Jubilee (1897), which adorns the Eastgate gateway.

Chester is home to a number of museums, including the **Grosvenor Museum**, whose collections explore the history of Chester, its art, silver heritage and natural history; the **Cheshire Military Museum** that tells the story of Cheshire Soldiers from the 17th Century; and the **Dewa Roman Experience**, featuring a superb collection of Roman artefacts from Chester and the wider Roman Empire.

Eastgate Street & Rows

Chester Castle

After you've had your fill of sightseeing, Chester offers a smorgasbord of great value eating and drinking establishments, from fine dining restaurants to fast food outlets. If you fancy some retail therapy, the medieval **Rows** (see box) are home to independent boutiques and high street

City Walls

Just outside the city walls overlooking the River Dee is **Grosvenor Park**, one of the country's finest Victorian parks with an open-air theatre, miniature railway and café, while on the opposite side of the Dee are **Chester Meadows**, a patchwork of grassland and wetlands that's a habitat for a wide range of flora and fauna. There are some lovely walks along the River Dee – you can also take a boat trip from The Groves – and along the Shropshire Union Canal towpath in the north of the city. Close to the city centre is **Chester Racecourse**, the oldest racecourse still in use in England, dating from the 16th century, while north of the city is superb **Chester Zoo**, one of the UK's largest zoos (125 acres) and the most-visited wildlife attraction in Britain.

favourites, while dedicated fashion fans head for **Cheshire Oaks** (10 minutes by car), a huge designer outlet village with some 150 stores.

Although it isn't noted for its dynamic nightlife, Chester has a number of excellent historic pubs, contemporary bars and music clubs. If you prefer something a bit more relaxing, the city stages an abundance of classical music concerts, including many in the cathedral, while there's also a handful of theatres and a cinema, including the **Storyhouse** award-winning cultural centre.

Today, beautiful Chester is one of the best-preserved walled cities in Britain with a number of medieval buildings, including the unique 13th-century **Rows**, the famous black-and-white two-storied galleried buildings in the city centre (although many are Victorian restorations).

Chichester

> **Address:** Chichester PO19 1LQ (visitchichester.org)
>
> **Getting there:** air (Southampton, 32mi), rail (Chichester, Southern), road (A27/A259)
>
> **Highlights:** Cathedral, Roman Walls, Georgian architecture, Novium Museum, Pallant House Gallery, Priory Park, Bishop's Palace Gardens
>
> **Nearby:** Arundel, Bosham, Bognor Regis, **Brighton**, Goodwood, Petworth, **Portsmouth**

Sleep

- **Luxury:** The Goodwood Hotel (4*), New Barn Hill, PO18 0QB (01243-775537).
- **Moderate:** The Vestry (3*), Southgate, PO19 1ES (01243-773358).
- **Budget:** Trents by Greene King Inns, 50 South St, PO19 1DS (01243-773714).

Situated on the River Lavant, 54 miles southwest of London, Chichester is the county town of West Sussex and its only city, despite having a population of less than 30,000. It has a long history as a Roman settlement (*Noviomagus Reginorum*) and was an important town in Saxon times. The plan of the city is inherited from the Romans, while the handsome Georgian streets – it's one of the UK's best-preserved Georgian cities – fan out from **Chichester (market) Cross**, which dates from 1501. It's a friendly, vibrant city, where ancient history and Georgian elegance combine with a 21st-century cosmopolitan vibe.

The best place to start a visit is at magnificent 12th-century **Chichester Cathedral**, consecrated in 1108. At the heart of the city's life for over 900 years, its unique architecture

Chichester Cathedral & Marc Chagall window

reflects just about every century of its life, where original medieval features sit alongside contemporary artworks. Look out for the Arundel Tomb (subject of a Philip Larkin poem) and two beautiful 12th-century carved stone panels (the Chichester Reliefs). There's a stained-glass window by Marc Chagall and a striking John Piper tapestry behind the high altar, too.

From the cathedral it's just a few steps to the award-winning **Novium Museum**, which contains three floors of exhibitions and artefacts and is a must-see for anyone with an interest in Chichester's fascinating history. Built on the site of the old Roman baths (which fill most of the ground floor) the museum tells the story of Roman Chichester. If you enjoy Roman history, a few miles west of the city is **Fishbourne Roman Palace**, once the largest Roman villa north of the Alps. A short distance away in North Pallant (lined with gorgeous Georgian buildings) is **Pallant House Gallery**, located in a handsome Queen Anne house. The modern airy extension houses a superb collection of 20th-century British art by the likes of Frank Auerbach, Peter Blake, Patrick Caulfield, Lucian Freud, Ben Nicholson, Eduardo Paolozzi, John Piper and Graham Sutherland, alongside temporary exhibitions. A bit further north is the

City Walls

One of the best ways to familiarise yourself with the city is to take a stroll around the 1,800-year-old city walls, some 80 per cent of which are still intact. The 1½-mile tree-lined trail around the walls encircles the historic centre of the city, visiting award-winning parks and offering lovely views.

Oxmarket Gallery in St Andrew's Court, a charity that stages over 150 exhibitions a year in a medieval church.

Chichester's main green space is glorious **Priory Park**, enclosed on two sides by the imposing **Roman City Walls** (see box), home to an aviary, lawn bowls and a nice café (see **Food & Drink**). The park also contains the **Guildhall**, dating from 1282, and the remains of a Norman motte. Next to Chichester Cathedral are the beautifully maintained **Bishop's Palace Gardens**, bordered by the city walls, from where you can enjoy superb views of the cathedral and gorgeous palace (private, but can be visited on 'behind the scenes' days).

Sleepy Chichester isn't noted for its sparkling entertainment or nightlife, but it does have the magnificent **Chichester**

Bishop's Palace Gardens

Pallant House Gallery

Festival Theatre, one of the country's best regional theatres with regular West End transfers. If it's music you're after, you can enjoy performances throughout the year by world-renowned musicians, orchestras and choirs. The city stages a celebrated four-week arts and music festival (**Festival of Chichester**) in June-July. Easy-going Chichester has a huge variety of restaurants and gastropubs. The local youth complain about the absence of clubs, although the Vestry and the Foundry (both on Southgate) stay open until 2am with DJs, acoustic nights and so on.

- **Crate & Apple:** Friendly pub serving tasty homemade food (14 Westgate, PO19 3EU, 01243-539336, 10am-11pm, £-££).
- **Purchases:** Bar & restaurant serving sophisticated modern European cuisine (31 North St, PO 19 1LY, 01243-771444, Mon-Sat 10.30am-11pm, Sun 10.30am-3.30pm, ££).
- **Viento de Levante:** Spanish restaurant serving delicious tapas and Mediterranean dishes (Victoria Ct, 24 St Pancras, PO19 7LT, 01243-788700, Tue-Thu noon-10pm, Fri 5.30-10.30pm, Sat-Sun noon-10/10.30pm, closed Mon, £).

The area around Chichester offers a wealth of attractions, including the world-famous Goodwood estate (2.4mi), charming Bosham village (5mi), the seaside resort of Bognor Regis (7mi) and Arundel (11mi) with its magnificent castle, to name just a few. Nature lovers will adore the glorious South Downs National Park to the north of the city, as well as Chichester Harbour, an area of outstanding natural beauty famous for its marine birdlife.

Chichester Harbour

Dundee

Address: Dundee DD1 1QE (dundee.com)

Getting there: air (Dundee, 2mi), rail (Dundee, Scotrail), road (A90/A92)

Highlights: V&A Museum of Design, Dudhope Castle, McManus Galleries, St Paul's Cathedral, Tay bridges, waterfront, statues, Scottish cuisine

Nearby: Arbroath, Carnoustie, Glamis Castle, Perth, St Andrews

Sleep

- **Luxury:** Apex City Quay Hotel & Spa (4*), 1 W Victoria Dock R, DD1 3JP (01382-202404).
- **Moderate:** Best Western Queens Hotel (3*), 160 Nethergate, DD1 4DU (01382-322515).
- **Budget:** Travelodge Dundee Central (2*), 152-158 W Marketgait, DD1 1NJ (0871-984 6301).

Scotland's fourth largest city, Dundee lies on the north bank of the Firth of Tay in the eastern Central Lowlands. The city developed into a burgh (borough) in the late 12th century and became an important east coast trading port. It expanded rapidly during the Industrial Revolution in the 19th century, when it was a world leader in the jute industry. With the decline of its traditional industries, Dundee has been busy regenerating its waterfront and reinventing itself as a cultural centre. Today, it's home to two universities and in 2014 was recognised as the UK's first UNESCO City of Design for its diverse contributions to architecture, medical research, comics and video games (etc.)

Dundee's oldest surviving building is Gothic **St Mary's Tower** (aka the Old Steeple), which dates from around 1480 and is now part of Steeple Church. Others include **Gardyne's Land** (1560), a late medieval merchant's house and the oldest domestic building in the city, while northwest of the centre **Dudhope Castle** (and its lovely parkland) dates from around 1590. A few centuries later are Gothic Revival

McManus Galleries (1867), designed by George Gilbert Scott, home to a museum and art gallery with a collection of fine and decorative art plus natural history, and **St Paul's Cathedral** (1855), also the work of Scott, with breathtaking Gothic interiors. Other architectural icons include the Flemish Neo-Gothic **Royal Exchange** (1850) and the **Courier Building** (early 1900s), an Edwardian sandstone wonder and HQ of publisher DC Thompson.

More recent landmarks include the **Bernard King Library** at the Abertay University, crowned the 'Best New Building in Scotland' in 1998; **Dundee Contemporary Arts (1999),** an arts centre with two galleries, a cinema

Dundee & River Tay

McManus Galleries

and print studio; and the otherworldly **V&A Museum of Design Dundee** opened in 2018 – the only V&A museum in the world outside London. This striking world-class building – which alone merits Dundee's inclusion in this chapter – is the brainchild of Japanese architect Kengo Kuma, a curved concrete three-storey edifice designed to complement its surroundings, devoid of straight external walls. Also worth a visit is the immaculately refurbished **Verdant Works**, the only dedicated jute museum in the UK. The city is also famous for its **statues**, which feature many characters from DC Thompson's cartoon comics, including Oor Wullie, Desperate Dan and Minnie the Minx.

The city centre isn't well endowed with parks and gardens, although this is compensated for by its glorious riverfront, while the city is surrounded by beautiful green

Dundee was the scene of one of the worst rail disasters in British history, when the first Tay Rail Bridge (1878) collapsed during a storm in 1879 as a passenger train passed over it, resulting in the loss of 75 lives.

Food & Drink

- **172 at the Caird:** highly rated bistro with river views and a patio (172 Nethergate, DD1 4EE, 01382-223934, see website for business hours, £-££).

- **Collinsons:** elegant fine dining Scottish-British cuisine using local produce (122-124 Brown St, DD5 1EN, 01382-776000, Tue-Sat noon-2pm, 7pm-midnight, closed Sun-Mon, ££).

- **The Tayberry:** upmarket contemporary British restaurant overlooking the Tay (594 Brook St, Broughty Ferry, DD5 2EA, 01382-698280, Wed-Sat noon-2pm, 6-9pm, Sun noon-3pm, closed Mon-Tue, ££).

spaces. If you fancy a spot of shopping, then Dundee's Overgate and Wellgate shopping centres should satisfy your desires, and when you're peckish you'll be pleased to know that the city is a surprising foodie haven, with an emphasis on modern Scottish cuisine and local produce. Come sundown, the city offers the usual spirited Scottish nightlife, with a surfeit of lively pubs, bars and clubs.

V&A Museum of Design

Durham

Address: Durham DH1 3NJ (thisisdurham.com)

Getting there: air (Newcastle, 25mi), rail (Durham, LNER/Northern), road (A1M, A167)

Highlights: Cathedral, Castle, old city centre, medieval churches, Town Hall, Durham Museum, Crook Hall, Market Hall, historic pubs

Nearby: Bishop Auckland, Barnard Castle, **Newcastle**, North Pennines, Sunderland

Sleep

• **Luxury:** The Town House (5*), 34 Old Elvet, DH1 3HN (0191-384 1037).

• **Moderate:** Hotel Indigo (4*), 9 Old Elvet, DH1 3HL (0191-329 3535).

• **Budget:** Honest Lawyer Hotel (3*), The Bridge, Croxdale, DH1 3SP (0191-378 3780).

The county town of County Durham – 'Land of the Prince Bishops' – stunning Durham city straddles a peninsula on the River Wear in the northeast of England. Its history can be traced back to AD995 when a group of monks from Lindisfarne settled there with the body of Saint Cuthbert. In 1083, a community of Benedictine monks was established following the Norman Conquest, and **Durham Cathedral** was built from 1093 by Bishop William of St Calais. As the final resting place of St Cuthbert – whose shrine is behind the high altar – and St Bede the Venerable, the cathedral is one of the most important religious sites in the UK (its cloisters have featured in two *Harry Potter* films). Today, it's recognised as one of the world's great buildings – the largest and most perfect example of Norman architecture in England – located in a dramatic setting high on a hill above the River Wear. The cathedral and adjacent 11th-century **Durham Castle** (see box on page 100) were designated a UNESCO World Heritage Site in 1986.

Durham contains an impressive collection of some 600 listed buildings, mostly located in the old city centre, including many historic churches such as **St Giles** (1112) and **St Oswald's**, also dating from the 12th century, along with the 14th-century **Town Hall**. One of the delights of Durham is simply wandering the city's maze of narrow cobbled streets and alleyways (called 'vennels'), lined with boutique shops, galleries, cafés, and the bustling Victorian

Durham from Predends Bridge

Durham Castle

Opposite the cathedral on Palace Green is **Durham Castle** (tours available), built on the site of a Saxon fortress in 1072. It was the ancient palace of the Prince Bishops of Durham, but since 1832 has been home to University College, one of the colleges of Durham University. It's one of only four English univesities, along with Cambridge, Oxford and York, to operate the collegiate system.

indoor **Market Hall**. Also worth a visit is **Durham Museum** housed in the beautiful former church of St Mary-le-Bow close to the cathedral, the **Museum of Archaeology** and **Palace Green Library**, home to historic collections and contemporary galleries.

Durham city isn't well endowed with parks and gardens, although there are some lovely walks along the riverside and just north of the centre is magnificent **Crook Hall**, a 13th-century medieval hall with beautiful gardens, while to the south is **Durham University Botanic Garden**. When you're done with sightseeing, Durham has an abundance of excellent restaurants and cafés, while nightlife revolves around the city's numerous bars, pubs and clubs.

Food & Drink

• **Bells Fish Restaurant:** legendary award-winning fish and chips (11 Market Pl, DH1 3NE, 0191-384 8974, 11.15am-8.30pm, Sun noon-3.30pm, £).

• **The Cellar Door:** fine dining British restaurant in a 13th-century cellar with riverside tables (41 Saddler St, DH1 3NU, 0191-383 1856, noon-9.30pm, ££).

• **Restaurant 17:** upscale European cuisine with a romantic ambience (17 Elvet Br, DH1 3AA, 0191-384 9050, Tue-Fri 5-11pm, Sat noon-11pm, closed Sun-Mon, ££).

If you have the time, a visit to **Barnard Castle** (25mi southwest) is well worthwhile, where the **Bowes Museum** has the best collection of European fine and decorative arts in the north of England, housed in a 19th-century French-style chateau.

Durham Castle & Cathedral (above)

Ely

Address: Ely CB7 4EG (visitely.org.uk)

Getting there: air (London Stansted, 46mi), rail (Ely, Greater Anglia), road (A10/A142)

Highlights: Cathedral, Oliver Cromwell's house, Dean's Meadow, Ely Museum, Stained Glass Museum, River Great Ouse, markets, galleries

Nearby: Bury St Edmunds, Cambridge, Newmarket, Thetford, Wicken Fen Nature Reserve

Sleep

- **Luxury:** Poets House (4*), 40 St Mary's St, CB7 4EY (01353-887777).

- **Moderate:** Lamb Hotel (3*), 2 Lynn Rd, CB7 4EJ (01353-663574).

- **Budget:** Travelodge Ely (2*), Witchford Rd, CB6 3NN (0871-984 6028).

One of England's most appealing cathedral cities, Ely (the name come from the eels harvested locally) in Cambridgeshire is around 80 miles north of London and 14 miles northeast of Cambridge (see page 27), which can be visited on the same trip.

Nestling under the big skies of the Fen countryside, Ely occupies the largest island in the Cambridgeshire Fens, the so-called 'Isle of Ely', which was accessible only by boat until the waterlogged Fens were drained in the 17th century. It's one of England's smallest cities and compact enough to explore on foot, but with sufficient attractions to easily fill a day.

Etheldreda (AD636-679) first founded an abbey at Ely in 673, which was destroyed in AD870 by Danish invaders and rebuilt in AD970 by Aethelwold, Bishop of Winchester. Today, the majestic Romanesque **Cathedral** towers over the Fens'

Ely Cathedral

skyline for miles around. One of England's most beautiful and largest Cathedrals – known locally as the 'Ship of the Fens' – it's a masterpiece of Norman architecture. Construction began in 1083 under Abbot Simeon and took over 300 years to complete. The famous octagonal lantern tower over the nave crossing – designed by Alan of Walsingham and built in 1322-28 – is one of the marvels of the medieval world. Many additions were made over the centuries, including the Galilee porch, the sumptuous 13th-century choir and the 14th-century Lady Chapel, built in an exuberant Decorated Gothic style. The cathedral was sympathetically restored in 1845-70 by George Gilbert Scott and is home to the only national museum dedicated to stained glass.

> The attractive parkland surrounding the cathedral in Cathedral Close contains one of the largest collections of medieval monastery buildings still in daily use, most by **King's Ely** (or King's School), a coeducational boarding school granted a royal charter in 1541 by Henry VIII, although a school is said to have existed since 970.

Ely's most famous resident was Oliver Cromwell (1599-1658), Lord Protector of the Commonwealth 1653-58, whose family lived in Ely for some ten years. You can visit **Cromwell's House** – recreated in 17th-century domestic style – which contains an exhibition about the civil war. **Ely Museum** – housed in a 13th-century gaol – is also worth a visit and tells the fascinating history of Ely and the Fens.

After you've done the sights, take a stroll through town – popping into some of the antiques shops and independent boutiques – through beautiful meadows

Food & Drink

- **Cutter Inn:** smart riverside pub and restaurant with outdoor terrace (42 Annesdale, CB7 4BN, 01353-662713, noon-11pm, Sun 10.30pm, £).
- **Old Fire Engine House:** welcoming restaurant serving creative British cuisine (25 St Mary's St, CBY 4ER, 01353-662582, Tue-Sat 10.30am-9pm, Sun 12.15-5.15pm, closed Mon, £-££).
- **Peacocks Tearoom:** family-run traditional tearoom with delightful garden (65 Waterside, CB7 4AU, 01353-661100, Wed-Sun 10.30am-5pm, closed Mon-Tue, £).

to the Waterside area on the River Great Ouse (boat trips to Cambridge in summer). Here you can enjoy lunch in one of the many cafés and restaurants and visit the galleries (including Babylon Arts). Ely has an award-winning farmers' market on the second and fourth Saturdays of the month, a Thursday general market, and a craft and collectables market on Saturdays.

River Great Ouse

Exeter

Sleep

A historic cathedral city on the River Exe with 2,000 years of history, Exeter is the county town of Devon. The site of a Roman fort (*Isca*) from around AD55, the Romans also built the city walls, some 70 per cent of which remain intact. The city was an important religious centre in the Middle Ages after the construction of Exeter Cathedral in the 11th century and was later a powerful city with an important wood and cloth trade. During the English Civil War it was one of the last Royalist cities to fall into Parliamentarian hands (in 1646). The city centre was badly damaged in the Second World War (rebuilt in the '50s) and today is the main centre of business and tourism for the West Country.

The only place to start a visit to Exeter is at beautiful **Exeter Cathedral** – officially known as the Cathedral Church of St Peter in Exeter – founded in 1050 but later rebuilt in Decorated Gothic style (completed round 1400). It's one of the great cathedrals of England and one of the finest examples of Gothic architecture in

Exeter Cathedral

Exeter Guildhall

the world. Among its notable features are an early group of misericords, minstrels' gallery, 14th-century bishop's throne, 15th-century astronomical clock, two Norman towers, striking west front carvings and the longest uninterrupted vaulted ceiling in the world. You can join a tour which includes the towers and roof.

Opposite the cathedral is handsome **Cathedral Close** overlooking Cathedral Green, home to the city's most beautiful buildings which include 11th-century **St Petrock's** church and 15th-century **St Martin's**, 16th-century **Mol's Coffee House**, and numbers 5, 8, 9, 9a and 10 Cathedral Close, along with the Royal Clarence Hotel in Cathedral Yard which overlooks the Green. In the north of the city is **Exeter Castle** (aka Rougemont Castle) built in the northern corner of the Roman city walls from 1068 after the city rebelled against William the Conqueror, offering superb views of the city. Nearby are medieval **Underground Passages** used to funnel clean drinking water from natural springs outside the

Food & Drink

- **The Galley Restaurant:** upscale, scruffy-chic fish-seafood restaurant in Topsham (41 Fore St, Topsham, EX3 0HU, 01392-876078, Tue-Sat noon-2.30pm, 6.30-9pm, closed Sun-Mon, ££).

- **Harry's Restaurant:** popular, long-established family-run restaurant (86 Longbrook St, EX4 6AP, 01392-202234, Tue-Fri noon-2.30pm, 5.45-9.30pm, Sat-Sun 9.30-11.30am, noon-2.30pm, 5.45-9.30pm, closed Mon, £-££).

- **The Old Firehouse:** Rustic pub with exposed beams serving great pizzas and real ales (50 New N Rd, EX4 4EP, 01392-277279, Mon-Wed 4pm-midnight, Thu-Sat noon-2/3am, Sun noon-11pm, £).

walled city. Remarkably, the tunnels are still intact and open for guided tours.

Exeter is a green city with many tranquil parks and beautiful gardens. **Northernhay Gardens** are the oldest public gardens in England (1612) and along with neighbouring **Rougemont Gardens** were originally part of the defences of Exeter Castle. The University of Exeter's (main) Streatham Campus is set within 300 acres of sublime **Botanical Gardens** (tour fee) established in the 1860s, and one of the most beautiful and interesting of any UK University. A visit to Exeter would be incomplete without visiting the city's historic **Quayside** – next to the River Exe

Cathedral Close

and the Exeter Ship Canal – one of the most attractive areas of the city with a fascinating history, interesting architecture, and lively pubs and restaurants. There are also numerous lovely walks along the river and canal.

You can discover more about the city's history at the excellent **Royal Albert Memorial Museum**, a local museum and art gallery whose collections include zoology, anthropology, fine art, archaeology and geology. Other local museums include **Tucker's Hall** (The Guild of Weavers, Fullers and Shearmen), the **Bill Douglas Cinema Museum** and **Topsham Museum** (housed in a group of late 17th-century buildings).

If you fancy some retail therapy, Exeter offers a wealth of shopping options. The main shopping area is extensively pedestrianised with a number of modern shopping centres such as the Guildhall – you can see the 14th-century **Guildhall** in the High Street – and Princesshay, plus several quaint little streets packed with independent boutiques. You can also happily while away a few hours browsing the boutique stores and antiques shops that dot the quayside.

The high proportion of students in Exeter makes for a lively nightlife scene, with an abundance of eateries, from fine dining to fast food, and a profusion of lively pubs and clubs. Whether your thing is theatre, live music or clubbing until the small hours, Exeter offers a wide variety of entertainment.

When you've exhausted all Exeter has to offer, allow some time to explore the surrounding area, such as the picturesque town of Topsham (4mi), the fine beaches of Exmouth (11mi) or a hike along the magnificent South West Coast Path (west from Dawlish Warren station or east from Exmouth).

Northernhay Gardens

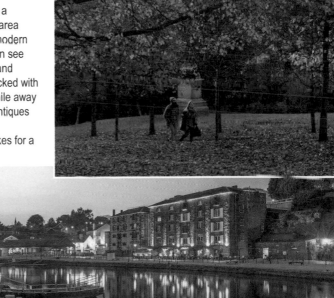

Exeter Quayside

Hereford

Address: Hereford HR1 2PJ (visitherefordshire.co.uk)

Getting there: air (Bristol, 47mi), rail (Hereford, West Midlands), road (A49, A438/A465)

Highlights: Cathedral, Bishop's Palace, Black & White House Museum, Hereford Museum & Art Gallery, River Wye, Castle Green

Nearby: Hay-on-Wye, Ledbury, Leominster, Ross-on-Wye

Sleep

- **Luxury:** Castle House (4*), Castle St, HR1 2NW (01432-356321).

- **Moderate:** Green Dragon Hotel (3*), Broad St, HR4 9BG (01432-272506).

- **Budget:** Hotel Three Counties (3*), Belmont Rd, Belmont, HR2 7BP (01432-299955).

The county town of Herefordshire situated on the River Wye, Hereford is located 16 miles east of the Welsh border (originally much of the county was Welsh-speaking). The city has been an important settlement since the 7th century AD and by the 8th century was the Saxon capital of West Mercia, but for the next few centuries was fought over by the Welsh and Anglo-Saxons. It has been an important religious centre and market town since the Middle Ages, particularly for agricultural produce.

Hereford is dominated by magnificent **Hereford Cathedral**, built 1079-1250 by Bishop Robert of Lorraine and dedicated to St Mary the Virgin and St Ethelbert the King (whose tomb resides in the cathedral). The cathedral is keeper of the famous 13th-century **Mappa Mundi** (world map), the oldest surviving British map in existence, and has a unique chained library, handsome cloisters, fine 14th-century misericords and six acres of award-winning gardens (tours May-Sep). The **Bishop's Palace** next to the Cathedral was built in 1180 and has been in continual use ever since, while **Hereford Cathedral School** is one of the oldest in England with records dating back to 1384. Hereford is also

Hereford Cathedral

home to a number of historic churches, including 14th-century **All Saints**.

Other important buildings include the half-timbered **Black and White House Museum**, housed in a beautiful 17th-century house (1621), which portrays domestic life in Jacobean times; the **St John Medieval Museum & Coningsby Hospital** in Widemarsh Street adjacent to the ruins of a Dominican Monastery, with a 13th-century chapel; grand **Shire Hall** (1817) with six Doric columns, now home to Hereford's Crown Court; and the terracotta Gothic **Town Hall** dating from 1904. Other places of interest include **Hereford Museum & Art Gallery**, a local history museum located in a Victorian Gothic building; the **Hereford Cider Museum** in a former Bulmer's cider factory; and the unique **Waterworks Museum**, housed in a Victorian pumping station, which tells the story of drinking water.

Food & Drink

- **The Beefy Boys:** casual dining restaurant specialising in great burgers (Old Market, HR4 9HU, 01432-359209, noon-8.30/9.30pm, £).

- **The Bookshop:** award-winning modern British restaurant – superb Sunday lunch (33 Aubrey St, HR4 0BU, 01432-343443, Mon-Tue 9am-3pm, Wed-Sat 9am-10pm, Sun 10am-6pm, £).

- **Cosy Club:** brunch, lunch, tapas, dinner – tasty food all day long (42 Widemarsh St, HR4 9EP, 01432-629031, daily 9am-11pm/midnight, £-££).

Sir Edward Elgar

In Cathedral Close is a striking life-size bronze (2005) of composer **Sir Edward Elgar** (1857-1934) – who lived in Hereford 1904-11 – leaning against his beloved Sunbeam bicycle.

Herefordshire is renowned for its beautiful countryside and parks, while the city has a number of green spaces, including the cathedral surrounds and gardens, **Castle Green** (where Hereford Castle once stood) and expansive **Bishop's Meadow,** a tranquil green oasis alongside the River Wye offering some lovely riverside walks. The main shopping centre is the new retail development, the Old Market, while the city's pedestrianised High Town has plenty of quirky independent shops and hosts a number of markets. Sleepy Hereford isn't noted for its lively nightlife, although it has some excellent restaurants, bars and pubs, two theatres, a cinema and a handful of nightclubs.

Black and White House Museum

Lichfield

Address: Lichfield WS13 6LU (visitlichfield.co.uk)

Getting there: air (Birmingham, 16mi), rail (Lichfield, West Midlands), road (A51/A38/A515)

Highlights: Cathedral, Church of St Chad, Samuel Johnson's Birthplace, Guildhall, Beacon Park, Minster & Stowe Pools, Garrick Theatre

Nearby: Birmingham, Cannock, National Memorial Arboretum, Stafford, Tamworth

Sleep

- **Luxury:** St Johns House (4* B&B), 28 St John St, WS13 6PB (01543-252080).
- **Moderate:** George Hotel (3*), 12-14 Bird St, WS13 6PR (01543-414822).
- **Budget:** Cathedral Hotel (3*), 62 Beacon St, WS13 7AR (01543-414500).

A beautiful cathedral city in Staffordshire, 18 miles north of Birmingham, Lichfield is famous as the birthplace of Samuel Johnson (1709-1784), author of *A Dictionary of the English Language* (1755), and the location of the **Staffordshire Hoard**, the most significant hoard of Anglo-Saxon gold and silver metalwork discovered in England (found four miles southwest of the city in 2009).

The city's recorded history dates from AD669 when Chad of Mercia established a bishopric, which became the ecclesiastical centre of Mercia. The town developed in the 12th century under Roger de Clinton, who fortified the Cathedral Close and laid out the town's ladder-shaped street pattern. Lichfield's heyday was the 18th century, when it was an important coaching stop and home to many eminent people, including Samuel Johnson, actor and playwright David Garrick, physician Erasmus Darwin and poet Anna Seward. Today, the city remains an important ecclesiastical centre and retains much of its historic character with over 230 listed buildings.

Lichfield's crowning glory is majestic **Lichfield Cathedral**, a Gothic Norman masterpiece built between 1195 and 1249, the only medieval three-spired – the 'ladies of the vale' – cathedral in

Lichfield Cathedral

Food & Drink

- **Ego Mediterranean:** smart waterside restaurant and bar serving tasty Greek, Italian and Spanish cuisine (New Minster House, Bird St, WS13 6PR, 01543-258234, daily 11am-11pm, £-££).

- **McKenzie's in the City:** modern European cuisine in a converted Victorian corn exchange (Corn Exchange, Conduit St, WS13 6JU, 01543-417371, Wed 5-10pm, Thu-Sat noon-3pm, 5-11pm, Sun noon-4pm, closed Mon-Tue, £).

- **Wine House:** fine dining restaurant and wine bar offering modern British cuisine (27 Bird St, WS13 6PW, 01543-419999, Mon-Sat noon-11pm/midnight, Sun noon-8pm, ££).

the country. It houses a number of treasures such as the 8th-century St Chad Gospels and the Herkenrode (stained) Glass, which dates from the 1530s (it came from the Abbey of Herkenrode in Belgium in 1801). Also worth a visit is the 12th-century **Church of St Chad** (to the north of Stowe Pool), where 7th-century St Chad's Well in the churchyard is a popular pilgrimage site.

Among the city's many attractions are the **Samuel Johnson Birthplace Museum**, a Georgian house (1707) built by his father; **Erasmus Darwin House** in Lichfield's idyllic Cathedral Close, dedicated to the life of the doctor, inventor and poet (1731-1802), grandfather of Charles Darwin; **Lichfield Guildhall**, where the Prison Cells at the rear of the building date from 1553;

Cathedral Close is home to a wealth of striking medieval buildings, where, on the north side, the 17th-century Bishop's Palace and charming 18th-century Deanery are now occupied by Lichfield Cathedral School.

and the **Staffordshire Regiment Museum**, three miles southeast of the city.

If you fancy a stroll, Lichfield boasts a number of beautiful parks and gardens, including stunning **Beacon Park** (70 acres) created in 1859, with beautiful gardens and lovely walks. At its eastern end the park adjoins **Minster Pool**, a former mill pond and fishery, while to the east of the city is **Stowe Pool** (14 acres), a former reservoir that's now a watersports' venue. Also not to be missed is the fabulous **National Memorial Arboretum** (6mi northeast of Lichfield), the UK's centre for honouring servicemen and women who died serving their country, with some 350 memorials.

After you've done the sights, you'll find the city's streets lined with tempting shops, quirky boutiques and markets, and when you're hungry, foodie Lichfield offers a host of fine restaurants and cafés. The city is home to many lively bars, pubs and clubs, along with superb Lichfield Garrick Theatre.

Stowe Pool

Lincoln

Address: Lincoln LN1 1DD (visitlincoln.com)

Getting there: air (Humberside, 30mi), rail (Lincoln, East Midlands), road (A15/A46/A57/A158)

Highlights: Cathedral, Castle, Old Bishop's Palace, Guildhall, High Bridge, Jews House, medieval churches, Museum of Lincolnshire Life, pubs

Nearby: Gainsborough, Grimsby, Lincolnshire Wolds, Newark, **Southwell**

Sleep

- **Luxury:** Doubletree by Hilton (4*), Brayford Wharf North, LN1 1YW (01522-565180).

- **Moderate:** Charlotte House (4*), The Lawn, Union Rd LN1 3BJ (01522-541000).

- **Budget:** Travelodge City Centre (2*), 16 Tentercroft St, LN5 7DB (08719-846543).

The county town of Lincolnshire on the River Witham in the East Midlands, Lincoln is one of England's most historic cathedral cities. The city developed from an Iron Age settlement conquered by the Romans in AD48, who built a legionary fortress (*Lindum Colonia*) at the northern end of the Fosse Way (now the A46). Lincoln fell into decline after the Romans left, but rose to prominence again under the Danes and at the time of the Norman Conquest was one of Britain's most important towns. By 1150, it was among the wealthiest towns in England, thanks to its cloth and wool exports, and a century later was the third-largest city in England. It continued to prosper until the Dissolution, which cut off its main source of income (pilgrimage) and patronage, leading to the city's relative decline. Lincoln's fortunes improved in the Georgian era and it boomed during the Industrial

Revolution, when it excelled in heavy engineering, building locomotives, steam shovels and all manner of machinery. Today, the city's economy is based mainly on public administration, commerce, arable farming and tourism, with relatively little industry.

Lincoln Cathedral

Lincoln is blessed with one of the world's great buildings, **Lincoln Cathedral** (free on Sundays), built between 1185 and 1311, which John Ruskin claimed was the 'most precious piece of architecture in Britain'. Built in English Gothic style, it was the tallest building in the world for 238 years (1311-1548) – until in 1548 its central spire collapsed and wasn't rebuilt – and remains the fourth-largest cathedral in Britain (after Liverpool, St Paul's and York Minster). The drawback is that you must haul yourself up, aptly named, Steep Hill to reach it (and the castle).

High Bridge

Magna Carta

The Bishop of Lincoln, Hugh of Wells, was one of the signatories to the *Magna Carta* in 1215 – which enshrined the liberty of the individual in English law – and for hundreds of years Lincoln Cathedral held one of the four remaining original copies (now displayed in Lincoln Castle).

The city's other outstanding landmark is **Lincoln Castle**, a Norman castle constructed in the late 11th century on the site of the existing Roman fortress. It's unusual in that it has two mottes, one of only two such castles in the country (the other being Lewes in East Sussex). The castle has been used as a prison and law court (ongoing) in modern times and is one of the best preserved in England. It's open to the public most days and offers sweeping views over the city and surrounding countryside.

Lincoln is awash with historic buildings, including the 12th-century **Old Bishop's Palace** in the shadow of the cathedral, once among the most important and impressive buildings in the country, and the administrative centre of the largest diocese in medieval England, stretching from the Humber to the Thames. The palace was damaged during the Civil War and subsequently largely abandoned. The most notable surviving feature is the East Hall, built over an undercroft and completed in the 1230s, along with an expanded chapel and the tower gatehouse built in the 1430s. The palace is now maintained by English Heritage (guided tours). Another fine building is **Lincoln Guildhall & Stonebow**, completed around 1520, which remains the meeting place of Lincoln City Council. The term 'Stonebow' refers to a stone archway that visitors entering the city from the south (along the High Street) passed through. South of the Guildhall is 16th-century **High Bridge** ('Glory Hole') over the River Witham, the oldest bridge in the UK still in use with a medieval building on it.

Jews House

Food & Drink

- **Bronze Pig:** acclaimed fine dining restaurant with rooms (4 Burton Rd, LN1 3LB, 01522-524817, Tue-Sat 6-10pm, Sun noon-2-30pm, closed Mon, ££).
- **Browns Pie Shop:** popular restaurant serving gourmet pies in a vaulted cellar (33 Steep Hill, LN2 1LU, 01522-527330, Wed-Fri 11.30am-2.30pm, 5-8.30/9.30pm, Sat 11.30am-9.30pm, Sun 11.30am-5pm, closed Mon-Tue, £).
- **Jews House:** upmarket British restaurant in a 12th-century building (15 The Strait, LN2 1JD, 01522-524851, Thu-Sat 6pm-midnight, Sun 1-5pm, closed Mon-Wed, ££).

One of the earliest surviving townhouses in England, **Jews House** – now a fine dining restaurant (see **Food & Drink** box) – is situated on Steep Hill next to Jews Court. It was associated with the thriving Jewish community in medieval Lincoln, but anti-Semitic hysteria in the 13th century led to the entire Jewish community being expelled from England in 1290. Lincoln is home to a number of ancient churches, including **St Mary le Wigford**, dating from the 10th century; **St Mary Magdalene** which was consecrated in 1317 and rebuilt in 1695; and **St Swithin's**, designed by James Fowler and completed in 1887. Lincoln isn't noted for its museums, but there are a few worth a visit, including the **Museum of Lincolnshire Life** – which celebrates the culture of Lincolnshire and its people from 1750 to the present day – and **The Collection**, the county museum and gallery.

If you fancy some fresh air and exercise, just a few minutes from the city centre is Lincoln Arboretum, with beautiful gardens, lakes and fountains, while on the opposite side of town is Brayford Waterfront on Brayford Pool, England's oldest inland harbour (created by the Romans). For such a small city, Lincoln has a surprising number of first class restaurants, historic pubs and lively nightclubs, while opera, dance, music and theatre can all be enjoyed at the Lincoln Theatre Royal and the Lincoln Performing Arts Centre.

Waterside & Empowerment Sculpture

Norwich

Address: Norwich NR2 1NH (visitnorwich.co.uk)

Getting there: air (Norwich, 4mi), rail (Norwich, Greater Anglia), road (A11/47/140)

Highlights: Cathedral, Castle, medieval Lanes & buildings, Castle Museum & Art Gallery, Norwich Museum, Sainsbury Centre, Riverside Walk

Nearby: Cromer, Great Yarmouth, Lowestoft, Norfolk Broads, **Southwold**, Thetford

Sleep

- **Luxury:** The Assembly House (5*), Theatre St, NR2 1RQ (01603-626402).
- **Moderate:** The Georgian Townhouse (3*), 30-34 Unthank Rd, NR2 2RB (01603-615655).
- **Budget:** Stracey Hotel (3*), 2 Stracey Rd, NR1 1EZ (01603-628093).

Norwich Cathedral

The county town of Norfolk, Norwich lies some 100 miles north of London on the River Wensum in East Anglia. Designated England's first UNESCO City of Literature in 2012, it's a popular tourist destination, widely considered to be one of the best small cities in the world. Following an uprising by the Iceni tribe (led by Boadicea) around AD60, the Caistor area of today's city became the Roman capital (*Venta Icenorum*) of East Anglia. After the Roman settlement fell into disuse around AD450, the Anglo-Saxons occupied the site in the 5th-7th centuries founding the town of *Northwic* (from which Norwich gets its name).

The Normans were responsible for the city's two most imposing buildings, **Norwich Castle** and **Norwich Cathedral**. The castle was built from around 1067 and is the only Norman castle in East Anglia; the stone keep, which still stands today, was probably built between 1095 and 1110 and since 1894 has been home to **Norwich Museum**. Magnificent Norwich Cathedral was begun in 1096 by Herbert de Losinga, Bishop of Thetford – who also founded **Norwich School**, where Admiral

Quayside

Horatio Nelson was educated – and is constructed of Caen (Normandy) limestone. Completed in 1145 with a wooden spire, the 315ft stone spire was erected in 1480, making it one of the largest cathedrals in England with the second-tallest spire and second-largest cloisters (after Salisbury Cathedral). Cathedral Close is home to over 80 listed buildings. Norwich also boasts **St John the Baptist Cathedral** (1882-1910), a beautiful Roman Catholic church designed by George Gilbert Scott Jr and the second-largest RC cathedral in England (after Westminster, London). The city has a wealth of medieval churches, too, including beautiful **St Peter Mancroft**, built between 1430 and 1455.

Norwich is the best preserved medieval city in the UK, where it's a delight to roam the ancient cobbled streets and alleyways, such as Elm Hill, Princes Street, Timber Hill and Tombland. Among its medieval gems are **St. Andrew's Hall** and **Blackfriars' Hall**, a magnificent group of church and convent flint buildings dating from the 14th century, comprising the most complete surviving friary complex in England. Nearby is **Norwich School** (formerly King Edward VI School), while northeast of the

Food & Drink

- **Benedicts:** acclaimed brasserie serving modern British cuisine (9 Benedicts St, NR2 4PE, 01603-926080, Tue-Thu 5-10pm, Fri-Sat noon-2pm, 5-10pm, closed Sun-Mon, ££).

- **Warwick St Social:** stylish British restaurant and bar with outdoor terrace (2 Warwick St, NR2 3LD, 01603-627687, Wed-Fri 4-8.30pm, Sat noon-8.30pm, Sun noon-5.30pm, closed Mon-Tue, £-££).

- **Woolf & Social:** contemporary restaurant with modern British menu (21-23 Nelson St, NR2 4DW, 01603-443658, Tue-Fri 6-11pm, Sat noon-3pm, 6pm-midnight, Sun noon-3pm, closed Mon, £).

centre is the **Great Hospital**, founded in 1249 and in continuous use as a caring institution ever since.

Other notable buildings include 14th-century **Strangers' Hall**, a former sanctuary for refugees and now a museum of domestic history; the splendid **Guildhall** (1407-1424); **Dragon Hall** (1427-1430), a half-timbered merchant's trading hall; the **Assembly House**

Elm Hill

Norwich Castle

(1754-1755), now a hotel and restaurant (see **Sleep** box); the Tudor Revival **Shirehall** (1823); handsome Art Nouveau **Royal Arcade** (1899); **Surrey House** (1900-1912), with a stunning marble hall and glass atrium; and imposing **Norwich City Hall** (1938)

> At the time of the Norman Conquest, Norwich was already one of the largest towns in England, with a population of 5,000-10,000, and from the Middle Ages until the Industrial Revolution it was the second-largest city in England after London.

Norwich Castle Museum & Art Gallery is home to outstanding collections of fine art, archaeology and natural history, while the **Museum of Norwich** at the Bridewell Museum explores the city's mercantile history. Another gallery well worth a visit is the **Sainsbury Centre for Visual Arts**, opened in 1978 on the campus of the University of East Anglia, which houses the world-renowned Robert and Lisa Sainsbury Collection (among others) in a purpose-built gallery designed by Norman Foster.

Norwich city isn't particularly well endowed with parks and gardens but **Chapelfield Gardens** and **Plantation Garden** – a lovely English garden with an Italianate terrace – are close to the centre. Three miles east of the city is **Whitlingham Country Park**, with 86 acres of stunning open parkland and water, while three miles to the southwest is popular **Eaton Park** (80 acres), a beautiful historic park with a host of attractions. The leafy **Riverside Walk** alongside the River Wensum offers rewarding views of the 14th-century defensive **Cow Tower**, the three-arched medieval **Bishop's Bridge**, and a watergate and ferry house called **Pull's Ferry**,

If shopping is your bag, then Norwich offers a wealth of options, from Castle Mall and Intu Chapelfield shopping centres to the mainly pedestrianised Lanes, Castle Quarter, Gentleman's Walk, Royal Arcade and Elm Hill (lined with antiques shops), plus a huge open-air **Market** (Mon-Sat) dating from the 11th century – the best in the country. When you're peckish, the city's compact centre is packed with foodie delights, from fine dining restaurants to street food and everything in between. After dark the city isn't the liveliest of places with relatively few nightclubs, although there's a wide choice of pubs and bars. There's also a number of cinemas (including an IMAX) and theatres and a host of live music venues.

Royal Arcade

Ripon

Address: Ripon HG4 1DB (discoverripon.org)

Getting there: air (Leeds Bradford, 19mi), rail (Ripon, NER), road (A61)

Highlights: Cathedral, Workhouse Museum & Garden, Wakeman's House, racecourse, riverside, Spa Gardens, Market Place, historic pubs

Nearby: Harrogate, Nidderdale AONB, Ripley, Studley Royal Park (Fountains Abbey), Thirsk

Sleep

- **Luxury:** The Old Deanery (3*), Minster Rd, HG4 1QS (01765-600003).
- **Moderate:** Ripon Spa (3*), Park St, HG4 2BU (01765-602172).
- **Budget:** The Unicorn (2*), Market Place E, HG4 1BP (01765-643410).

Located in North Yorkshire (historically part of the West Riding) at the confluence of two tributaries of the River Ure (the Laver and Skell), Ripon is most famous for its imposing cathedral. Originally known as *Inhrypum*, the settlement was founded by Saint Wilfrid during the time of the Anglian Kingdom of Northumbria, who built a monastery. In the 12th century Ripon established a prosperous wool trade, which was supplemented in the 16th century by the manufacture of spurs. During the Georgian era, the city wasn't significantly influenced by the Industrial Revolution, despite the existence of various guilds. Today, it's a prosperous market town whose main business is tourism.

Majestic **Ripon Cathedral** is the fourth church on the site, begun by Roger de Pont l'Évêque, Archbishop of York (1154-81). It's built over Wilfrid's 7th-century crypt (he's buried in the church near the high altar) – a significant example of early Christian architecture in England – in order to promote pilgrimages to his tomb. The cathedral was constructed between 1160 and 1547 and is notable for its Gothic west front in the Early English style, along with its medieval Geometric east window and beautifully-carved, 15th-century choir stalls and misericords (said to have inspired Lewis Carroll's *Alice in Wonderland*).

Ripon is noted for its 'law & order' museums (not for the faint hearted), which include the grim Victorian **Workhouse Museum & Garden**, the **Prison & Police Museum**, housed in the former Ripon Liberty Prison, and the elegant **Courthouse Museum**, built in 1830 and virtually unchanged since. Also worth a visit is 16th-century **Thorpe Prebend House**, a historic residence in

Ripon Cathedral

the cathedral's shadow, which is now a heritage centre for the cathedral with a charming garden.

Wakeman

Opposite Market Place is 14th-century timber-framed **Wakeman's House** (now home to a café) associated with Hugh Ripley, last Wakeman and first Mayor of Ripon. A ceremony known as 'setting the watch' has been performed for over 1,000 years (ongoing) and entails the blowing of a horn by the Wakeman at 9pm each evening at the four corners of the obelisk in Market Place.

If you want to stretch your legs, look no further than **Spa Gardens** (alongside Ripon Spa Baths), a beautiful park in the heart of the city, where summer concerts are held in the Victorian bandstand. The area around the cathedral is also a tranquil place to relax, while there are some lovely walks along the rivers and Ripley Canal. If you fancy a bit of retail therapy, you'll find Ripon's shopping streets – lined with medieval and Georgian buildings – a delightful experience, where you'll find the usual high street chains alongside a bounty of independent retailers. Be sure to visit Ripon's beautiful **Market Place** (main market, Thu 9am-4pm), which Daniel Defoe described as 'the finest and most beautiful square of its kind in England'. Ripon isn't renowned for its eateries or nightlife, but has sufficient restaurants, bars, pubs and clubs to satisfy most visitors.

Nearby attractions include Ripon Racecourse (Apr-Sep), the UNESCO World Heritage Site of Fountains

- **Mario's:** popular family-run Italian restaurant established in 2004 (27 Kirkgate, HG4 1PB, 01765-608688, Mon-Sat 5-10pm, closed Sun, £).
- **Royal Oak:** friendly gastropub in a beautiful 18th-century coaching Inn (36 Kirkgate, HG4 1PB, 01765-602284, daily 8am-10/11pm, £-££).
- **Water Rat:** homely riverside pub offering traditional home-cooked food (Bondgate Green, HG4 1QW, 01765-602251, daily 11am-11pm, £).

Abbey and Studley Royal Park, 18th-century Newby Hall and its award-winning gardens, 14th-century Ripley Castle and Norton Conyers, a late medieval manor house.

Ripon Market

St Albans

> **ℹ**
>
> **Address:** St Albans AL1 3JE (enjoystalbans.com)
>
> **Getting there:** air (Luton, 12mi), rail (St Albans City, Thameslink), road (M1/A1, A414)
>
> **Highlights:** Cathedral, Roman remains, St Michael's Church, Great Gateway, Roman Theatre, St Alban's Museum, Verulamium Museum & Park
>
> **Nearby:** Hatfield House, Knebworth House, Woburn Safari Park

St Albans in Hertfordshire is a historic market town situated 20 miles northwest of London on the River Ver. It was the first major Roman town (*Verulamium*) on the old Roman Watling Street and the second-largest in Britain after London (*Londinium*). St Albans takes its name from the first recorded British saint, Alban, who lived in the town during the 3rd or 4th century AD and was executed by the Romans for his Christian beliefs.

Sleep

• **Luxury:** St Michael's Manor (4*), Fishpool St, AL3 4RY (01727-864444).

• **Moderate:** The White Hart (3*), 23-25 Holywell Hill, AL1 1EZ (01727-853624).

• **Budget:** Premier Inn (3*), 1 Adelaide St, AL3 5BH (0871-527 9464).

He was commemorated by an abbey, founded in the 8th century and built on the site where he was buried, making it one of the oldest sites of continuous Christian worship in Britain.

St Albans' skyline is dominated by the spectacular **Cathedral and Abbey Church of St Alban**, which officially ceased to be an abbey in the 16th century and became a cathedral in 1877. Built 1077-89, its

St Alban

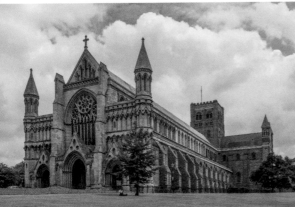

St Albans Cathedral

Great Gateway of the Monastery

architecture is a blend of Norman, Gothic and Victorian era restoration, with the longest nave in England. The great tower contains bricks salvaged from the ruins of Roman *Verulamium* and is the only 11th-century great crossing tower remaining in England.

Other historic buildings in St Albans include charming **St Michael's Church**, close to Verulamium Park, built in the 10th or early 11th century and the most significant surviving Saxon building in Britain. On the High Street, the **Clock Tower** was completed in 1405 and is the only medieval town belfry in England, while close to the cathedral is the imposing **Great Gateway of the Monastery**. Built in 1365 and the last remaining building (except for the cathedral itself) of the Benedictine

monastery, it's now the entrance to St Albans School, a public school dating back to the 10th century.

Not surprisingly, the city contains a host of Roman ruins, including a **Roman Theatre** built around AD140 and unearthed in 1847; it's the only visible example of its kind in Britain, being a theatre with a stage rather than an amphitheatre. Subsequent excavations have revealed a row of Roman shop foundations, a villa and a secret shrine, all thought to date from the 1st century AD. Nearby, **Verulamium Park** contains remains of the city's ancient **Roman Wall** and the **Hypocaust**, part of a large AD200 Roman townhouse showing the early sophisticated heating system that allowed hot air to circulate beneath the mosaic floors and through the walls of a building. Iconic later buildings include the Neo-Classical Court House (1830), aka the **Old Town Hall**.

Saint Alban

The cathedral's shrine to St Alban attracts pilgrims from far and wide, and on the Saturday closest to 22nd June – St Alban's Day – there's a spectacular Pilgrimage Procession of giant puppets that tells the story of the saint's martyrdom.

There are two main museums in St Albans, the **St Albans Museum + Gallery**, opened in 2018 in the magnificent Old Town Hall, and the **Verulamium Museum**. Set over three floors, the St Albans Museum showcases over 2,000 years of heritage and contemporary artworks, including the building's historic rooms, while at the Verulamium Museum you can explore Roman life, view recreated Roman rooms and admire some of the finest mosaics outside the

St Michael's Church

Mediterranean. You can also see recent discoveries such as the Sandridge Hoard, a collection of 159 Roman gold coins found in a nearby field in 2012.

The largest green space in St Albans is magnificent **Verulamium Park** (100 acres), where remains of the city's Roman walls and the outline of the London Gate can still be seen. An outstanding feature of the park is ornamental Verulam Lake, alongside the River Ver, constructed in 1929 and home to flocks of water birds, including one of the few heronries in Hertfordshire. Close to the cathedral is historic **Vintry Garden**, a walled garden and vineyard originally tended by medieval monks.

The main entertainment centre in St Albans is the **Alban Arena** (formerly St Albans City Hall), a theatre and music venue. Other venues include the **Maltings Arts Theatre**, a lively fringe theatre; the **Abbey Theatre**, a 230-seat theatre and studio space; and **St Albans Organ Theatre**, which has a unique collection of mechanical (self-playing) musical instruments.

St Albans has been an important market town for over 1,000 years, with the street market (Wed, Sat) in St Peter's Street dating from the 9th century, complemented by a host of independent shops. When

Food & Drink

• **Lussmanns:** overlooking Vintry Garden, serving modern British cuisine (Waxhouse Gate, AL3 4EW, 01727-851941, Tue-Sun 11.30am-10pm, closed Mon, £-££).

• **Thompson St Albans:** affordable fine dining offering modern British cuisine (2 Hatfield Rd, AL1 3RP, 01727-730777, daily noon-2pm, 6-9/9.30pm, ££).

• **Ye Olde Fighting Cocks:** claims to be Britain's oldest pub, YOFC offers tasty pub grub (16 Abbey Mill Ln, AL3 4HE, 01727-869152, noon-10.30pm/midnight, £-££).

you need sustenance, the city offers a profusion of excellent restaurants, cafés and pubs – plus street food on market days. St Albans also has a lively nightlife, with a number of clubs and live music venues.

Verulamium Park

Salisbury

Address: Salisbury SP1 1EJ (visitwiltshire.co.uk/salisbury)

Getting there: air (Southampton, 21mi), rail (Salisbury, SWR), road (A30/A36/A338/A354)

Highlights: Cathedral, Cathedral Close, medieval buildings, Mompesson House, Arundells, St Thomas' Church, Salisbury Museum, Water Meadows, Charter Market, historic pubs

Nearby: Cranborne Chase AONB, **New Forest**, Old Sarum, Stonehenge, Wilton

Most famous for its beautiful 13th-century cathedral, Salisbury is located in Wiltshire on the edge of Salisbury Plain, 80 miles southwest of London. The original site of the city (called **Old Sarum**) is two miles north and consisted of an Iron Age hill fort that was reused by the Romans, Saxons and Normans; remnants of the old fort remain, along with castle ruins and the foundations of the original cathedral. Tensions between the church and army led to the cathedral being relocated two miles south to New Sarum, around which Salisbury grew up.

Salisbury Cathedral (1220-1258) is renowned for its magnificent soaring spire – dating from 1549 and the tallest in the UK (404ft) – one of the UK's best examples of Early English architecture. The cathedral has the UK's largest cloisters and is set within the country's largest cathedral close (80 acres), while the cathedral clock (allegedly dating from 1386) is among the oldest working examples in the world. It's free to visit the cathedral, although there's a fee to climb the tower.

The main entrance to Cathedral Close is guarded by the splendid 14th-century **High Street Gate** – still

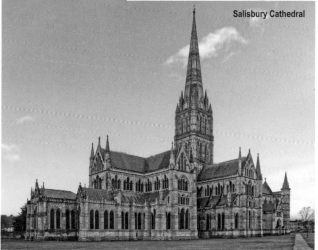

Salisbury Cathedral

High Street Gate

locked at night (11pm-6am) – which once housed a small jail for those convicted of misdeeds within the Liberty of the Close. Just inside the gate stands the **College of Matrons**, founded in 1682 for the widows and unmarried daughters of clergymen. The magnificent **Cathedral Close** contains a host of splendid historic buildings, including **Mompesson House** (National Trust), an 18th-century mansion; attractive **Arundells**, dating back to the 13th century (though extensively rebuilt in the 18th century), the former home of Prime Minister Sir Edward Heath (1916-2005); and the 13th-century **Medieval Hall**, the setting for splendid banquets just 200yds from the Cathedral. South of the cathedral is the **Bishop's Palace**, now the private Cathedral School, parts of which date back to 1220. The Close is also home to several museums (see below).

Magna Carta

Displayed in the cathedral's **Chapter House** is the best preserved of the four surviving original copies of the *Magna Carta*, a charter of rights agreed to by King John at Runnymede on 15th June 1215.

Sleep

- **Luxury:** Milford Hall Hotel & Spa (4*), 206 Castle St, SP1 3TE (01722-417411).
- **Moderate:** The Legacy Rose & Crown (4*), Harnham Rd, SP2 8JQ (01722-328615).
- **Budget:** The Old Mill (3*), Town Path, W Harnham, SP2 8EU (01722-327517).

Other important buildings and sites in Salisbury include charming **St Thomas's Church**, the original of which was built for cathedral workmen in 1219 and named after Thomas Becket. The current church dates from the 15th century and features a celebrated **Doom Painting** above the chancel arch, painted around 1475, depicting Christ on the Day of Judgement. The **Poultry Cross** at the junction of Silver and Minster Streets is a 14th-century market cross. **Salisbury Museum** is an excellent local history museum housed in 13th-century King's House within Cathedral Close, while nearby the **Rifles Berkshire & Wiltshire Museum** is situated in

Arundells

The Wardrobe, a 15th-century building used to store the robes of the Bishops of Salisbury. The city also has a number of galleries, including the Young Gallery in the central library, Gallery 21, Whitewall Galleries and **Fisherton Mill**, a former Victorian grain mill housing galleries, artists' studios and a popular café.

If you wish to stretch your legs, Salisbury offers a number of parks and gardens. Among the most popular is **Queen Elizabeth Gardens**, a glorious formal garden with famous views of the cathedral to the east and the River Avon to the south. From here you can access the Town Path leading to **Harnham Water Meadows** and on to Harnham village – a serene and lovely walk. Around a mile to the southeast is **Churchill Gardens**, also bordered by the Avon, home to a wide variety of shrubs and trees. Close to the town centre are the **Greencroft** and **Bourne Hill Gardens**, while to the north is pretty **Victoria Park**, the oldest park in Salisbury (1887), with attractive formal planting.

Salisbury offers a bounty of places to eat and drink, while if you fancy a bit of shopping the city has scores of independent shops, along with the historic **Charter Market** (Tue, Sat, 9am-3/4pm) in Market Place. The city's traditional entertainment venues include **City Hall**, which stages music, comedy and other performances, **Salisbury Playhouse**, one of Britain's leading provincial theatres, and the bijou **Studio Theatre** (just 92 seats), which offers a more intimate experience. Salisbury also stages the celebrated annual **Salisbury International Arts Festival** at the end of May/beginning of June. For those who prefer something more lively, the city has plenty of pubs, bars and clubs.

If you have a few hours to spare, the UNESCO Heritage Site of **Stonehenge** – just eight miles north of the city – is a must-see.

Salisbury Cathedral from the Water Meadows

Shrewsbury

Address: Shrewsbury SY1 2AS (originalshrewsbury.co.uk)

Getting there: air (Birmingham, 50mi), rail (Shrewsbury, Transport for Wales/W Midlands), road (A5/A49/A458)

Highlights: Castle, Abbey, half-timbered medieval buildings, Shrewsbury Library, Shrewsbury Museum & Art Gallery, River Severn, Quarry Park & Dingle

Nearby: Ironbridge, **Ludlow & Shropshire Hills**, Oswestry, Telford, Wroxeter

Sleep

- **Luxury:** Prince Rupert (4*), Butcher Row, SY1 1UQ (01743-499955).
- **Moderate:** The Loopy Shrew, 15-17 Bellstone, SY1 1HU (01743-366505).
- **Budget:** Lion Hotel, Wyle Cop, SY1 1UY (01743-353107).

The county town of Shropshire on the River Severn, Shrewsbury (pronounced 'Shrowsbury' or 'Shroosbry' by locals) is located nine miles east of the Welsh border and 47 miles northwest of Birmingham. The town is noted for its largely unspoilt medieval street plan and over 650 listed buildings, including many 15th/16th-century timber-framed buildings.

The area was important during the Roman era, when Wroxeter (5 miles to the southeast) was the site of *Viroconium*, the fourth largest town in Roman Britain. The early capital of the Kingdom of Powys, Shrewsbury has been the site of many conflicts, notably between the English and Welsh. The Angles, under King Offa of Mercia, took possession in AD778 at the beginning of the town's known history, while the Normans built Shrewsbury castle in 1074. The town reached its commercial zenith in the late Middle Ages, when it was an important centre of wool production, while in the 18th century it was a major market town and staging post for travellers between London and Holyhead.

Red sandstone **Shrewsbury Castle** – occupying a commanding position on a hill overlooking the River Severn directly above the railway station – was built around 1074 by Roger de Montgomery (now home to the Shropshire Regimental Museum). Shrewsbury

Shrewsbury Panorama

Shrewsbury Castle

Food & Drink

- **Henry Tudor House:** modern British restaurant and bar in 15th-century Tudor building (Barracks Passage, Wyle Cop, SY1 1XA, 01743-361666, Wed-Thu 5-11pm, Fri-Sat noon-11pm, Sun noon-7pm, closed Mon-Tue, £).

- **House of the Rising Sun:** contemporary Australian fusion cuisine in striking building (8 Butcher Row, SY1 1UW, 01743-588040, daily 9.30am-11pm/1am, £-££).

- **Lion + Pheasant:** creative fine dining in a 16th-century coaching inn (49-50 Wyle Cop, SY1 1XJ, 01743-770345, telephone for meal times, ££).

has a number of important churches – in addition to **Shrewsbury Abbey** (see box on page 126) – including 12th-century **St Mary's**, the town's largest church (now redundant), which boasted the tallest spire in England for over 500 years, **St Chad's** built in 1792 in a distinctive round design, and Roman Catholic **Shrewsbury Cathedral** (1856), designed by Edward Pugin (son of Augustus Pugin).

Shrewsbury Library is housed in the former home of Shrewsbury School from 1552 until 1882 (fronted by a statue of former student, Charles Darwin, who was born in Shrewsbury); founded by Edward VI in 1552, the school moved to its present site on the south bank of the River Severn in 1882, where its imposing main building is a former workhouse. Other notable buildings include the town's defensive walls, built between 1110 and 1135, now mostly demolished apart from the 14th-century **Town Walls Tower** (National Trust); **Ireland's Mansion** (1575), a beautiful timber-framed, 'black and white' house on

the High Street; the **Old Market Hall** (1596), where wool merchants sold their fleeces; **Draper's Hall** (1658), now a hotel and restaurant; and **Ditherington Flat Mill** (just north of the town), the oldest iron-framed building in the world.

English Bridge & River Severn

Shrewsbury is home to a number of museums and galleries, including **Shrewsbury Museum & Art Gallery**, founded in 1835 and housed in the Victorian Music Hall, which tells the story of Shropshire and Shrewsbury from Roman times to the present day, while the **Shropshire Regimental Museum** in Shrewsbury Castle houses the absorbing collection of the Shropshire Regiment. Also worth a visit is **Bear Steps Art Gallery**, set in a stunning medieval building, where local artists exhibit their work.

Shrewsbury has a number of parks and gardens, including magnificent **Quarry Park** (29 acres), established in the 16th century and encircled by a majestic loop of the River Severn, which offers some lovely walks. At its heart is the **Dingle**, a floral masterpiece created by world-renowned gardener Percy Thrower (Parks Superintendent for 28 years), with a delightful sunken garden. Two miles southeast of the town is **Attingham Park**, a splendid 18th-century mansion and estate owned by the National Trust.

The town is a shoppers' delight, with a couple of modern shopping centres (Darwin and Pride Hill) and Market Hall (Tue-Sat), although it's the town's wealth of independent shops and traditional food market that set it apart (Wyle Cop is lined with a series of independent

Shrewsbury Abbey

Founded in 1083 as a Benedictine monastery, Shrewsbury Abbey was one of the most influential in England and an important centre of pilgrimage. Much of the Abbey was destroyed after the Reformation in the 16th century, but the nave survived as a parish church and today serves as the mother church for the Parish of Holy Cross.

shops). Shrewsbury has an abundance of outstanding restaurants and cafés, while for night owls there are dozens of lively pubs, bars, clubs and music venues. The town's traditional entertainment venues include the neo-Classical **Buttermarket** (a former 1835 butter warehouse) and **Theatre Severn**, a modern riverside theatre with two auditoriums staging musicals, drama, comedy, dance and live concerts.

Shrewsbury Square

Southwell

Address: Southwell NG25 0EP (visit-nottinghamshire.co.uk/explore/market-towns/southwell)

Getting there: air (East Midlands, 24mi), rail (Southwell, Midland), road (A617, B6386)

Highlights: Minster, Workhouse, Archbishop's Palace, Prebendal Houses, racecourse, festivals

Nearby: Mansfield, Newark, **Nottingham**

- **Luxury:** Old Vicarage Boutique Hotel (4*), Westhorpe, NG25 0NB (01836-815989).

- **Moderate:** Saracens Head (3*), Market Pl, NG25 0HE (01636-812701).

- **Budget:** Crown Hotel (3*), 11 Market Pl, NG25 0HE (01636-918153).

One of the prettiest towns in the Midlands, Southwell in Nottinghamshire lies on the River Greet 14 miles northeast of Nottingham, the birthplace (75 Church Street) of the Bramley apple, first propagated here in 1809. The area was occupied by the Romans and was an important Saxon town, while in the 12th century the Normans built Southwell Minster on the site of an earlier Anglo-Saxon church. In 1530, the **Archbishop's Palace** (see box on page 128) sheltered Cardinal Wolsey (Archbishop of York) and during the English Civil War Charles I spent his last night in Southwell before surrendering to the Scottish Army at nearby Kelham.

First stop for visitors has to be stunning **Southwell Minster**, built by the Normans between 1108 and ca. 1300, an outstanding example of severe Romanesque design with one of the finest Norman naves in Europe. Among the Minster's many outstanding features are its 13th-century stone carvings of leaves (the 'leaves of Southwell'), animals and green men in the beautiful Chapter House. Also exemplary are the sanctuary stained glass windows dating from 1528 and the Great War Memorial window (2014) by Nicholas Mynheer, dedicated to the men of Nottinghamshire and Derbyshire who lost their lives in the First World War.

The other main attraction in Southwell, of a very different order to the Minster, is austere **Southwell Workhouse** – just east of the town centre – built in 1824. Now owned by the National Trust, the workhouse is the most complete in existence, restored and redecorated as it would have been in the 19th century.

Southwell Minster

Archbishop's Palace

Behind the Minster is the partly ruined 14th-century **Archbishop's Palace**, once the residence of Cardinal Wolsey (1473-1530), Archbishop of York, where you can see the restored State Chamber (Great Hall) and the recently created Education Garden.

Its architecture was influenced by prison design and its harsh regime became a blueprint for workhouses throughout the country. Other historic buildings include the **Prebendal Houses** in Church Street and Westgate – dating from the 11th century to 1291 – ten of which survive today. They belonged to the Minster and were built for the parish canons of the outlying villages. The 15th-century, timber-framed **Saracens Head Hotel** (previously called the King's Head), was where Charles I spent his last night as a free man in May 1646. Three miles to the east is the **Museum of Timekeeping** in Upton, which houses a unique collection of artefacts at the home of the British Horological Institute, while nearby is **Southwell Racecourse** (meetings throughout the year).

If you fancy a stroll, Southwell has some outstanding walks, including six heritage trails that highlight the history and attractions of the town. When you've done the sights and had a walk, Southwell has an array of independent shops, restaurants and pubs, and a Saturday market (8.30am-4pm). The town is

Food & Drink

- **La Parisienne:** popular French-style bistro offering gluten-free and vegan options (12 King St, NG25 0EN, 01636-816573, Tue-Sat 9.30am-4/4.30pm, closed Sun-Mon, £-££).

- **Piano:** family-run Italian restaurant in 18th-century Georgian townhouse (1 Westgate, NG25 0JN, 01636-816770, Tue-Thu 5.30-9.30pm, Fri-Sat noon-3pm, 5.30-9.30pm, closed Sun-Mon, £-££).

- **Saracens Head:** upmarket bistro dining in an elegant 17th-century room (Market Pl, NG25 0HE, 01636-812701, Daily noon-2.30/3pm, 5/6-9pm, Sun 6-8pm bar food only, ££).

famous for its festivals, which include the Bramley Apple Festival (Oct), the Gate to Southwell Festival (June, roots and acoustic music) and the Southwell Music Festival (August, classical music), in addition to music in the Minster every month.

Southwell Workhouse

Stamford

Address: Stamford PE9 2DR (stamford.co.uk)

Getting there: air (Norwich, 29mi), rail (Stamford, East Midlands), road (A1, A43/A606/A1175)

Highlights: Georgian architecture, medieval churches, Burghley House & Park, Browne's Hospital, Town Hall, Town Meadows, brewery

Nearby: Grantham, Melton Mowbray, Peterborough, Rutland Water

Sleep

- **Luxury:** George Hotel (4*), 71 High St, PE9 2LB (01780-750750).
- **Moderate:** William Cecil (4*), St Martins, PE9 2LJ (01780-750070).
- **Budget:** The Green Man (3*), 29 Scotgate, PE9 2YQ (01780-753598).

Located on the River Welland in Lincolnshire, pretty Stamford is a small market town famous for its wealth of 17th and 18th-century stone buildings – dubbed the 'finest stone town in England' – older timber-framed buildings, medieval parish churches and cobbled streets. The town was the first designated conservation area in England, home to over 600 listed buildings. It's a popular location for filming period dramas: George Elliot's *Middlemarch*, the 2004 film version of Jane Austen's *Pride and Prejudice*, and scenes from the *Da Vinci Code* were all filmed in and around Stamford.

Romans built Ermine Street across what's now Burghley Park and forded the River Welland to the west of Stamford, while the Danes occupied the area before being ousted by the Anglo-Saxons in the 10th century. By the Middle Ages, Stamford was famous for its pottery, wool and woollen cloth (haberget). Today, the economy is based on light industry, services, agriculture and tourism.

The town's most famous building – and its main draw – is magnificent **Burghley House** (see box on page 130)

in Burghley Park, one mile south of the town centre. Other notable buildings include delightful 13th century **All Saints Church**, where you can climb the tower; **St Martin's Church**, founded in the 12th century but rebuilt in Perpendicular style in the 15th century, where the North Chapel houses the tombs of the Cecil family (including the 1st Lord Burghley); **Browne's Hospital** (open at weekends), one of the country's best medieval almshouses founded in 1485 by wealthy wool merchant William Browne; and the buildings of **Stamford School**, established in 1532 by William Radcliffe.

Town Centre

Burghley House

A grand 16th-century country mansion, Burghley is England's finest Elizabethan house, built 1555-1587 by Sir William Cecil, 1st Baron Burghley (1520-1598), Lord High Treasurer and chief advisor to Elizabeth I. The house is still occupied by the Cecil family. The deer park was laid out by Lancelot 'Capability' Brown in the 18th century.

Food & Drink

- **Oak Room, George Hotel:** atmospheric fine dining at Stamford's finest hotel (71 High St, PE9 2LB, 01780-750750, telephone for meal times, ££-£££).
- **Tobie Norris:** unique Kneads pub in 13th-century building serving tasty pub grub (12 St Paul's St, PE9 2BE, 01780-753800, Mon-Sat noon-11pm, Sun noon-8pm, £-££).
- **Zada Restaurant:** Delicious Turkish cuisine in rustic surroundings with belly dancing! (13 St Mary's Hill, PE9 2DP, 01780-766848, Mon-Fri 5.30-11pm, Sat-Sun noon-11pm, £).

Also of note is **Stamford Town Hall**, completed in 1779 and home to an impressive collection of paintings and period furniture; the **Eleanor Cross** – one of twelve lavishly decorated stone monuments erected between 1291 and 1295 in memory of Eleanor of Castile, wife of Edward I; the ruins of **St Leonard's Priory**, built in AD658 and re-founded in 1082 before being destroyed in the Dissolution in 1538; and **All Saints Brewery** (est. 1825), which offers guided tours.

The town has a number of inviting green spaces, including the **Town Meadows**, an oasis of green between two forks of the River Welland, **Stamford Recreation Ground** created in 1871, with a bandstand, tennis courts and skatepark, and splendid **Burghley Park** (8am to dusk).

Stamford is a popular market town with an abundance of interesting independent shops and a bustling Friday market (8.30am-4pm), and when you fancy a bite to eat there's a wide choice of restaurants, pubs (try the Tobie Norris) and cafés. If you desire some culture there's the Stamford Corn Exchange Theatre and Stamford Arts Centre (former Assembly Rooms), which features a theatre, art-house cinema and art gallery.

Town Bridge & River Welland

Wells

Sleep

- **Luxury:** Beryl Country House (4*B&B), Top of Hawkers Ln, BA5 3JP (01749-678738).
- **Moderate:** Swan Hotel (4*), 11 Sadler St, BA5 2RX (01749-836300).
- **Budget:** Premier Inn (3*), Rowdens Rd, BA5 1UA (0333-234 6496).

England's smallest city (not counting the City of London) with a population of around 12,000, charming Wells in Somerset is located at the foot of the Mendip Hills. Unlike many English cities, Wells has a treasure trove of secular buildings which survived the Reformation almost intact, including its Cathedral, Bishop's Palace and Vicars' Close.

The city gets its name from three wells around which a former Roman settlement grew in importance under the Anglo-Saxons, who founded a minster church in

704. With the construction of the Cathedral and Bishop's Palace in the 13th century, Wells became the principal seat of the diocese of Bath and Wells and in the Middle Ages was an important cloth trading centre. The city featured prominently in both the English Civil War (1642-51) – when it backed the Royalists and was besieged by the Parliamentarians – and the Monmouth Rebellion (1685), when the 1st Duke of Monmouth attempted to

Wells Cathedral

Bishop's Palace

Front containing 300 sculpted figures, the ingenious 'scissor arches' in the crossing, a superb astronomical clock (the second-oldest clock mechanism in Britain), the fascinating octagonal Chapter House, gorgeous 'Tree of Jesse' Window (one of the finest examples of medieval stained glass in Europe) and one of only four chained libraries in the country. Opposite the cathedral is 14th-century **Vicars' Close**, the most complete example of a medieval close in the UK. It's said to be the oldest purely residential street with intact original buildings in Europe, comprising 27 dwellings (originally 44), a chapel and library at the north end, and a hall at the south end over the arched entrance gate from St Andrew Street.

Just north of the Close is **Wells Cathedral School** with links to a school founded in AD909 – one of the oldest extant schools in the world – which specialises in high-level musical tuition. The school's 15th-century Music School on Cathedral Green was previously

Bishop's Palace & Gardens

The unique moated Bishop's Palace was begun around 1210; the chapel and great hall (partly ruined) were added between 1275 and 1292, while the walls, gatehouse and moat (complete with resident swans trained to ring a bell for food!) were completed in the 14th century and the Bishops House in the 15th century. The delightful 14-acre gardens are a haven of tranquillity.

overthrow James II. Wells was the final location of the Bloody Assizes on 23rd September 1685, when, on one day, over 500 men were tried and the majority sentenced to death.

First port of call in Wells has to be majestic **Wells Cathedral** – built between 1176 and 1450 – one of the country's most beautiful and poetic cathedrals. England's first Gothic cathedral (mostly in Early English style), it's noted for its breathtaking West

Vicars' Close

Food & Drink

- **Anton's Bistrot:** popular atmospheric venue in a 15th-century coaching inn (Market Place, BA5 2RP, 01749-673457, daily 7am-10/10.30pm, £).

- **Courtyard:** good value, family-run restaurant with mainly gluten-free menu (9, Heritage Courtyard, Sadler St, BA5 2RR, 01749-077772, Thu-Sat 5-8.30/9pm, Sun 11.30am-6pm, closed Mon-Wed, £).

- **Goodfellows:** smart restaurant-café specialising in fish and seafood (5-5b Sadler St, BA5 2RR, 01749-673866, Tue noon-4pm, Wed, Fri-Sat noon-10pm, Sun 1-3pm, closed Mon, Thu, ££).

afield is the beautiful **Mendip Hills** AONB, where the famous Wookey Hole Caves, Ebbor Gorge and dramatic Cheddar Gorge are popular sights.

Back in town, the cobbled **Market Place** has been a focal point of the city for over 800 years and still holds a bustling twice weekly market (Wed & Sat) and a farmers' market on Wednesdays. Off the Market Place is the **Georgian Town Hall** and, on the eastern side, two 15th-century gateways – the **Bishop's Eye** leading to the Bishop's Palace and the **Penniless Porch** (where beggars would come for alms) into the cathedral. While it isn't noted for its shopping, Wells has a good selection of independent shops and boutiques, and when you fancy a break from sightseeing there's a variety of restaurants, cafés and pubs. Wells is also home to the Little Theatre and Wells Film centre, while Wells Cathedral holds regular choral concerts.

the house of the Archdeacon of Wells, while next door is the **Wells & Mendip Museum**, housed in the former Chancellors' House (mostly 17th-18th-century) and the 12th-century **Old Deanery & Garden** of the diocese of Bath & Wells. Also worth a visit is imposing Perpendicular **St Cuthbert's** church at the southern end of the High Street, dating from the 13th century and grand enough to be mistaken for the cathedral.

In addition to the enchanting **Bishop's Palace Gardens**, nearby is Wells Recreation Ground, where you'll find The Bishop's Barn, a 15th-century tithe barn donated to the city by Bishop Lord Arthur Hervey in 1887. Just north of the town centre is **Stoberry House & Garden**, a stunning six-acre garden offering panoramic views over the city, and Arts & Craft **Milton Lodge Gardens** a stone's throw away. A bit further

Bishop's Palace Gardens

Worcester

Sleep

Address: Worcester WR1 2EY (visitworcestershire.org/worcester)

Getting there: air (Birmingham, 35mi), rail (Worcester Foregate Street, West Midlands/GWR), road (M5, A44/A38)

Highlights: Cathedral, The Commandery, Tudor House Museum, City Art Gallery & Museum, River Severn, parks, market

Nearby: Cotswolds, Evesham, **Great Malvern & Malvern Hills**, Ledbury, **Stratford-upon-Avon**, Tewkesbury

- **Luxury:** Stanbrook Abbey Hotel (4*), Jennett Tree Ln, Callow End, WR2 4TY (01905-832940).
- **Moderate:** Worcester Whitehouse (4*), Foregate St, WR1 1EA (01905-24308).
- **Budget:** Fownes Hotel (3*), City Walls Rd, WR1 2AP (01905-613151).

One of England's great cathedral cities, Worcester is the county town of Worcestershire situated 31 miles southwest of Birmingham on the River Severn. The city has long been an important trading place and centre of monastic learning and church power (the Diocese of Worcester was created in AD680). It was the site of the final battle of the English Civil War in September 1651 – the Battle of Worcester – when Oliver Cromwell defeated Charles II's Royalists. In the late medieval period it was a cloth trading centre and in the late 18th/early 19th centuries was noted for its glove-making industry.

Majestic **Worcester Cathedral** was built between 1084 and 1504 and represents every style of English architecture from Norman to Perpendicular Gothic. Its many outstanding features include its Norman crypt, unique chapter house, unusual transitional Gothic bays, fine wood carvings and exquisite central tower. Both King John and Prince Arthur, eldest son of Henry VII and Henry VIII's brother, are buried in the Cathedral.

Other notable buildings in Worcester include **The Commandery**, a historic 15th-century building and Civil War museum that was Charles II's headquarters during the English Civil War; **St Oswald's Hospital** (which survived the Dissolution), an ancient

Worcester Cathedral

Food & Drink

- **Anchor Pub & Kitchen:** cosy pub with all-day British menu and garden seating (54 Diglis Rd, WR5 3BW, 01905-351094, daily 9.30am-10/11.30pm, £-££).
- **Browns at the Quay:** international menu with fish specials in riverside warehouse with terrace (24 Quay St, WR1 2JJ, 01905-25800, Tue-Sat noon-11pm, Sun noon-7pm, closed Mon, ££).
- **Old Rectifying House:** stylish modern British fine dining with bar and terrace garden (N Parade, WR1 3NN, 01905-619622, Wed-Fri noon-3pm, 6-9pm, Sat noon-9pm, Sun noon-4pm, closed Mon-Tue, ££).

The renowned **Museum of Royal Worcester**, a ceramics museum located in the former Royal Worcester porcelain factory, houses the world's largest collection of Royal Worcester porcelain dating back to 1751.

almshouse now located in Victorian buildings around a courtyard; and the **Guildhall**, a beautiful Queen Anne style building dating from 1721. In Friar Street there's a cluster of 16th-century houses, including the **Tudor House Museum**, where you can explore 500 years of the city's history, while **Greyfriars House & Garden** (National Trust) is a wealthy merchant's house built circa 1480-90. The **City Art Gallery & Museum** (founded 1833) houses an eclectic local history collection, while the **Infirmary Museum** at the University of Worcester's City Campus explores the history of Worcester Royal Infirmary, where the British Medical Association was founded in Castle Street in 1832.

Worcester and its surrounds are blessed with an abundance of green spaces, including **Cripplegate Park** just over Worcester Bridge, a verdant riverside park with a lovely garden opposite picturesque Worcestershire County Cricket Club; **Chapter Meadows** to the south, a tranquil natural area with marked trails and abundant wildlife; the **Pitchcroft** (100 acres), home of Worcester Racecourse, where horse racing has taken place since 1718; **Gheluvelt Park** to the north of the city, a beautiful memorial park straddling Barbourne Brook; and, to the east, **Fort Royal Park**, the site of the Battle of Worcester in 1651. There's also a number of pleasant walks along the River Severn.

Worcester Bridge

After you've done the sights, Worcester has a multitude of restaurants, cafés and pubs, and if you fancy a bit of shopping there's the usual high street names plus a profusion of independent boutiques, along with a general market in Angel Place (Wed-Sat 9am-4.30pm). Worcester has a lively nightlife with variety of theatres, cinemas, bars and clubs, including an outpost of London's Tramps nightclub.

Bradford City Hall (see page 138)

3.
Unexpected Pleasures

This chapter highlights some of the UK's largely unheralded cities, which offer a surprising treasure trove of sights and attractions. They include the ancient Roman cities of Carlisle, Colchester and Rochester, the historic ports of Hull, Plymouth and Portsmouth, and the Victorian industrial powerhouses of Bradford, Coventry, Nottingham and Sheffield. Here you can revel in Britain's glorious past, from Roman castles and medieval abbeys to Tudor forts and stately homes, from grandiose Victorian civic masterpieces to the legacies of the country's proud industrial heritage, when Britain ruled the world.

Bradford

Address: Bradford BD1 1HY (visitbradford.com)

Getting there: air (Leeds-Bradford, 7mi), rail (Bradford Forster Sq, West Yorkshire Metro), road (M62/M606, A629/A647/A658)

Highlights: Cathedral, Wool Exchange, Cartwright Hall, Boiling Hall, Lister Mills, Bradford Industrial Museum, National Science & Media Museum, Bradford City Park, Alhambra Theatre

Nearby: Halifax, Haworth, Ilkley, Keighley, **Leeds**, Saltaire Village, Shipley

Sleep

- **Luxury:** Great Victoria Hotel (4*), Bridge St, BD1 1JX (01274-728706).
- **Moderate:** Jurys Inn (4*), 2 Thornton Rd, BD1 2DH (01274-848500).
- **Budget:** Midland Hotel (3*), Forster Sq, BD1 4HU (01274-735735).

Historically part of the West Riding of Yorkshire, Bradford is located nine miles west of Leeds in the foothills of the Pennines. It's the third largest city (it received city status in 1974) in Yorkshire and the Humber, after Leeds and Sheffield. From a small town in the Middle Ages, Bradford grew to become an important manufacturing town in the 18th century and by the 19th century was a prominent centre of textile manufacture, rapidly becoming the 'wool capital of the world'. After a decline in manufacturing from the mid-20th century, the city has made a strong recovery and became the first UNESCO City of Film in 2009 due to its long history of film and filmmaking.

What better way to begin than with a visit to handsome **Bradford Cathedral**, set in tranquil gardens. Dating from the 14th century and much enlarged since (becoming a cathedral in 1919), it's packed with interesting features including some of William Morris's earliest stained glass; bronze and embroidery by Ernest Sichel; and sculpture by John Flaxman. Other notable buildings include majestic Italianate **Bradford City Hall** (1873) overlooking Centenary Square, noted for its 220ft Venetian-style bell/clock tower; the Gothic Revival **Wool Exchange Building** (1867), now a Waterstones bookshop; **Cartwright Hall** (1904), the city's civic art gallery in the Manningham district, with a gallery dedicated to Bradford-born David Hockney; **St George's Hall** (1853), the UK's oldest concert hall that's still in use; **Boiling Hall**, the oldest building in Bradford dating from the 14th century, now a museum and education centre; Italianate **Lister Mills** (1838) in attractive Lister

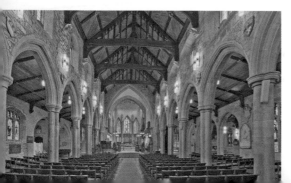

Bradford Cathedral

Park, once the world's largest silk factory; and the magnificent **Alhambra Theatre** (1913), named after the Alhambra Palace in Granada (Spain).

Bradford is home to a number of museums and galleries, including the **National Science and Media Museum**, focusing on photography, cinema, television, animation, videogaming and the internet (etc.); the **Peace Museum** – the only UK museum dedicated to the history and stories of peace, peacemakers and peace movements – **Bradford Industrial Museum**, established 1974 in Moorside Mills, which specialises in local industry, particularly printing and textile machinery; and the **Impressions Gallery**, a renowned independent contemporary photography gallery.

- **Akbars:** popular South Asian restaurant serving classic dishes (1272-1280 Leeds Rd, BD3 8LF, 01274-773311, Mon-Fri 5pm-midnight, Sun 4.30pm-12.30am, closed Sat, £),

- **Cona Restaurant:** steakhouse offering prime beef cuts and seasonal dishes (20 E Parade, BD1 5HD, 01274-727747, Wed-Sat 5-10pm, Sun noon-5pm, closed Mon-Tue, ££).

- **My Lahore:** South Asian café-bar serving Indian and eclectic dishes (52 Great Horton Rd, BD7 1AL, 01274-308508, daily 11am/noon-midnight, 1am Fri-Sat, £).

Saltaire Village

Don't neglect to visit magnificent **Saltaire Village** (3mi north in Shipley), a UNESCO World Heritage Site, where Titus Salt (1803-1876) built a vast mill and model workers' village in 1853.

---

usual big names. When it comes to leisure, the city offers a multitude of restaurants, particularly if you like Indian food (it's the 'curry capital of Britain'), while there's sufficient pubs (try City Vaults), bars, clubs, theatres and cinemas to satisfy most visitors.

As for green spaces, the city centre offers a number of parks and gardens with many more on the outskirts. Don't miss the award-winning, high-tech water feature in **Bradford City Park** (adjacent to City Hall) where 100 fountains, laser lights, mist and water effects create an amazing display. Bradford is an exciting shopping destination, particularly for Asian wares (try Bombay Stores), while the unique subterranean **Sunbridge Wells** and the **Broadway** shopping centre offer the

Alhambra Theatre

Carlisle

Address: Carlisle CA3 8JE (discovercarlisle.co.uk)

Getting there: air (Carlisle Lake District, 6mi), rail (Carlisle, Northern), road (M6, A7, A689)

Highlights: Cathedral, Castle, City Walls, Citadel, Old Town Hall, Guildhall Museum, Tullie House Museum & Art Gallery, Market Hall, rivers

Nearby: Gretna Green, Hadrian's Wall, Kielder Forest Park, **Kendal & Lake District**, North Pennines, Penrith, Solway Coast

The county town of Cumbria, Carlisle – at the confluence of the rivers Eden, Caldew and Petteril – is located in northwest England ten miles south of the Scottish border. The city has a turbulent 2,000-year history of wars and invasions, having been fought over for centuries between the English and Scots (and everyone else), culminating in the Jacobite rising in 1745. The city began life as a Roman settlement, established to serve the forts on Hadrian's Wall, although at the time of the Norman Conquest in 1066 it was part of Scotland and wasn't even recorded in

- **Luxury:** Crown & Mitre (3*), English St, CA3 8HZ (01228-525491).
- **Moderate:** County Hotel (3*), 9 Botchergate, CA1 1QP (01228-531316).
- **Budget:** Hallmark Hotel (3*), Court Sq, CA1 1QY (0330-028 3401).

the 1086 *Domesday Book* (Carlisle was captured by the Normans in 1092). During the Industrial Revolution Carlisle was transformed into a densely populated mill town. Today, it has some 350 listed buildings and is the main cultural, commercial and industrial centre for north Cumbria.

Carlisle Castle (English Heritage) – built by William Rufus, son of William the Conqueror, in 1093 – remains relatively intact and once served as a prison for Mary, Queen of Scots. Since 1932 it has housed the **Museum of Military Life**, spanning over 300 years of local military history. Also of note is a section of the 12th-century **City Walls**, which has been preserved and incorporated into a row of buildings (10-22 West Walls), and the **Citadel** (1541), used as courts until recently, a group of impressive oval towers at the southern end of the city walls built to replace the medieval Botcher Gate. Other historic buildings include the **Old Town Hall**, which dates back to 1668; **St Cuthbert's Church** (1778-79), a Georgian church with red sandstone brickwork whose church hall is a splendid **Tithe Barn** dating from 1480; the **Guildhall Museum** – believed to date from the late

Carlisle Castle

14th century – with exhibits related to the city's medieval trade guilds; **Tullie House Museum & Art Gallery** (1893), housed in a handsome converted Jacobean mansion; and striking **Carlisle Railway Station**, built in 1847 by Sir William Tite in Tudor-Gothic style.

Carlisle has a number of spacious green spaces, including beautiful **Bitts Park** north of the castle adjoining the River Eden, and nearby **Eden Bridge Gardens**, an Italian garden designed by Thomas Mawson. If you fancy a spot of retail therapy, Carlisle has a number of shopping centres (the Lanes and Carlyle's Court) and the **Victorian Market Hall** (Mon-Sat 8am-5pm), plus a profusion of independent shops. When you're famished, the city offers many outstanding restaurants and cafés, while night owls will love the array of lively pubs, bars, clubs and music venues, along with the **Sands Centre**, offering a theatre, music, variety and comedy.

Carlisle Cathedral

Food & Drink

- **Alexandros Greek Restaurant:** classic and original Greek dishes plus a deli (68 Warwick Rd, CA1 1DR, 01228-592227, Tue-Sat noon-1.30pm, 5-10pm, closed Sun-Mon, £).

- **David's Restaurant:** refined, seasonal British-European cuisine (62 Warwick Rd, CA1 1DR, 01228-523678, Tue-Sat noon-3.30pm, 6-11pm, closed Sun-Mon, ££).

- **Penny Blue:** stylish bar/restaurant serving tapas and grill dishes (20-34 Warwick Rd, CA1 1AB, 01228-210241, Wed-Fri, Sun noon-8pm, Sat noon-10pm, closed Mon-Tue, £-££).

Carlisle Cathedral

The handsome cathedral was founded as an Augustinian priory in 1122 and became a cathedral in 1133. It's the second smallest of England's ancient cathedrals, noted for its figurative stone carving, medieval choir stalls and misericords, magnificent choir ceiling and its beautiful east window, the largest Flowering Decorated Gothic window in England.

Colchester

Sleep

i

Address: Colchester CO1 1PJ (visitcolchester. com)

Getting there: air (Southend, 24mi), rail (Colchester, Greater Anglia), road (A12/A120, A133/134)

Highlights: Castle & Museum, Roman Walls, Dutch Quarter, Water Tower, Town Hall, Hollytrees Museum, Castle Park, Zoo, Arts Centre, theatres

Nearby: Clacton-on-Sea, East Bergholt, Dedham Vale AONB, Mersea Island

- **Luxury:** Greyfriars (4*), High St, CO1 1UG (01206-575913).
- **Moderate:** Wivenhoe House (4*), Park Rd, Wivenhoe, CO4 3SQ (01206-863666).
- **Budget:** Holiday Inn Colchester (3*), Abbotts Ln, 8 Ash Green, CO6 3QL (0333-320 9326).

Situated on the River Colne in Essex, Colchester is a historic market town 50 miles northeast of London, the second-largest town (after Norwich) in East Anglia. Dating from 43AD, it's the oldest recorded Roman town (*Camulodunum*) in Britain – allegedly the oldest town in Britain full stop – and for a period was the capital of Roman Britain. Burnt to the ground by Boadicea's Iceni tribe in AD60, it never regained its former prominence,

and after the fall of the Roman Empire in AD410 it passed through the hands of the Saxons, Vikings and Normans.

Colchester was granted its first royal charter in 1189 and was the largest town in Essex throughout the Middle Ages. Its woollen cloth industry developed rapidly from the late 14th century and by the 16th century it was one of the most prosperous wool towns in England (boosted by an influx of Flemish weavers). The town suffered dreadfully during the English Civil War and the Great Plague in 1665, but by the 18th century was once again

Castle Museum

Colchester Castle

Roman Theatre, Colchester (artist's impression)

Food & Drink

- **Greyfriars:** superb 'Art Deco' hotel restaurant serving modern European cuisine (High St, CO1 1UG, 01206-575913, all day/evening dining, open 7 days a week, ££).
- **Loofer's:** popular café offering Mediterranean influenced food (1 Culver St, CO1 1JG, 01206-573500, Mon-Sat 8am-6pm, Sun 10am-5pm, £).
- **Purple Dog:** pub dating from 1647 offering award-winning ales and home-made food (42 Eld Ln, CO1 1LS, 01206-564995, Sun-Thu 11am-11pm, Fri 10am-midnight, Sat 9.30am-1am, £).

prosperous, although its cloth industry went into terminal decline. An economic recovery in the Victorian era was led by new industries such as engineering, when the population more than trebled. Today, it's the fastest growing town in the east of England and a popular tourist destination.

Where better to start than with the Romans, whose history can be seen throughout the town. Colchester's Roman wall is the oldest and longest surviving town wall in Britain, built 65-80AD to defend the town after the Boudiccan rebellion, which includes Balkerne Gate, the original main entrance to the town. A circular walk of two miles follows the course of the wall and its surviving parts. Off Maidenburgh Street are the remains of a **Roman Theatre**, while the only known Roman circus in Britain was discovered in 2005 just north of Abbey Field, seating 8,000 spectators.

The town's most prominent historic building and main attraction is **Colchester Castle**, built on the remains of the Roman Temple of Claudius. Founded by William the Conqueror, the castle was built around the same time as the Tower of London (1078). The **Castle Museum** features a superb exhibition of Roman history and artefacts, including the stunning Fenwick Hoard of Roman jewellery discovered in 2014. The town also boasts Saxon and Norman churches, and countless timber-framed buildings, some of which still bear the scars of the English Civil War. More recent buildings include Britain's oldest Victorian **Water Tower** (1883),

Castle Park

Dutch Quarter

Some of Colchester's most picturesque streets are in the so-called **Dutch Quarter**. In the 16th century Colchester was home to many Flemish Protestant refugees fleeing religious persecution, although the houses actually pre-date their arrival and were formerly inhabited by the Jewish community and other immigrants. Today, it's a quiet residential area just north of the High Street.

close to the Balkerne Gate, and the splendid Baroque **Town Hall** (1902), which features a 162ft tower and magnificent function rooms.

Colchester is home to a number of museums in addition to the **Castle Museum.** Also in Colchester Castle Park is **Hollytrees Museum**, a social history museum located in a handsome 18th-century Georgian townhouse, while nearby on the High Street is the **Natural History Museum**, housed in the former All Saints' Church. Also worth a visit is **Firstsite**, an innovative arts and cultural centre in a striking curved building, designed by the Uruguayan architect Rafael Viñoly. Nearby, **Minories Galleries** (run by the Colchester School of Art) is a contemporary art gallery housed in a Georgian building.

Colchester Castle Park is blessed with over 600 mature trees, with the River Colne flowing through its northern section, where there are some lovely waterside walks. It also features a number of beautiful gardens, including **Avignon Garden** commemorating the twinning of Colchester with Avignon in France in 1972, and **Wetzlar Garden** (1979) – located to the side of Hollytrees Museum – which celebrates the city's twinning with the German city of Wetzlar in 1969. Around four miles outside the town is **Colchester Zoo**, home to many rare and endangered species, while the world-famous **Beth Chatto Gardens** are six miles away.

If it's entertainment you're after, the flourishing **Colchester Arts Centre**, a multi-function arts venue housed in former St Mary-at-the-Walls church (1872), is home to the repertory **Mercury Theatre**, offering a comprehensive programme of music, performance and comedy. Colchester also has two amateur theatres, the **Headgate Theatre** and the university **Lakeside Theatre**.

There's plenty to keep your tastebuds tickled in Colchester, from traditional pubs to inviting cafés, fast food to fine dining, while shopping fans will be delighted with the town's big name outlets, wide variety of independent shops and weekly market (Fri-Sat). For night owls, Colchester offers an abundance of lively pubs, bars, clubs, music venues and two cinemas.

Coventry

Address: Coventry CV1 5RR (visitcoventry.co.uk, coventrycitycentre.co.uk)

Getting there: air (Birmingham, 10mi), rail (Coventry, West Midlands), road (M6/69, A45/46, A444)

Highlights: Cathedral, medieval buildings, Holy Trinity Church, Guildhall, Bond's Hospital, Herbert Art Gallery & Museum, Lady Herbert's Gardens

Nearby: **Birmingham**, Kenilworth Castle, Nuneaton, Royal Leamington Spa, Rugby

An ancient cathedral city in the West Midlands, 19 miles south east of Birmingham, Coventry is the 12th largest city in the UK. It suffered severe bomb damage in 1940 during the Second World War, when over 4,000 homes were destroyed along with the city's medieval centre and the cathedral. (Coventry is dubbed the 'City of Peace and Reconciliation' due to its forgiveness for this act – coventrycityofpeace.uk.) However, despite the destruction, Coventry still boasts a rich heritage of historic buildings and was the UK City of Culture in 2021.

The Romans founded a settlement in Baginton (south of today's city) next to the River Sowe and the area was later occupied by Saxons and Danes. In the 12th century the Normans constructed a castle, later demolished and St Mary's Guildhall built on the site. By the 14th century Coventry was a major cloth trading centre and throughout the Middle Ages was one of the largest and most important towns in England. In the 18th and 19th centuries it was a leading watch and clock-making centre, and later had important bicycle, motorcycle, automobile (it's the birthplace of Britain's motor industry), machine tool and aircraft industries.

Today's modernist **Coventry Cathedral** – designed by Sir Basil Spence and consecrated in 1962 – sits alongside the ruins of the old 14th-century Gothic

Sleep

• **Luxury:** Ramada Hotel & Suites (4*), The Butts, CV1 3GG (024-7623 8110).

• **Moderate:** Doubletree by Hilton (4), Paradise Way, CV2 2ST (024-7660 3000).

• **Budget:** Hotel Quality Coventry (3*), Birmingham Rd, Allesley, CV5 9BA (024-7640 3835).

Coventry Cathedral

Coventry Council House

cathedral, destroyed by German bombs in 1940. The cathedral's interior is notable for its huge tapestry of Christ designed by Graham Sutherland, the emotive sculpture of the *Mater Dolorosa* by John Bridgeman in the east end, the striking abstract baptistry window designed by John Piper, and Sir Jacob Epstein's triumphant sculpture of St Michael and the Devil on the exterior. Also worth a visit is majestic 12th-century **Holy Trinity Church**, the only complete medieval church remaining in Coventry, with one of the tallest (236ft) non-cathedral spires in the UK. Another significant church is **St John the Baptist Church**, an imposing 14th-century building with some splendid medieval stone carvings.

The remnants of the **City Walls & Gates** are a rare 14th-century survivor, which include Cook Street and Swanswell Gate and the best-preserved section of the wall in the grounds of Lady Herbert's Gardens. Other notable historic buildings include **St Mary's Guildhall**, built 1340-42 (much altered and extended in 1460), which houses a collection of royal portraits from the 17th-19th centuries, arms and armour, fine stained glass and an important tapestry dating from around 1500. One of Coventry's best-preserved historic buildings is 15th-century, timber-framed **Lychgate Cottages**,

- **Antalya:** casual restaurant serving superb Turkish cuisine (124 Walsgrave Rd, CV2 4AX, 024-7627 8488, daily 11am-11pm, £).
- **Ristorante Da Vinci:** elegant restaurant offering classic Italian cuisine (50 Earlsdon St, CV5 6EJ, 024-7671 3554, daily 10am-10/10.30pm, £-££).
- **Turmeric Gold:** award-winning Indian cuisine in cosy dining room (166 Spon St, CV1 3BB, 024-7622 6603, daily 5.30-9.30pm, 8.30pm Sun, £-££).

close to Holy Trinity Church, while on Hill Street stands timber-framed **Old Bablake School & Bond's Hospital**, one of the city's most intriguing groups of buildings dating back to at least the 14th century. Just south of

the centre is **Cheylesmore Manor House**, the remnants of a medieval royal palace thought to date from 1237, which includes a magnificent timber-framed building now better known as the Register Office. Also worthy of mention is **Ford's Hospital** off New Union Street, an early 16th-century, timber-framed almshouse, and **Spon Street**, with its profusion of medieval and Tudor buildings.

Lady Godiva Statue

Coventry's museums include the **Herbert Art Gallery & Museum,** endowed by industrialist Sir Alfred Herbert and housed in an imposing refurbished building, whose collection includes Old Masters, modern art, and local and natural history. Fittingly, the city is also home to **Coventry Transport Museum**, which houses the UK's largest collection of British-made road transport 'vehicles', including some 240 cars and commercial vehicles, 100 motorcycles and 200 bicycles.

In the west of the city is **Weaver's House**, a living museum in a row of 15th-century workers' cottages, while in the east of the city is **Whitefriars Monastery**, the surviving buildings of a Carmelite friary founded in 1342, along with **Charterhouse**, a Carthusian monastery (founded 1385) surrounded by parkland. Later buildings include the handsome Tudor Revival **Council House** (1013–17); the controversial **Elephant Building** (1975), aka Coventry Sports Centre; stunning **Lanchester Library** (2001) and the weird and wonderful futuristic **Engineering and Computing Building** (2012), both at Coventry University. Also of note is the **Lady Godiva Statue** (1949) in Broadgate by Sir William Reid Dick; she allegedly road naked through the streets of Coventry in the 11th century in protest at oppressive taxation imposed by her husband, Leofric, Earl of Mercia.

Coventry isn't blessed with an abundance of green spaces, but has a number of charming small parks and gardens, including **Lady Herbert's Gardens** (1930), nearby historic Swanswell Park and pool, Naul's Mill Park in the north of the city and Greyfriars Green. South of the city is beautiful **War Memorial Park** (48 acres), which commemorates the Coventrians who died in the First World War, while 4½ miles east of the city is magnificent 500-acre **Coombe Country Park** and Cistercian Coombe Abbey, built in 1150 and once owned by Henry VIII. Back in the city there are some inviting walks along Coventry Canal and the **Coventry Canal Basin** in the north of the city.

After you've done the sights you'll find that Coventry is a popular shopping destination with a number of shopping centres (such as the Cathedral Lanes Centre), designer boutiques, independent retailers and markets, and when you're hungry the city has a host of restaurants, cafés, pubs and bars, offering cuisines from around the world. The city also has a number of cinemas and theatres, a casino, and a range of nightclubs and music venues.

City Centre

Hull

Address: Hull HU1 3RQ (visithull.org, visithullandeastyorkshire.com)

Getting there: air (Humberside, 11mi), rail (Hull Paragon, Northern), road (A15/A63/A164/A165/A1079)

Highlights: Minster, Hull & East Riding Museum, Hull Maritime Museum, Wilberforce House, Ferens Art Gallery, The Deep Aquarium, Humber River & Bridge, Trinity Market, Philip Larkin Trail

Nearby: **Beverley**, Grimsby, Scunthorpe, Yorkshire Wolds

A port city in the East Riding of Yorkshire, Kingston-upon-Hull (usually abbreviated to just Hull) lies on the north bank of the Humber Estuary at the mouth of the River Hull, 25 miles inland from the North Sea. The city has some 500 listed buildings and structures and in 2017 was the UK's second City of Culture.

Founded as Wyke on Hull in the late 12th century by the monks of Cistercian Meaux Abbey, it was

Sleep

• **Luxury:** Doubletree by Hilton (4*), 24 Ferensway, HU2 8NH (01482-755500).

• **Moderate:** Kingston Theatre Hotel (3*), 1-2 Kingston Sq, HU2 8DA (01482-225828).

• **Budget:** Ibis Hull City Centre (2*), Osbourne St, HU1 2NL (01482-947950).

renamed Kings-town on Hull in 1299. The chief exports from medieval Hull were wool and cloth, which continued until the 17th century when fishing and shipbuilding were also important industries. The city's rapid growth in the 19th century led to Hull becoming the third largest port in Britain (the main outlet for manufactured goods from the

Hull Minster

fast-growing towns of Yorkshire) and a major passenger port. Hull's prosperity peaked in the decades before the First World War and it suffered widespread destruction

Hull City Hall

Food & Drink

- **Ambiente Tapas:** elegant Spanish restaurant and bar in a former warehouse (5 Humber St, HU1 1TG, 01482-426126, daily 11.30am-10pm, £).

- **Humber Fish Co:** relaxed fish and seafood restaurant (Humber St, HU1 1TU, 01482-326130, Thu-Sat noon-10pm, Sun noon-6pm, closed Mon-Wed, £-££).

- **Marco Pierre White Steakhouse Bar & Grill:** traditional steakhouse from the former Michelin-starred chef (24 Ferensway, HU2 8NH, 01482-947459, daily noon-4pm, 5-10pm, ££).

from bombing in the Second World War. However, after a period of post-industrial decline, the city has been regenerated and is now a popular place to live and visit.

One of Hull's finest historic buildings is **Hull Minster** in the city's Old Town; dating from around 1300, it's the largest parish church in England by area, containing some of the finest medieval brickwork in the country. It's also noted for its stained-glass windows, colourful nave and chancel roof, pew carvings and grand organ (parts of which date from 1622). While in the Old Town, take some time to explore its cobbled streets, such as Prince Street and its colourful Georgian houses. Other notable buildings include 15th-century **St Mary's Church**, restored by Sir Gilbert Scott in the 19th century; handsome **Maister House** (National Trust), a Palladian merchant's house rebuilt in 1743 after a fire; **St Charles**

Borromio church, a splendid Roman Catholic church consecrated in 1829; imposing **Hull City Hall**, a Baroque Revival building constructed 1903-09 with a grand central hall that's now a popular concert venue; and the grand **Guildhall** (1914), the headquarters of Hull City Council.

Hull is noted for its museums, many of which are located in the city's Museum Quarter on the High Street in the Old Town. The **Hull and East Riding Museum** (1925) is housed in a former Customs House and displays items from the prehistoric to the medieval periods; the **Streetlife Museum** is a transport museum, including veteran cars, horse-drawn carriages and vehicles relating to local public transport; while **Wilberforce House** – the birthplace of William Wilberforce MP (1759-1833), a leader of the movement to abolish slavery in the British Empire – traces the history of slavery. Other museums and galleries include the **Hull People's Memorial**, which tells the story of Hull, its residents and soldiers during both World Wars; **Hull Maritime Museum** which explores the seafaring heritage of the city and its environs; and the **Hands on**

History Museum that tells the story of Hull and its people. The latter museum is housed in the old grammar school (1766-1878) – built in 1583 as the Hull Merchant Adventurers' Hall, where William Wilberforce

Old Town

The **Ferens Art Gallery** (1927), named after its benefactor Thomas Ferens, houses an impressive collection of paintings and sculptures, including European Old Masters, portraiture, marine painting, and modern and contemporary British art, while the **Humber Street Gallery** is a contemporary art gallery opened in 2017.

The Deep

studied. Other popular attractions include **The Deep** (2002), one of the UK's most spectacular aquariums (designed by Sir Terry Farrell) containing over 3,000 sea creatures. Nearby on the River Hull is the 212-tonne **Tidal Surge Barrier**, opened in 1980 to protect the city from flooding.

Hull isn't noted for its city centre parks, but the surrounding area offers a wealth of stately homes, parks and gardens. The city's largest park is 130-acre **East Park** (1887), three miles northeast of the centre, containing a 16-acre boating lake and an Animal Education Centre (children's zoo), while **Pickering Park** in the western suburbs boasts a beautiful fishing lake, ornamental gardens and a fine collection of native and exotic trees. A mile north of the centre is attractive **Pearson Park**, Hull's first public park, with ornamental and sensory gardens and aviaries. There are some interesting walks around the old docks and quays, and along the River Hull and Humber waterfront. Also of note is the **Philip Larkin Trail** (thelarkintrail.co.uk), which explores the city through the eyes of the celebrated poet, who lived the greater part of his life in Hull.

Hull has a number of shopping centres, including St Stephens and Princes Quay, which has a Vue Cinema, 12-lane bowling alley and an abundance of eateries, along with Hepworth and Paragon Victorian Arcades, home to some attractive traditional boutiques, and the superb **Trinity Indoor Market** (Mon-Sat). The city's gastronomic and nightlife scene has come on in leaps and bounds in recent years, and Hull now boasts a host of excellent restaurants, cafés, pubs, bars and clubs, along with a number of theatres, cinemas and two casinos.

Humber Bridge

Nottingham

Address: Nottingham NG2 3NG (visit-nottinghamshire.co.uk)

Getting there: air (East Midlands, 12mi), rail (Nottingham, East Midlands), road (M1, A52/A60/A606/A610)

Highlights: Castle, Cathedral, Victorian architecture, Lace Market, National Justice Museum, Nottingham Contemporary, City of Caves, River Trent, Arboretum, The Exchange, pubs

Nearby: Derby, Leicester, Newark, Newstead Abbey, Mansfield, Peak District, **Southwell**

- **Luxury:** Hart's Hotel (4*), Standard Hill, Park Row, NG1 6GN (0115-988 1900).
- **Moderate:** Hilton (4*), Milton St, NG1 3PZ (0115-934 9700).
- **Budget:** Ibis Nottingham Centre (2*), 16 Fletcher Gate, NG1 2FS (0115-985 3600).

The county town of Nottinghamshire, Nottingham is situated on the River Trent in the East Midlands, 45 miles northeast of Birmingham. Some 15 miles to the west, on the other side of the M1 motorway, is Derby, with which Nottingham forms an almost continuous conurbation (although the cities are fierce rivals). Nottingham was granted city status in 1897 and is a major sporting centre, dubbed the 'Home of English Sport'.

There's no evidence of Roman occupation in Nottingham, despite the Roman Fosse Way passing just six miles to the south. The city began life as a small Anglo-Saxon settlement in the 6th century called Snotta inga ham, captured by Danish Vikings in the 9th century. Following the Norman Conquest the Saxon settlement developed into the Borough of Nottingham. Today although little remains of the city's proud industrial past (apart from museums), Nottingham is a thriving modern city – with an award-winning public transport system (including trams reintroduced in 2004) – a UNESCO City of Literature (2015), and a major tourist destination and sports centre.

The city's most prominent building is 12th-century **Nottingham Castle** (see box on page 153), home to the city's Museum & Art Gallery. The Roman Catholic **Cathedral Church of St Barnabas** was designed by Augustus Pugin (of Palace of Westminster fame) and built 1841-44, but the city's oldest church and largest

Old Market Square & Town Hall

St Mary's Church

medieval building is **St Mary's Church** – mentioned in the *Domesday Book* (1086) – although the present church dates from the 14th century and is notable for its Gothic Perpendicular style.

Once the hub of the British Empire's lace industry, the **Lace Market** quarter features a number of handsome red-brick Victorian warehouses, including the **Adams Building** and the **Birkin Building** (re-purposed as fashion boutiques, gastropubs, and creative agencies).

Trent Building

Here you'll also find the **National Justice Museum** (which, bizarrely, displays Oscar Wilde's cell door from Reading Gaol), housed in 14th-century courtrooms, while nearby is the **City of Caves** – a network of sandstone caves in use for over 1,000 years – **St Mary's Church** (see above) and **Nottingham Contemporary**, a vast modern art gallery opened in 2009.

Other museums include the **Museum of Nottingham Life** (social history), the **Brewhouse Yard Museum**, the **William Booth Birthplace Museum** (founder of the Salvation Army) and the **Nottingham Industrial Museum** (in Wollaton Park – see below).

Other buildings of note include the majestic **Theatre Royal & Royal Concert Hall** (1865); **Jesse Boot's Shop** (1882) at 16-22 Goose Gate (now the Larder on Goosegate restaurant – see **Food & Drink** box), the birthplace of the vast Boots pharmacy conglomerate; the

Food & Drink

• **The Cod's Scallops:** superb fish and seafood restaurant (311-313 Mansfield Rd, NG5 2D, 0115-708 0251, Mon-Sat 11.30am-9/9.30pm, closed Sun, £).

• **The Larder on Goosegate:** fine dining restaurant serving classic British-European cuisine (16-22 Goose Gate, NG1 1FF, 0115-950 0111, Tue-Sat 5.30pm-midnight, Fri-Sat noon-2.30pm, closed Sun-Mon, ££).

• **Petit Paris:** casual, Parisienne-style French restaurant from Gordon Ramsay (2 King's Walk, NG1 2AE, 0115-947 3767, telephone for meal times, £-££).

Theatre Royal

Prudential Assurance Building (1893-8); the iconic Art Deco **Trent Building** (1928) at Nottingham University; and the Neo-Baroque **Nottingham Council House** (1929).

The city centre isn't exactly awash with green spaces, although to the north is the enchanting **Arboretum**, the city's oldest public park (1852), home to over 800 trees. Three miles to the west is splendid **Wollaton Hall** Gardens & Deer Park, one of the country's finest Elizabethan mansions set in 500 acres of rolling parkland, while nearby is lovely **Highfields Park** (121 acres) and boating lake close to Nottingham University. Twelve miles to the north is **Newstead Abbey**, a former Augustinian priory founded in 1170, better known as the ancestral home of Lord Byron (1788-1024), while even further north are the remnants (450 acres) of legendary **Sherwood Forest**, home to some of Britain's oldest oak trees.

From high street labels to independent stores and luxury boutiques, Nottingham caters for most shopping desires and all styles, tastes and budgets. The city has a number of shopping malls, including **The Exchange**, the city's first (and most handsome) shopping centre opened in 1929 and the intu Broadmarsh & intu Victoria Centres, while the Lace Market and Hockley Village are home to dozens of independent boutiques. And when you fancy a bite to eat, the city's abundance of fine restaurants is guaranteed to tickle your tastebuds.

Nottingham's legendary nightlife offers something for everyone, with a multitude of pubs – including several, such as **Ye Olde Trip to Jerusalem**, claiming to be the oldest in Britain (1189 in this case) – bars, music venues and clubs, to theatres, cinemas and classical concert venues.

Lace Market

Plymouth

Address: Plymouth PL1 1RJ (visitplymouth.co.uk)

Getting there: air (Exeter, 47mi), rail (Plymouth, GWR), road (A38, A386/A388)

Highlights: Plymouth Hoe, Royal Citadel, Mayflower Museum, Aquarium, beaches, marinas, River Tamar, Beaumont Park, Barbican

Nearby: Buckland Abbey, Dartmoor National Park, **Exeter**, Saltram House, South Devon AONB, Tamar Valley, Tavistock

A port city situated on the south coast of Devon 37 miles southwest of Exeter, Plymouth lies at the mouths of the rivers Plym and Tamar, which along with Plymouth Sound forms the boundary with Cornwall. A Roman trading post developed into the Saxon settlement of Sutton in the 9th century, later renamed Plymouth. With its natural harbour and open access to the Atlantic and English Channel, Plymouth became an important port from the late Middle Ages, from where the Pilgrim

Plymouth Hoe

Sleep

- **Luxury:** Crowne Plaza (4*), Armada Way, PL1 2HJ (01752-639988).
- **Moderate:** Jurys Inn (4*), 50 Exeter St, PL4 0AZ (01752-631000).
- **Budget:** New Continental Hotel (3*), Millbay Rd, PL1 3LD (01752-220782).

Fathers sailed in 1620 to establish the second English colony in America. Throughout the Industrial Revolution, Plymouth grew as a commercial shipping port, while the neighbouring town of Devonport became a strategic Royal Naval shipbuilding and dockyard town. The city's naval importance resulted in widespread destruction by German bombing in World War Two, which led to the city centre being almost completely rebuilt. Plymouth's economy remains strongly influenced by shipbuilding and seafaring – HMNB Devonport is the largest operational naval base in Western Europe – including ferry links to France and Spain.

The best place to start a visit to Plymouth is at **Plymouth Hoe** (Hoe Park), which offers commanding views of Plymouth Sound, Drake's Island and Mount Edgcumbe in Cornwall. The most prominent landmark on the Hoe is **Smeaton's Tower**, John Smeaton's Eddystone Lighhouse originally built on Eddystone Rocks (14 miles to the south) in 1759; dismantled in 1877 it was re-erected on the Hoe. The tower overlooks **Tinside Lido**, an unusual 1930s outdoor lido that sits on the limestone shoreline at the base of the cliff. Also

Barbican Waterfront

on the Hoe is a **Statue of Sir Francis Drake** by Joseph Boehm (1884) and several war memorials, including one commemorating Royal Navy personnel who died in the two world wars and the Armada Memorial (1888), celebrating the tercentenary of the Spanish Armada.

To the east of the Hoe is the dramatic **Royal Citadel** fortress (English Heritage), constructed 1665-75 on the site of Drake's Fort, built 1592-1598 by Sir Francis Drake. The Citadel was the most important English defence for over 100 years, with 70ft-high walls regularly strengthened over the years, particularly in the 1750s when it was equipped with 113 guns. It's still occupied by the military but guided tours are offered. Nearby is the **Mayflower Steps Memorial**, close to where the Pilgrim Fathers set sail on the *Mayflower* for the New World in 1620, and the **Mayflower Museum**, which explores the area's seafaring history and the *Mayflower's* voyage. The memorial is located at the entrance to bustling **Sutton Harbour**, where a nearby footbridge leads to the **National Marine Aquarium** (1998), the UK's largest aquarium home to over 4,000 ocean creatures. Just north of the Mayflower Museum in New Street is **Elizabethan House** (National Trust) and gardens, a rare surviving late 16th-century merchants' house, now a museum. The city's latest attraction is **The Box**, a cultural centre that opened in Spring 2020, incorporating the former Plymouth City Museum and Art Gallery.

Royal Citadel

Sir Francis Drake

Plymouth's most famous resident (born in Tavistock), navigator, privateer and vice-admiral of the Royal Navy, Drake (1540-1596) was mayor of Plymouth 1581-1582. He completed the second circumnavigation of the world in a single expedition from 1577 to 1580, but is better known as second-in-command of the English fleet that defeated the Spanish Armada in 1588.

To the west of Sutton Harbour is **Merchant House Museum**, a fine example of a 16th/17th-century property that was home to three Plymouth mayors, now a local history museum, while just north of the museum is **Prysten House**, Plymouth's oldest building (1487) that's now a restaurant (see **Food & Drink** box). Also nearby is 15th-century **St Andrew's Church**, the original parish church of Sutton; the largest parish church in Devon, it was designated a minster church in 2009. To the west of the city in Stonehouse is **Royal William Yard** (1825-31), a vast former Royal Navy victualling depot that's now one of Plymouth's premier entertainment centres.

When you've done the sights and fancy a spot of shopping, the city centre's West End is home to an abundance of independent shops and indoor Plymouth Market, while to the east is Drake Circus shopping centre with over 70 stores. Sutton Harbour also offers a variety of art galleries, antiques shops and quirky independent boutiques. Plymouth has a host of outstanding restaurants, pubs and cafés, and when the sun goes down there are scores of bars, clubs and live music venues (including Plymouth Pavilions), along with a number of theatres and cinemas.

Also worth a visit is beautiful **Beaumont Park** to the north of Sutton Harbour; **Saltram House** (National Trust) and park, three miles east of the city centre, a splendid Georgian house designed by Robert Adam, sprawling **Mount Edgcumbe Country Park** (885 acres) on the Rame Peninsula overlooking Plymouth Sound (reachable by ferry from the Barbican) and magnificent 700-year-old **Buckland Abbey** (National Trust), Sir Francis Drake's former home, ten miles north of the city.

National Marine Aquarium

Portsmouth

Sleep

Address: Portsmouth PO1 2AB (visitportsmouth. co.uk)

Getting there: air (Southampton, 20mi), rail (Portsmouth, SWR/Southern), road (M27/A3M, A27)

Highlights: Historic Dockyard & ships, medieval buildings, Cathedral, Guildhall, forts, Royal Navy Museum, Portsmouth Museum, D-Day Story, Blue Reef Aquarium, Southsea beach, Gunwharf Quays

Nearby: Brighton, Cowes, Gosport, **Isle of Wight, New Forest,** South Downs, Southampton

- **Luxury:** Marriott Hotel (4*), Southampton Rd, PO6 4SH (023-9238 3151).
- **Moderate:** Queens Hotel (3*), Clarence Parade, Osborne Rd, PO5 3LJ (023-9282 2466).
- **Budget:** Duke of Buckingham, 119 High St, PO1 2HW (023-9282 7067).

A historic port city in Hampshire, Portsmouth (nicknamed Pompey) is located 70 miles southwest of London and 19 miles southeast of Southampton. The city is mainly built on Portsea Island, a low-lying island measuring 9mi^2, the only island city in the UK, while the 'suburb' of Southsea is a popular seaside resort.

Portsmouth's history dates back to Roman times, when they built a fort (*Portus Adurni*) at nearby Portchester in the late 3rd century. After the Romans left Britain in the 5th century the south coast had a turbulent history and was regularly invaded by the Danes. Portsmouth came to prominence as an important port in the late 12th century, receiving a royal charter in 1194, and has been a significant naval port ever since, with the

world's oldest dry dock (built in the 10th century). It was England's first line of defence during the French invasion of 1545 and the world's most heavily fortified town and greatest naval port at the height of the British Empire. Portsmouth – which became a city in 1926 – was heavily bombed during the Second World War, when it was the main embarkation point for the D-Day landings in 1944. Today, it remains the home of the Royal Navy and the

Old Portsmouth

base for around two-thirds of the UK's surface fleet, while the cruise ship and ferry port is the second-busiest (after Dover) in the UK.

The first port of call for anyone visiting Portsmouth should be the **Historic Dockyard**, home to the *Mary Rose* (see box), *HMS Victory* – Lord Nelson's flagship at the Battle of Trafalgar, where he was mortally wounded – and *HMS Warrior*, a 40-gun, steam-powered frigate built in 1859-61, among other important ships. You can purchase a 'Full Navy Ticket' which includes all of Portsmouth's naval attractions except for the *Mary Rose*. The Dockyard is also home to the **National Museum of the Royal Navy**, founded in 1911. Today, the waterfront and Portsmouth Harbour are dominated by the Emirates **Spinnaker Tower** (2005, 560ft), an observation tower affording panoramic views over the city and harbour.

Other attractions in Portsmouth include beautiful **Portsmouth Cathedral** in Old Portsmouth, founded in 1180 (the chancel and transepts remain) and rebuilt in the 17th and 18th centuries. The city is also home to the Roman Catholic **Cathedral of St John the Evangelist**,

Mary Rose

The fascinating **Mary Rose Museum** contains the wreck of the *Mary Rose*, Henry VIII's flagship, which sank in the Solent in 1545 when confronting a French invasion fleet, and was raised in 1982. The museum contains a multitude of artefacts from the ship, including weapons, sailing equipment, naval supplies and personal objects used by the crew.

dedicated in 1882. A short distance from Portsmouth Cathedral is the **Royal Garrison Church** near Clarence Pier, originally called Domus Dei (Hospital of Saint Nicholas and Saint John the Baptist), an almshouse and hospice built around 1212. The nearby **Square Tower** was constructed in 1494 as part of the dockyard's fortifications and served as the home of the Governor of Portsmouth, while the **Round Tower** was constructed in 1490. Further fortifications include **Southsea Castle** (1544), **Fort Cumberland** (1785-1812) and **Lumps Fort** (1859-61). Another building of note is splendid Neo-Classical **Portsmouth Guildhall** (1890), designed by William Hill, now a concert, wedding and conference venue.

The city's wealth of museums includes **Portsmouth Museum** (local history), housed in an imposing building previously part of the Clarence and Victoria Barracks complex; the **D-Day Story**, close to Southsea Castle, which tells the story of Operation Overlord and the Normandy D-Day landings; **Charles Dickens'**

HMS Victory

Spinnaker Tower

Birthplace Museum, Cumberland House Natural History Museum and **Southsea Model Village**.

Although densely populated, Portsmouth has a large number of parks and open spaces, including **Victoria Park** (15 acres), the city's first public park founded in 1878; **Ravelin Park** (4 acres) at the University of Portsmouth; **Baffins Pond** (a wildlife refuge) to the east of the city; **Canoe Lake** and **Rose Garden** on Southsea Seafront; and **Southsea Common**, a large expanse of grassland adjacent to Clarence Esplanade, home to the **Blue Reef Aquarium**.

When it comes to shopping, Portsmouth's biggest draw is **Gunwharf Quays**, a designer outlet shopping mall offering some 90 leading brands at discount prices. High street favourites can be found in Commercial Road and the Cascades Shopping Centre, while Palmerston Road hosts a number of markets. Portsmouth offers an abundance of eateries (although it's short on fine dining), and when the sun goes down there's a profusion of lively pubs, bars, clubs and music venues to while away the night (Guildhall Walk and Palmerston Road are popular nightlife scenes). For theatre lovers there's Kings Theatre and the New Theatre Royal, while Gunwharf Quays is home to a cinema, bowling alley, casino and more.

Food & Drink

• **Algarve's Grill:** popular Portuguese restaurant serving tapas, steaks & seafood (48 Osborne Rd, PO5 3LT, 023-9307 6062, Mon-Sat noon-10pm, Sun noon-8pm, £-££).

• **Becketts:** one of Southsea's most popular British restaurants (with rooms) and a bar (11 Bellvue Ter, Southsea, PO5 3AT, 023-9286 5000, Tue-Fri 5-11pm/midnight, Sat 9am-midnight, Sun 9am-6pm, closed Mon, £).

• **Restaurant 27:** Fine dining French cuisine with set-price and tasting menus (27a S Parade, Southsea, PO5 2JF, 023-9287 6272, Wed-Sat 6.30-9.30pm, Sun noon-2.30pm, closed Mon-Tue, ££).

Also worth a visit is **Gosport**, a 4-minute ferry ride across the harbour, where highlights include the Royal Navy Submarine Museum and the Solent Beach Path.

Portsmouth Cathedral

Rochester

Address: Rochester ME1 1YD (visitmedway.org/see-and-do/destinations/rochester)

Getting there: air (London City, 31mi), rail (Chichester, Southeastern), road (M2, A2/A229)

Highlights: Cathedral, Castle, medieval buildings, Guildhall, Huguenot Museum, River Medway, Castle Gardens & Garth, Charles Dickens' associations

Nearby: Chatham, Gillingham, Kent Downs AONB, Maidstone

Sleep

• **Luxury:** Ship & Trades (3*), Maritime, St Mary's Island, Chatham ME4 3ER (01634-895200).

• **Moderate:** Golden Lion, 147-149 High St, ME1 1EL (01634-880521).

• **Budget:** Travelodge (2*), 11 Corey's Rd, ME1 1GR (0871-984 8484).

Historic Rochester, with its Norman castle and ancient cathedral, is tucked into a bend of the River Medway in Kent, 30 miles southeast of London. Along with its neighbours – Chatham, Gillingham, Strood and a number of villages – it forms an area known as the Medway Towns. For centuries Rochester has been of vital strategic importance due to its position near the confluence of the Thames and the Medway. Neolithic remains have been found in the vicinity of the city, which has been occupied by Celts, Romans (who arrived in 43AD), Jutes, Saxons and Normans.

At the heart of the town is magnificent **Rochester Cathedral**, the second-oldest cathedral in England (after Canterbury), founded in 604 by Bishop Justus. The current Norman building dates from 1080 – built by the French monk Gundulf – and has one of the finest Romanesque façades in England. It features fine examples of later Gothic architecture, along with a glorious 14th-century chapter library door. Just south of the cathedral is the **King's School**, which refers to Henry VIII, although there has been a school here since 604, making it the second-oldest continuously operating school in the world.

Just across the road from the cathedral is one of the best-preserved and finest examples of Norman architecture in England, **Rochester Castle**, whose great keep towers over the River Medway, where the

Rochester Cathedral

Rochester Castle

Romans built the first bridge. Like the cathedral, the castle was begun by Bishop Gundulf (in 1087), incorporating the remains of the Roman city walls which guarded the river crossing. The castle has a chequered history, having been subject to siege three times and partly demolished by King John in 1215. Just one mile from Rochester is the **Historic Dockyard** in Chatham – the most complete surviving dockyard from the age of sail in the world – which is well worth a visit. Established in the mid-1500s, Chatham witnessed the beginning of the Royal Navy's long period of supremacy, and many famous warships were built here, including Nelson's flagship *HMS Victory* (which you can see in Portsmouth, see page 158).

Food & Drink

• **Coopers Arms:** A characterful pub in a 12th-century building (10 St Margaret's St, ME1 1TL, 01634-404298, Sun-Thu noon-11pm, Fri-Sat noon-midnight, £).

• **Don Vincenzo:** Family-run Italian restaurant serving classic and modern dishes (108 High St, ME1 1JT, 01634-408373, Mon-Sat noon-3pm, 6-10pm, Sun noon-8pm, £).

• **Tiny Tim's Tea Rooms:** Popular café offering everything from breakfast and lunch to afternoon tea (5 Northgate, ME1 1LS, 01634-939031, Wed-Sun 10am-4pm, closed Mon-Tue, £).

Other buildings of note include **Restoration House**, a notable city mansion where Charles II stayed on the eve of the restoration of the monarchy in 1660; it served as the model for Miss Havisham's Satis House in Charles Dickens' (see box on page 162) novel *Great Expectations*. Also immortalised by Dickens was the **Six**

Rochester Skyline

HMS Gannet, Chatham

Poor Travellers' House, a Tudor charity 'hotel'; **Eastgate House**, a 16th-17th-century townhouse with a rich history; **Dickens' Swiss Chalet**, where the author wrote some of his greatest works, located in the gardens of Eastgate House; and **Rochester Guildhall**, built in 1687, with a magnificent plaster ceiling and an intricate weather vane featuring a fully-rigged, 18th-century warship. Across the river from Rochester (in Strood) is 13th-century **Temple Manor**, a rare surviving house that once belonged to the Knights Templar.

The Guildhall is home to the excellent **Guildhall Museum** of local history founded in 1897, which tells the fascinating history of the Medway, including the life and times of Charles Dickens. Rochester is also home to the **Huguenot Museum**, Britain's only museum of Huguenot history, while in nearby Gillingham is the **Royal Engineers Museum**, Kent's largest military museum.

Rochester has some delightful green spaces, including **Castle Gardens** and the **Garth**, a tranquil place for reflection near the cathedral where Bishop Gundulf built his priory. **The Esplanade** and **Churchfields** bordering the Medway comprise a large expanse of grassland with some attractive walks, while

The Vines next to Restoration House (see above) is an attractive small park with majestic trees. In the south of the city are the expansive green spaces of **Jackson's Field** and **Victoria Gardens**, while nature lovers may wish to visit nearby spectacular **North Kent Marshes**, one of the most important natural wetlands in northern Europe for migrating birds.

Rochester isn't particularly noted for its cultural activities (the Georgian Royal Theatre is now an events centre), although the amateur **Medway Little Theatre** on the High Street keeps theatrical traditions alive. The city hosts a number of concerts and festivals throughout the year, including the celebrated **Sweeps Festival** in May, which recreates the chimney sweeps' traditional holiday, and two **Dickens' Festivals**. Rochester (and the Medway district) offers a wide range of restaurants to suit every pocket and taste, plus an abundance of historic pubs, while the quaint Victorian High Street contains many original independent shops and a nearby monthly farmers' market.

Charles Dickens

Rochester is closely associated with novelist Charles Dickens (1812-1870), who spent part of his childhood in Chatham and returned to the area in later life as a successful writer. He featured the town in many of his works and many buildings he depicted can still be seen today.

Sheffield

Address: Sheffield S1 2HH (welcometosheffield.co.uk)

Getting there: air (Doncaster-Sheffield, 20mi), rail (Doncaster, Northern), road (M1, A61/A57)

Highlights: Cathedral, industrial heritage, Town Hall, Weston Park Museum, Kelham Island Museum, Millonnium Gallery, Graves Art Gallery, Peace Gardens

Nearby: Barnsley, Chesterfield, Doncaster, Peak District, Rotherham, Worksop

Located in South Yorkshire on the rivers Sheaf (from which it gets its name) and Don, underrated Sheffield ('Steel City') is the seventh largest English metropolitan district by population. The area has been inhabited for at least 10,000 years and was home to a Roman settlement in the first century AD. The Normans built a castle in Sheffield around which a small market town developed. The town was already known for the production of knives by the 14th century and in the early 17th century was the main centre of cutlery production in England outside London. Sheffield played an important role in the Industrial Revolution, when many significant inventions and technologies were developed in the city, particularly regarding stainless and crucible steel. International competition caused a decline in the steel industry in the '70s, which coincided with the collapse of coal mining in the area. Today, post-industrial Sheffield is a friendly, modern city with a modern tram system and much to entertain visitors.

Sleep

- **Luxury:** Leopold Hotel (4*), 2 Leopold St, S1 2GZ (0114-252 4000).
- **Moderate:** Mercure Sheffield Kenwood Hall (4*), Kenwood Rd, S7 1NQ (0114-258 3811).
- **Budget:** OYO Sheffield Metropolitan (3*), Blonk St, S1 2AU (020-8089 8579).

The city is noted for its fine architecture, although it's home to few Grade I listed buildings, one of which is **Sheffield Cathedral**, originally a parish church elevated to cathedral status in 1914 (Sheffield was granted its city charter in 1893). Parts of the cathedral date from a 13th-century church, while the sanctuary and chancel are from the 15th century. Sheffield also boasts the **Cathedral Church of St Mario**, built 1846-50 in Gothic Revival style and a superb example of an English Roman Catholic cathedral with much fine interior decoration.

Sheffield Cathedral

Food & Drink

- **Ego:** Mediterranean restaurant & bar offering everything from tagines to mezze and tapas (88 Surrey St, S1 2LH, 0114-278 2004, daily 11am-11pm, £-££).

- **The Milestone:** contemporary gastropub with exposed beams serving locally-sourced British cuisine (84 Green Ln, S3 8SE, 0114-272 8327, Mon, Thu-Sat noon-11/11.30pm, Sun noon-8pm, closed Tue-Wed, £-££).

- **Silversmiths:** contemporary Yorkshire cuisine in former cutlery works (111 Arundel St, S1 2NT, 0114-270 6160, Wed-Fri 5-10pm, Sat noon-3pm, 5-10pm, Sun noon-5pm, closed Mon-Tue, ££).

Another majestic building is **Sheffield Town Hall** (1890-97), which was criticised during its construction for its expensive embellishments, including carvings by F. W. Pomeroy and friezes depicting Sheffield industries, along with a 210ft clock tower surmounted by a statue of Vulcan. The impressive interior is well worth a look. Other handsome buildings include **Sheffield City Hall** (1932), a Neo-Classical concert hall with a giant portico dominating Barker's Pool, while **Cutlers' Hall** (1832) is the HQ of the Company of Cutlers

in Hallamshire. The city is also known for its wealth of Brutalist and Modernist buildings.

Sheffield is celebrated for its museums, particularly those relating to its industrial heritage, including **Kelham Island Museum** (see box opposite). Four miles south of the city centre is **Abbeydale Industrial Hamlet**, a museum located on a former steel-working site on the River Sheaf, with a history going back to the 13th century. It consists of a number of dwellings and workshops that comprised the Abbeydale Works, a scythe-making plant in operation until the 1930s. The third of Sheffield's industrial museums is **Shepherd Wheel**, a working museum and water wheel in a former grinding workshop located on Porter Brook to the southwest of the city centre.

Other museums include **Weston Park Museum** (1875), Sheffield's largest museum, one mile west of the city centre in picturesque Weston Park. The museum houses a wide range of collections, including archaeology, ivories, metalwork, natural history, social history, visual art and world cultures. The **Millennium Gallery** (2001) in Arundel Gate is a modern art gallery and museum, whose permanent displays include the (John) Ruskin Collection and the Metalwork Collection

Sheffield Town Hall

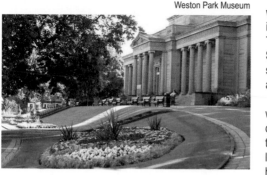

Weston Park Museum

comprising over 13,000 objects made in Sheffield. The nearby **Graves Art Gallery**, located above the Central Library, houses the city's collection of British and European art, including works by JMW Turner, Alfred Sisley and Sir Stanley Spencer. Sheffield is also home to the **National Emergency Services Museum** and the **National Videogame Museum**, the 'home of videogames', housed in iconic Castle House.

Somewhat surprisingly, some 60 per cent of Sheffield's metropolitan area is green space, a third of which lies within the Peak District National Park,

with over 250 parks, woodlands and gardens. These include the **Peace Gardens** (city square) opposite the Town Hall, the nearby indoor **Sheffield Winter Garden**, **Sheffield Botanical Gardens** (19 acres), two miles southwest of the centre, Norfolk Heritage Park (1848) and Graves Park & Animal Farm south of the city.

Sheffield has a number of shopping centres along with an abundance of appealing independent shops and quirky shopping districts, while three miles northeast of the city is the vast **Meadowhall** shopping centre, the largest in Yorkshire. When you fancy a break, the city has a vast range of excellent restaurants, pubs and cafés catering for all budgets and tastes, while its lively night-time scene can compete with the best, with a number of theatres (including the Crucible and Victorian Lyceum in Tudor Square), a plethora of great pubs and bars, and an abundance of nightclubs and live music venues, including the City Hall, O2 Academy, Foundry, Leadmill and Corporation.

Kelham Island Museum

Situated alongside the River Don, Kelham Island is a man-made island resulting from the construction of a mill race in the 12th century. The museum tells the story of Sheffield's industry, from light trades and skilled workmanship to mass production during the Industrial Revolution.

Women of Steel statue

Portmeirion (see page 191)

4.

Gateway Gems

The towns included in this chapter – although worthy of inclusion in their own right – are gateways to some of the country's most magnificent national parks and areas of outstanding natural beauty. They include the delightful towns of Bakewell and Buxton in the Derbyshire Dales and Peak District; historic Cirencester in the Cotswolds and beautiful Beaulieu in the New Forest; charming Great Malvern and Ludlow in the Malvern and Shropshire Hills respectively; handsome Harrogate in the Yorkshire Dales and invigorating Inverness in the Scottish Highlands; captivating Kendal – 'Gateway to the Lake District' – and enchanting Portmeirion and Snowdonia National Park.

Bakewell & the Derbyshire Dales

Sleep

- **Luxury:** Fischer's Baslow Hall (4*), Calver Rd, Baslow, DE45 1RR (01246-583259).
- **Moderate:** Rutland Arms (3*), The Square, DE45 1BT (01629-812812).
- **Budget:** Castle Inn (3*), Castle St, DE45 1DU (01629-812103).

Address: Bakewell DE45 1BT (visitpeakdistrict.com/explore/towns-and-villages/bakewell-p680091)

Getting there: air (East Midlands, 17mi), rail (Bakewell, Midland), road (A6, A619)

Highlights: All Saints Church, Old House Museum, Bakewell Bridge, River Wye, historic stately homes, tea rooms, quirky shops, Bakewell tart & pudding

Nearby: Buxton, Chatsworth House, Chesterfield, Haddon Hall, Matlock, Rowsley

A small market town in the Derbyshire Dales (the southern part of the Peak District National Park), picturesque Bakewell ('Capital of the Peak') lies on the River Wye, 13 miles southwest of Sheffield. Famous for its Bakewell pudding (and tart – not the same!), the town dates back to Anglo-Saxon times when it was part of the Kingdom of Mercia. By Norman times, Bakewell had gained some importance and was mentioned in the *Domesday Book*. A market was established in 1254 and the town developed as a trading centre; today, it's an important agricultural and market town and a popular tourist centre.

The best place to start a visit is with a tour of the town's delightful traffic-free labyrinth of narrow streets, alleyways, courtyards and arcades – not forgetting Bath Gardens – dotted with quirky shops and eateries. Among the town's most important buildings is **All Saints Church**, founded in AD920 – the churchyard contains two Saxon crosses – although the present church was constructed in the 12th-13th centuries and rebuilt in the 1840s. **Bakewell Bridge**, a five-arched bridge over the River Wye, was constructed in the 13th century, while the local history **Old House Museum** is housed in a 16th-century Tudor cottage, which later became a gentleman's residence. North of the town is **Lumford Mill** (1777), a former cotton mill (now a business park) built by Richard Arkwright, while a little further northwest up the River Wye is charming **Ashford-in-the-Water**, a village with a handsome packhorse bridge, home to Ashford Hall estate, an elegant Palladian mansion and Victorian landscaped park.

Bakewell

Chatsworth House

Located on the banks of the River Derwent, 4½ miles northeast of Bakewell, Chatsworth is the seat of the Dukes of Devonshire, home to the Cavendish family since 1549. It contains an important collection of paintings, furniture, Old Master drawings, neoclassical sculptures, books and other artefacts. You can also explore the estate's 105-acre garden, including an arboretum, rock garden, fountains and sculptures.

Although Bakewell is a charming town, one of the main reasons people flock here is to explore the surrounding **Derbyshire Dales** and **Peak District National Park** (see also **Buxton** on page 173), and to visit Chatsworth House and Haddon Hall (see below). The Peak District is Britain's oldest National Park with 555mi² of high moorland hills, rocky tors and serene river valleys. One of the park's most beautiful trails, the Monsal Trail (for cyclists and walkers), runs along the former Midland Railway line for 8½ miles from Coombs Viaduct (1mi south of Bakewell) along the Wye Valley to Topley Pike junction in Wyedale (3mi east of Buxton).

Northeast of Bakewell is glorious **Chatsworth House** (see box), one of England's most famous stately homes, while three miles south is **Haddon Hall**, which dates back to the 11th century with later medieval and Tudor additions. The former seat of the Dukes of Rutland, it has been described as 'the most perfect house to survive from the Middle Ages' by Simon Jenkins (in

Food & Drink

- **The Manners:** traditional pub (with rooms) serving excellent food (Haddon Rd, DE45 1EP, 01629-812756, telephone for meal times, £-££).
- **Piedaniel's:** refined French-accented cooking in intimate dining room (Bath St, Bakewell DE45 1BX, 01629-812687, Tue-Sat noon-3pm, 7-11pm, closed Sun-Mon, ££).
- **White Lion:** laid-back gastropub with classic British menu (Main St, Great Longstone, DE45 1TA, 01629-640252, Tue-Fri noon-2.30pm, 5-9pm, Sat noon-9pm, Sun noon-6pm, closed Mon, £).

England's Thousand Best Houses), with a spectacular banqueting hall and minstrels' gallery, magnificent tapestries, chapel frescos and impressive long gallery – not forgetting its lovely gardens. Nearby Lathkill Dale is one of the prettiest of the **Derbyshire Dales.**

After a day's hiking or touring, why not head back to Bakewell for afternoon tea and some delicious Bakewell pudding at the Old Original Bakewell Pudding Shop?

Haddon Hall

Beaulieu & the New Forest

Sleep

- **Luxury:** Montagu Arms (4*), Palace Ln, SO42 7ZL (01590-624467).
- **Moderate:** Beaulieu Inn (3*), Beaulieu Rd, SO42 7YQ (0800-444441).
- **Budget:** The Turfcutters Arms, East Boldre Rd, East Boldre, SO42 7WL (01590-612003).

Charming Beaulieu village – the name, pronounced 'Bewley', derives from the Latin *bellus locus regis*, meaning 'beautiful place of the king' – is situated in the southeast of the New Forest National Park in Hampshire, at the heart of the 7,000-acre Beaulieu estate. A National Park (England's smallest) since 2005, the New Forest (see below) is a nature lover's paradise, noted for its heathland and open moors, ancient woodland and forest trails, cliff-top walks, native free-roaming ponies and charming villages where life proceeds at a leisurely pace.

The **Beaulieu Estate** is home to the National Motor Museum, Palace House, Beaulieu Abbey ruins and much more, which you can explore via unlimited rides on the 'Skytrain' monorail and a replica 1912 open-top bus. Situated at the head of the picturesque Beaulieu River, the village dates back to the 13th century, when it grew up around the abbey founded in 1204 by Cistercian monks on land granted to them by King John, who had a royal hunting lodge at Beaulieu. The king had quarrelled with the Cistercian order early in his reign and established the abbey to atone for his past oppressions.

Palace House, originally the 13th-century gatehouse of **Beaulieu Abbey**, has been the ancestral home of a branch of

Beaulieu Palace House

National Motor Museum

The NMM contains a collection of over 250 iconic cars and motorcycles from the early days of the motor car to today. Exhibits include vehicles used to set world land-speed records and Formula 1 racing cars, while *Top Gear* fans will enjoy exploring the **World of Top Gear**, featuring vehicles that have appeared in the popular BBC series.

the Montagu family since 1538, when it was purchased from the crown by Sir Thomas Wriothesley (later 1st Earl of Southampton) following the Dissolution of the Monasteries by Henry VIII. The house was extended in the 16th century and again in the 19th century and today is a fine example of a Victorian Gothic country house (it's no longer the home of Lord and Lady Montagu, who live in a modern villa on the estate). The house and its attractive gardens are open to the public, while the tranquil remains of **Beaulieu Abbey** are beautifully preserved and an oasis of calm. Among the surviving monastery buildings are the domus – once the lay brothers' living quarters, now used for functions and exhibitions – and the monks' refectory, which became **Beaulieu Parish Church** after the abbey was destroyed.

One of Beaulieu's main attractions is the **National Motor Museum** (see box), opened in 1952 as the Montagu Motor Museum. Beaulieu also has a **Secret Army Exhibition** that tells the story of its role as a top-secret training establishment for special agents of the Special Operations Executive (SOE) during the Second World War. Also part of the Beaulieu Estate is **Buckler's Hard** (2½ miles south of the village), a hamlet on the banks of the Beaulieu River famous for shipbuilding in the 18th century. After you've exhausted the delights of Beaulieu, the New Forest offers a wealth of interesting places to explore.

New Forest: Once a royal hunting ground for William the Conqueror, the New Forest covers an area of around 220mi^2, encompassing parts of Dorset, Hampshire and Wiltshire. In fact, it isn't actually a forest at all but a patchwork of heaths, coastal marshes, mudflats, grassland and farmland, where deer, ponies and cattle roam free. It's recognised as one of the most unique and important 'wilderness' areas in Western Europe – home to thousands of common and rare species of flora and fauna – and a haven for walkers, cyclists and horse-riders.

Beaulieu Abbey

Beaulieu Village

Food & Drink

- **Monty's Inn:** quaint pub serving traditional local dishes (Palace Ln, SO42 7ZL, 01590-614986, Wed-Sun noon-2.30pm, 7-9pm, closed Mon-Tue, £-££).

- **Old Bakehouse:** cosy tea rooms serving tasty food (61 High St, Beaulieu SO42 7YA, 01590-612777, Mon-Sat 8.30/9am-2pm, closed Sun, £).

- **Terrace Restaurant:** superb seasonal/regional British cuisine in handsome hotel (Montagu Arms, Palace Ln, Beaulieu SO42 7ZL, 01590-612324, Wed-Sun noon-2.30pm, 7-9pm, closed Mon-Tue, ££-£££).

from where you can hop aboard a ferry to Yarmouth (40 mins) on the Isle of Wight, or visit Hythe (in the east of the park) and cross Southampton Water to Southampton.

When you fancy a break from sightseeing, the New Forest offers an abundance of superb hotels and restaurants, cosy cafés and historic pubs, and a host of delightful independent shops, boutiques and markets.

Among the many delights of the New Forest are the magnificent 200-acre **Exbury Gardens** and steam railway, the **New Forest Wildlife Park**, **Bolderwood Deer Sanctuary** and **Paulton's** (theme) **Park** – all of which offer the perfect outing if you have kids to entertain – and a bounty of picturesque villages such as Brockenhurst, Burley, Lymington and Lyndhurst. Lymington is a major yachting centre on the Solent,

Ancient Woodland

New Forest Ponies

Acres Down

Buxton & the Peak District

Sleep

- **Luxury:** Palace Hotel & Spa (4*), Palace Rd, SK17 6AG (0871-221 0253).
- **Moderate:** Old Hall Hotel (3*), The Square, SK17 6BD (01298-22841).
- **Budget:** Lee Wood Hotel (Best Western), The Park, Park Rd, SK17 6TQ (01298-23002).

Address: Buxton SK17 6DZ (visitbuxton.co.uk, visitpeakdistrict.com)

Getting there: air (Manchester, 17mi), rail (Buxton, Northern), road (A6, A53, A515)

Highlights: Georgian & Victorian architecture, spas, The Crescent, Pump Room, Museum & Art Gallery, Opera House, River Wye, Pavilion Gdns

Nearby: Bakewell, Castleton, Chesterfield, Edale, Macclesfield, Tideswell

A market and spa town on the River Wye in the Peak District National Park (see box on page 174 and **Bakewell** on page 168) in Derbyshire, regal Buxton has the highest elevation (1,000ft) of any market town in England. Dubbed the 'gateway to the Peak District National Park', it's one of the area's most popular tourist destinations, where its outstanding Georgian and Victorian architecture provides an impressive backdrop to its vibrant range of art, music, theatre and festivals. The Romans established a settlement and baths (*Aquae Arnemetiae*) here in around AD80 and the town became popular with pilgrims wishing to take the waters in the Middle Ages (Mary, Queen of Scots was a notable visitor).

The 18th century saw the town develop into a fashionable spa town with the construction of striking **Crescent** in 1780-89 (it enjoyed another period of development during the Victorian period). Designed by John Carr and based on Bath's Royal Crescent, it was the centrepiece of the 5th Duke of Devonshire's development of Buxton and is one of the most architecturally significant buildings in the country. The Crescent faces the site of St Ann's Well (aka 'the lion's head'), the source of the spa's warm spring water which has flowed for thousands of years. Opposite the

Pavilion Gardens

Peak District National Park

The UK's first National Park (created in 1951), the Peak District is situated mostly in northern Derbyshire, but includes parts of Cheshire, Greater Manchester, Staffordshire and Yorkshire. An area of great diversity, it's mostly split into the southern White Peak and the northern Dark Peak, where most of the moorland – including stark plateaus such as Kinder Scout, the park's highest point – is found and the geology is gritstone. The southern White Peak area is characterised by steep limestone valleys such as Dovedale, with its famous stepping stones, and Lathkill Dale. The park is popular with adventures sports enthusiasts and has an extensive network of public footpaths and cycle trails, rock climbing and caving. The village of Edale, nine miles northeast of Buxton, marks the southern end of the iconic 268-mile Pennine Way hiking route, while nearby is the Blue John Cavern (tours) at Castleton, where Blue John stone is mined. A walking circuit on Mam Tor affords marvellous views over the area.

Crescent is the elegant **Pump Room**, built in 1894 by Henry Curry to ease overcrowding at the previous well in the Natural Baths, now home to **Buxton Visitor Centre**. Nearby is the historic **Old Hall Hotel**, the oldest hotel building in England, parts of which date back to 1573 when the captive Mary, Queen of Scots stayed in the Tudor 'Talbot Tower'. A short walk away is the stunning **Buxton Opera House**, designed by Britain's finest theatre architect Frank Matcham (built in 1903). Now an entertainment centre, it hosts the annual **Buxton Festival** in July.

North of the Crescent is the grand **Devonshire Dome** building (previously known as the Devonshire Royal Hospital), a former stable block built by John Carr (1780-89) and extended by Robert Rippon Duke in 1881, who added what was then the world's largest unsupported dome with a diameter of 145ft. In 1859, part of the building was converted into a charity hospital, which became the Devonshire Royal Hospital in 1934 (closed in 2000). It's now the Buxton campus of the University of Derby and open to the public with a restaurant, café and award-winning spa. Nearby, on the opposite side of Devonshire Road is the **Palace Hotel**, a spectacular Victorian building constructed in 1868, set in five acres of landscaped gardens. Among the town's attractions are **Buxton Museum & Art Gallery**, where you can discover the geology, archaeology and history of the Peak District, while nearby is the **Green Man Gallery**, an independent contemporary gallery and arts centre. After you've seen the sights, Buxton offers a host of independent shops and boutiques, including beautiful Cavendish Arcade (the former thermal baths), a wide choice of

The Crescent

Opera House

Food & Drink

- **Columbine Restaurant:** upmarket dining with a refined menu (7 Hall Bank, SK17 6EW, 01298-78752, Mon, Wed-Sat 7-10pm, Sun noon-3pm, closed Tue, ££).
- **Flamenco Tapas Bar:** cosy venue for tapas, paella and Spanish specialities (7-9 Concert Pl, SK17 6EE, 01298-27392, Tue-Sun 6-11pm, closed Mon, £).
- **St Moritz:** Italian restaurant with Alpine interior serving classic Italian dishes and pizzas (7 Cavendish Circus, SK17 6AT, 01298-22225, Mon-Wed 5-10pm, Thu-Sun noon-10/11pm, £).

cafés, restaurants, pubs and bars, along with an annual programme of fairs and markets.

The town's green spaces include the superb 23-acre **Pavilion Gardens** (1871), designed by Sir Joseph Paxton, featuring lakes, flower beds, shaded walks (the Serpentine Walks) and a bandstand, along with children's play areas, an adventure playground, outdoor gym, miniature railway, boating lake and café. Also in the gardens is the **Octagon Concert Hall** (1871) and the **Pavilion Arts Centre**, Buxton's second theatre and conference venue. South of the town in Buxton Country Park is **Poole's Cavern**, an extensive limestone cavern that's one of the finest show caves in England, boasting strange and wonderful formations sculpted over millions of years.

Winnats Pass, Peak District

Ladybower Reservoir, Peak District

Cirencester & the Cotswolds

Address: Cirencester GL7 2PP (cirencester.co.uk, cotswolds.com)

Getting there: air (Bristol, 40mi, Cotswold, 7mi), rail (Cirencester, GWR), road (A429, A417, A419)

Highlights: church of St John the Baptist, Corinium Museum & Amphitheatre, New Brewery Arts, Cirencester Park, Abbey Grounds, Charter Market

Nearby: Bibury, Burford, Cheltenham, Cotswold Way, Gloucester, Nailsworth, Stroud, Tetbury

- **Luxury:** King's Head (4*), 24 Market Pl, GL7 2NW (01285-700900).
- **Moderate:** Golden Cross Inn (3*), 20 Black Jack St, GL7 2AA (01285-652137).
- **Budget:** Crown of Crucis Hotel (3*), Ampney Crucis, GL7 5RS (01285-851806).

Our chosen base for a weekend in the Cotswolds is the historic market town of **Cirencester** – dubbed the 'capital of the Cotswolds' – 80 miles west of London. It's an excellent example of a town that flourished from the wool trade in the Middle Ages, with its huge wool church and wealth of Cotswold stone buildings. Today, it's one of the largest towns in the Cotswolds (see below), perfectly placed at the centre of the region where a number of trunk roads meet.

Situated on the River Churn, a tributary of the River Thames, Cirencester is steeped in history going back 2,000 years to when it was the Roman town of *Corinium*, which in the 2nd century AD was the second-largest city by area (after London) in Britain. You can discover the town's Roman history at the fascinating **Corinium Museum**, while to the southwest of the town is a partly excavated **Roman Amphitheatre**.

After the Norman Conquest, Cirencester was granted to the Earl of Hereford and then to Augustinian Cirencester Abbey in 1189 (founded in 1117), which was dissolved in 1539. The magnificent **Church of St John the Baptist** on Market Place – one of the largest parish churches in England, aka the 'Cathedral of the Cotswolds' – was constructed around the same time (1115) as the abbey. Much altered and enlarged over

Church of St John the Baptist

the centuries, it's notable for its fan vaults, stained glass and merchants' tombs, while its nave (rebuilt 1515-30) is a superb example of Late Perpendicular Gothic architecture.

If you plan to tour the Cotswolds by car, then look no further than our sister publication *Touring the Cotswolds* (see page 222), a unique guide to exploring the region through eight carefully planned tours by car or bicycle.

To the west of the town centre is 3,000-acre **Cirencester Park**, one of the country's largest private parks with Grade I listed gardens. The park and mansion is the seat of the Earls of Bathurst and is unusual for a stately home in that it's located within the town of Cirencester, screened from prying eyes by the tallest yew hedge in the world. Situated behind the parish church are the **Abbey Grounds**, the site of Cirencester Abbey, now a public park extending down to the River Churn. Also worth a visit is the **New Brewery Arts**, a former Victorian brewery housing a contemporary art gallery, craft shop, studios and café.

Cirencester is packed with interesting independent shops and has a number of markets, including the **Charter Market** (Mon & Fri), a farmers' market on the second and fourth Saturdays of the month, along with antiques and arts & crafts markets. When you fancy a break from shopping the town is a foodie favourite, with an abundance of excellent restaurants, cafés, pubs and bars. Once you feel you have seen all that Cirencester has to offer, the town is the perfect base from which to explore the Cotswolds' wealth of picturesque towns, villages and countryside.

Market Place

The Cotswolds: The glorious sweep of the Cotswold Hills begins in the meadows of the upper Thames and rises to an escarpment known as the Cotswold Edge, just southeast of the Severn Valley and Evesham Vale. Designated an Area of Outstanding Natural Beauty (AONB) in 1966 – the largest in the UK – the Cotswolds cover an area of 787mi², some 25 miles wide and 90 miles long, stretching southwest from Stratford-upon-Avon (Warks) to Bath (Somerset), but mostly situated within Gloucestershire and Oxfordshire. One of the loveliest regions in the UK, the Cotswolds is noted for its rural charm, lush countryside, idyllic picture-postcard villages and vibrant market towns. Its ancient landscapes are crisscrossed by some 4,000 miles of historic stone walls – a legacy of the wool trade – and characterised

Cirencester Park

by houses built from local honey-coloured limestone. The region is the perfect place for walking, cycling, riding or simply relaxing. Wherever you are in the Cotswolds you're never more than a few steps away from unspoilt countryside, with over 3,000 miles of footpaths and bridleways, including the delightful 102-mile Cotswold Way running northeast from Bath to Chipping Camden.

The region's treasure trove of chocolate-box towns and villages includes Broadway, Chipping Campden, Moreton-in-Marsh and Stow-on-the-Wold in the north, Bibury and Burford in the east, Nailsworth and Stroud (and Laurie Lee's Slad Valley) in the west, and Malmesbury and Castle Combe in the south – so many, in fact, that it's difficult to know which way to turn. Not far from Cirencester is the National Arboretum at Westonbirt near Tetbury (noted for its antiques shops), the Cotswold Wildlife Park near beautiful Burford, and the Cotswold Country Park & Beach at South Cerney, just 3 miles south of Cirencester.

Food & Drink

- **Made by Bob:** buzzing bistro and deli serving chic Euro-English cuisine (6-8 The Corn Hall, 26 Market Pl, GL7 2NY, 01285-641818, Mon-Sat 8am-10pm, Sun noon-10pm, £-££).

- **Malt & Anchor:** contemporary eatery offering fish & chips, seafood and savoury pies (4 Castle St, GL7 1QA, 01285-646343, Mon-Fri noon-2.30pm, 4/5-9/9.30pm, Sat noon-9.30pm, Sun noon-3pm, £).

- **Tierra & Mar:** fine dining European & Spanish style tapas, plus seven-course menu (29 Sheep St, GL7 1QW, 01285-642777, Tue-Sat noon-2pm, 6-8.30pm, closed Sun-Mon, £-££).

Broadway

Burford

Great Malvern & the Malvern Hills

Address: Great Malvern WR14 4PZ
(visitthemalverns.org, malvernhills.org.uk)

Getting there: air (Birmingham, 45mi), rail (Great Malvern, West Midlands/GWR), road (A449, A4103)

Highlights: Great Malvern Priory, Malvern Museum, gas lamps, Malvern Theatres, Priory Park, Rose Bank Gardens, music festivals

Nearby: **Hereford**, Ledbury, **Ludlow**, Tewkesbury, **Worcester**

Sleep

- **Luxury:** Abbey Hotel (4*), Abbey Rd, WR14 3ET (01684-892332).
- **Moderate:** Mount Pleasant Hotel (3*), 50 Bellevue Ter, WR14 4PZ (01684-561837).
- **Budget:** Foley Arms (3*), 14 Worcester Rd, WR14 4QS (01684-580350).

A spa town in Worcestershire at the foot of the Malvern Hills, Great Malvern is located 39 miles southwest of Birmingham and nine miles southwest of Worcester. The modern town is largely Victorian, although its roots go back to the Iron and Bronze Ages. Malvern was founded in the 11th century by Benedictine monks, who established a priory here, but it remained a collection of small cottages until the Middle Ages. Great Malvern is a historic conservation area – the town and the surrounding district is collectively known as the Malverns – which grew dramatically in Victorian times thanks to its popularity as a hydrotherapy spa based on the local spring waters. Among the town's claims to fame are its bottled water (favoured by Queen Elizabeth II) and the home of the Morgan Motor Company.

One of your first stops should be the magnificent Norman **Great Malvern Priory**, constructed from 1085 as a Benedictine monastery, which has the largest number of 15th-century stained glass windows in England, splendid 15th-16th-century misericords, and the country's largest collection of medieval floor and wall tiles. The priory's nearby former gatehouse (known as the **Abbey Gateway**) was built around 1480 and is now home to **Malvern Museum**, the town's fascinating local history museum. Nearby on Belle Vue Island is the **Malvhina Fountain**, a modern fountain fed with Malvern Water, while close by is a **Statue of Sir Edward Elgar** (see below). A glimpse of Malvern's glorious Victorian history can be seen in the town's many working **Gas Lamps** (it originally had some 1,250!), which are Grade II listed.

Great Malvern Priory

Malvern Hills AONB

One of the most spectacular landscapes in the country, the Malvern Hills are mainly located in the counties of Worcestershire and Herefordshire, along with a small area of north Gloucestershire. The Hills dominate the surrounding countryside and the towns and villages of the district of Malvern, where the highest point (Worcestershire Beacon, 1,394ft) offers panoramic views of the Wye and Severn Valleys as far as the Cotswolds, the hills of Herefordshire and the Welsh mountains.

Malvern has a proud history as a centre for the performing arts, since George Bernard Shaw and Edward Elgar brought Malvern into the 20th Century with their music and theatre festivals, held in the Edwardian Winter Gardens overlooking Priory Park (see below). The Winter Gardens were re-invented as the **Malvern Theatres** in the late '90s, comprising the 850-seat Festival Theatre, the Forum Theatre, a 400-seat cinema, and a bar and restaurant. Malvern is also home to the **Theatre of Small Convenience** (a former Victorian

Food & Drink

- **Anupam:** long-established Indian restaurant serving tasty food (85 Church St, WR14 2AE, 01684-573814, Mon-Sat 5.30-11/11.15pm, Sun 1-9pm, £).
- **L'amuse Bouche:** award-winning fine dining British restaurant (Cotford Hotel, 51 Graham Rd, WR14 2HU, 01684-572427, telephone for meal times, ££).
- **Nag's Head:** traditional pub serving tasty classic pub grub (19-21 Bank St, WR14 2JG, 01684-574373, Mon-Sat 11am-11.15/11.30pm, Sun noon-11pm, £).

Gentlemen's Lavatory!), which seats 12 and is officially the smallest theatre in the world.

Priory Park, formerly the gardens of Priory Mansion (1874), now the **Council House**, is home to many majestic trees surrounding a large pond spanned by a couple of bridges, while **Rose Bank Gardens** on the edge of town offer access to the Malvern Hills, where a well-trodden path leads to **St Ann's Well** and Café. Great Malvern is a lovely town to wander around, its intimate streets packed with cafés, restaurants, pubs and a good selection of independent boutiques, galleries and antiques shops, along with the usual high street names.

Malvern Hills

Harrogate & the Yorkshire Dales

Sleep

- **Luxury:** Hotel du Vin (4*), Prospect Pl, HG1 1LB (01423-608121).
- **Moderate:** Yorkshire Hotel (4*), Prospect Pl, HG1 1LA (01423-706700).
- **Budget:** Crown Hotel (3*), Crown Place, HG1 2RZ (01423-567755).

Address: Harrogate HG1 2AE (visitharrogate.co.uk)

Getting there: air (Leeds-Bradford, 10mi), rail (Harrogate, LNER), road (A1, A59/A61)

Highlights: Royal Baths, Georgian Theatre, Bath Hospital, Royal Pump Room Museum, Mercer Art Gallery, Theatre, Royal Hall, Valley Gardens

Nearby: Boroughbridge, Knaresborough, Nidderdale AONB, Pateley Bridge, Ripley, **Ripon**, Wetherby

A historic spa town in North Yorkshire, Harrogate is located 17 miles north of Leeds and 21 miles west of York, while a short distance to the northwest is Nidderdale AONB and the Yorkshire Dales National Park. The town grew out of two smaller settlements in the 17th century, High Harrogate and Low Harrogate, and became known as 'The English Spa' in the Georgian era, due to its 'chalybeate' (containing iron) waters, first discovered in the 16th century. During the late 19th and early 20th centuries, Harrogate was popular among the English élite and even frequented by Europe's nobility, although its popularity declined after the First World War.

Today, it's a thriving, laid-back market town and popular visitor centre, at the heart of one of Yorkshire's most beautiful areas – taking in Ripon, Boroughbridge, Knaresborough and Wetherby – and rated one of the 'happiest places to live in Britain'. Although the original spa has long since closed, Harrogate offers a number of modern 21st-century spas and glorious renovated 19th-century **Turkish Baths** (located in the **Royal Baths** building, opened in 1897), one of the best-preserved Victorian Turkish baths in the world.

To provide for the increasing numbers of visitors, the **Georgian Theatre** was built in 1788, the **Bath Hospital** (later the Royal Bath Hospital) in 1826, a leading centre for hydrotherapy and spa treatments, and the **Royal Pump Room** in 1842. The latter closed shortly after the start of the Second World War and now houses the **Royal Pump Room Museum** (1953), which tells the

Montpellier Quarter

Knaresborough

A trip to Harrogate would be incomplete without visiting the neighbouring medieval town of Knaresborough, perched on the cliffs above the River Nidd with an dramatic railway viaduct spanning the Nidd Gorge, where a warren of medieval streets and stone staircases tumbling down the hill.

story of Harrogate as a spa town through its collection of some 20,000 artefacts. Nearby, the **Mercer Art Gallery** is home to Harrogate district's fine art collection, consisting of around 2,000 works, mainly from the 19th and 20th centuries. The imposing Anglican **St Wilfrid's Church** (1904) on Duchy Road is the greatest work of Temple Lushington Moore, and one of the largest parish churches in England. Other prominent buildings include the 300-year-old **Crown Hotel** next to the Royal Pump Room Museum; 250-year-old **White Hart Hotel**, which architectural expert Nikolaus Pevsner regarded as Harrogate's best building; **Harrogate Theatre** (1900), a typical example of

a late Victorian proscenium arch venue built over five floors; and the splendid Edwardian **Royal Hall** (1903).

If you fancy a walk, then spectacular **Valley Gardens** in regal Low Harrogate is the perfect spot, comprising 17 acres of park, woodland and wonderful floral displays (including a Japanese garden), while adjacent to the gardens are a further 96 acres of semi-natural woodland. It's believed that the largest number of mineral springs (36) in the world come to the surface in Valley Gardens. To the east of town is **The Stray** (describes unenclosed land), created in 1778 – 200 acres of public parkland linking the town's curative springs and wells. Southwest of the town is **RHS Gardens Harlow Carr** (58 acres), one of only a handful of gardens in Britain run by the Royal Horticultural Society. If you're visiting in July you may wish to time your visit to take in the **Great Yorkshire Show** (greatyorkshireshow.co.uk) – one of the largest agricultural shows in England – held just southeast of the town.

After you've done the sights and enjoyed the gardens, why not browse the elegant shops and boutiques in

The Stray in spring

Bettys Tea Room

the town's fashionable Montpellier Quarter, home to over 50 exclusive independent shops and boutiques, galleries, antiques shops and pavement cafés – including legendary **Bettys Café Tea Rooms**, a splendid traditional tea room opened in 1919 – bars, pubs and award-winning restaurants. Harrogate also boasts a host of galleries, from prestigious commercial galleries to working artists' studios and workshops, while if it's high street names you're after then you need look no further than the elegant **Victoria Shopping Centre**.

When you've exhausted all Harrogate has to offer, it's time to explore some of the surrounding towns and attractions, such as Knaresborough (see box opposite), Boroughbridge, Masham, Pateley Bridge, Ripley (and its 14th-century castle), Ripon (see page 116) and Wetherby – not forgetting the Yorkshire Dales.

Yorkshire Dales & Nidderdale AONB: To the west of Harrogate lies the magnificent Yorkshire Dales National Park (established in 1954), covering an area of 041mi^2 mostly within North Yorkshire. The Dales comprise river valleys and hills rising from the Vale of York westwards to the hilltops of the Pennine watershed, with numerous walking trails, while the area's extensive limestone cave systems are one of the country's major caving areas. The Nidderdale AONB (233mi^2), bordering the Yorkshire Dales to the west, comprises most of Nidderdale itself, part of lower Wharfedale, the Washburn Valley and part of lower Wensleydale. Among the area's most popular sites are Aysgarth Falls, Malham Cove, Ingleborough and Ribblehead Viaduct.

Food & Drink

- **Fat Badger:** stylish pub with terrace offering up-market modern pub grub (Cold Bath Rd, HG2 0N, 01423-505681, daily noon-9/10pm, £-££).

- **Graveley's:** family-run restaurant with traditional fish and seafood menu (8-12 Cheltenham Parade, HG1 1DB, 01423-507093, Mon-Sat 11.30am-9/9.30pm, Sun noon-8pm, £).

- **William & Victoria:** Popular British dishes in classy dining room and buzzy bistro (6 Cold Bath Rd, Harrogate, HG2 0NA, 01423-521510, Mon-Thu noon-11pm, Fri-Sun 10am-11pm, £-££).

Yorkshire Dales National Park

Inverness & the Scottish Highlands

Address: Inverness IV2 3PY (explore-inverness.com, visitscotland.com/destinations-maps/highlands)

Getting there: air (Inverness, 8mi), rail (Inverness, Scotrail), road (A9/A82)

Highlights: Castle, Cathedral, River Ness, Town House, Museum & Art Gallery, River Ness & Caledonian canal, Scottish cuisine, pubs

Nearby: Cairngorms, Culloden, Fort George, Loch Ness, Moray Firth, Speyside (distilleries)

Capital of the Scottish Highlands region, Inverness is the northernmost city of Scotland – situated at the mouth of the River Ness and the end of the Great Glen – and the perfect base for touring the Highlands. One of Europe's fastest growing cities, it has the highest quality

- **Luxury:** Ness Walk (5*), 12 Ness Walk, IV3 5SQ (01463-215215).
- **Moderate:** Best Western Inverness Palace (3*), 8 Ness Walk, IV3 5NG (01463-223243).
- **Budget:** Glen Mhor Hotel (3*), 7-17 Ness Bank, IV2 4SG (01463-234308).

of life in Scotland and enjoys rapid economic growth; it's also claimed to be the happiest place in Scotland.

A settlement was established by the 6th century with the first royal charter granted by Dabíd mac Maíl Choluim (King David I, reigned 1124-1153) in the 12th century. Inverness lies near two important battle sites: the 11th-century battle of Blàr nam Fèinne (Battlefield of the Fingalians) against Norway, and the 18th-century Battle of **Culloden** (see box opposite).

Inverness Castle sits on a clifftop overlooking the River Ness, where a succession of castles have stood since 1057. The red sandstone structure you see today was built in 1836 by William Burn and houses the Inverness Sheriff Court, part of which is open to the public and offers fabulous views over the city. **Inverness Cathedral**, aka the Cathedral Church of St Andrew, of the Scottish Episcopal Church, was the first Protestant cathedral built in Britain since the Reformation, consecrated in 1869. The city also has a number of historic churches, including the Old High Church, which was used as a prison for captured Jacobites. Other buildings of note include the **Inverness Town House**

Inverness Castle

Inverness Cathedral

(now the local town hall) – a fairy-tale Flemish-Baronial style townhouse constructed 1878-82 by local architect William Lawrie, with lavish interior decoration – and the **Inverness Museum and Art Gallery**, which houses a fascinating range of artefacts celebrating Highland life and heritage.

Inverness is home to many parks and gardens, particularly along the River Ness and Caledonian Canal, including the Inverness Botanic Gardens. Not the best

---

Culloden

Three miles east of Inverness, the **Culloden Battlefield** bore witness to one of the greatest battles on Scottish soil, where in 1746 the clans – who supported the restoration of the Catholic Stuarts to the Scottish throne – rallied behind Prince Charles Edward Stuart (aka Bonnie Prince Charlie) in the Jacobite cause. The hour-long battle – in which the British 'redcoats' defeated the Scots, killing over 1,000 – led to the 'pacification' of the Highlands, the banning of clan chiefs and tartans, and the attempted destruction of Highland culture.

Food & Drink

• **Café One:** classic European and Scottish dishes featuring local produce (75 Castle St, IV2 3EA, 01463-226200, 5-9.30pm, closed Sun, ££).

• **Kitchen Brasserie:** acclaimed restaurant with creative Scottish menu (15 Huntly St, IV3 5PR, 01463-259119, noon-3pm, 5-10pm, £-££).

• **Rocpool Restaurant:** contemporary fine dining highlighting modern Scottish cuisine (1 Ness Walk, IV3 5NE, 01463-717274, noon-2.30pm, 5.45-10pm, closed Sun, ££-£££).

---

place for shopaholics, the Eastgate Centre is good for high street stalwarts and the handsome indoor **Victorian Market** (1876) contains independent boutiques. When you've worked up an appetite you'll find Inverness has an abundance of quality restaurants, many specialising in Scottish cuisine and local produce, and plenty of hostelries where you can enjoy a wee dram or two.

Highlights of the Scottish Highlands region include **Loch Ness**, home to the 'legendary' Loch Ness Monster; the **Moray Firth** north of the City (noted for its dolphins); the magnificent **Cairngorms National Park** – a popular hiking, climbing, fishing, shooting and winter sports area – **Fort George & The Highlanders' Museum**, the best example of an 18th-century military fortification in Europe; and the historic **Speyside** whisky distilleries along the River Spey.

Kendal & the Lake District

Address: Kendal LA9 4DL (visit-kendal.co.uk, golakes.co.uk)

Getting there: air (Carlisle, 43mi), rail (Kendal, Northern), road (A6, A684/A591)

Highlights: Parish Church, Abbot Hall Art Gallery, Town Hall, Kendal Museum, Museum of Lakeland Life & Industry, Sizergh Castle, Levens Hall

Nearby: Ambleside, Cartmel Priory, Grasmere (Dove Cottage), Keswick, Ullswater, Windermere

- **Luxury:** Castle Green (4*), Castle Green Ln, LA9 6RG (01539-734000).
- **Moderate:** Riverside Hotel (3*), Stramongate Br, Beezon Rd, LA9 6EL (01539-734861).
- **Budget:** Premier Inn (3*), Maude St, LA9 4QG (0871-527 8562).

A market town in Cumbria, Kendal – dubbed the 'Gateway to the Lakes' – lies on the River Kent (from which it gets its name) 19 miles north of Lancaster. One of the region's main manufacturing towns from the 14th-19th centuries, with many woollen mills on the River Kent, today it's mainly a tourist centre, the home of Kendal Mint Cake, and pipe tobacco and snuff production. The town was the home of Alfred Wainwright (1907-1991) – the celebrated author and illustrator of walking guidebooks – who lived and worked in Kendal for 50 years.

Among Kendal's most prominent buildings is handsome **Kendal Parish Church**, aka Holy Trinity Church, a place of worship since the 13th century, although the current church is mostly 18th-century. It's Cumbria's largest parish church and one of the largest in England, with a fine western tower and a peel of ten bells. Also of interest is the Roman Catholic **Church of Holy Trinity & St George** (1837) in Blackhall Road. Beside the Parish Church is **Abbot Hall Art Gallery**, Kendal's fine art gallery containing one of the northwest's best collections of 18th- and 19th-century art – including an important collection of paintings by local artist George Romney – housed in an attractive Georgian (1759) building. The gallery occupies a beautiful setting beside the River Kent, surrounded by a park and overlooked by the ruins of **Kendal Castle**. Not far away on Highgate is the **Brewery Arts Centre**, a multi-purpose arts complex offering theatre, music, comedy, films, lectures and exhibitions.

Kendal Parish Church

Miller Bridge

Back in the town centre, imposing **Kendal Town Hall** was designed by Francis Webster and built as the Whitehall Assembly Rooms in 1827, which was replaced as the town council meeting place when Kendal County Hall was built in 1939. There are five road bridges over the River Kent in Kendal, the most notable being **Millor Bridge**, a stone arch structure erected in 1818 by John Rennie. The town is home to a number of museums, including the **Kendal Museum of Natural History and Archaeology** founded in 1796, containing archaeology, history, geology and natural history collections. Others include the **Museum of Lakeland Life & Industry**, depicting how Cumbrian people have lived, worked and entertained themselves since the 18th century, and the **Quaker Tapestry Museum**, home of the Quaker Tapestry, an embroidery created by over 4,000 people in 15 countries over 15 years.

Stately homes close to Kendal include **Sizergh Castle & Garden** (National Trust), four miles south of the town, a handsome medieval house with splendid gardens and a 1,600-acre estate, and **Levens Hall** (a few miles further south), an Elizabethan manor house that's home to ten acres of spectacular gardens, including the world's oldest topiary garden.

If you plan to tour the Lakes by car, then look no further than our sister publication ***Touring the Lake District*** (see page 222), a unique guide to exploring the region through eight carefully planned tours.

Kendal has an abundance of green spaces, including the riverside parks of Abbot Hall and Goosehulme, along with many lovely walking trails (indicated by signs around the town). When you fancy a bite to eat, the town offers a wide choice of restaurants, cafés and pubs to suit every taste and budget, and has a lively nightlife scene, offering live music, theatre, comedy, film and festivals. After you've exhausted the town's attractions, you'll find Kendal is an excellent base from which to explore the rest of the Lake District.

Lake District National Park: Also known as the Lakes or Lakeland, the park was established in 1951 – the largest in England and Wales covering an area of

Sizergh Castle

912mi² – and belatedly designated a UNESCO World Heritage Site in 2017. Britain's most popular National Park, it's celebrated for its glacial ribbon lakes, rugged fell mountains (or 'fells'), forests and historic literary associations, including poets William Wordsworth and Samuel Taylor Coleridge, authors Arthur Ransome and Beatrix Potter, and art critic John Ruskin. The Lake District lies entirely within the county of Cumbria and contains all land in England above 3,000 feet, including Scafell Pike (3,209ft), the highest mountain in England. It also contains the deepest and largest natural lakes in England: Wastwater (deepest) and Windermere (largest).

Whether you tour by car or follow in the footsteps of Alfred Wainwright and hike up Scafell Pike, the Lake District offers something for everyone. It's one of the best places in Britain to enjoy the great outdoors with sufficient trails to keep keen hikers busy for a month of Sundays. There's also plenty to offer the less active visitor, including lake cruises, a host of picturesque villages, historic houses and museums, and a feast of superb restaurants and pubs.

Food & Drink

• **Baba Ganoush:** popular breakfast-lunch spot for tasty food (Unit 4, Berrys Yd, 27 Finkle St, LA9 4AB, 01539-738210, Tue-Sat 10am-3pm, closed Sun-Mon, £).

• **The Moon Highgate:** fine dining modern British cuisine in cosy building (129 Highgate, LA9 4EN, 01539-729254, Thu-Sat 5-9pm, Sun noon-3.30pm, closed Mon-Wed, £-££).

• **Romneys:** traditional, stone-built gastropub and carvery (72 Milnthorpe Rd, LA9 5HG, 01539-720956, daily 9am-midnight, £-££).

Derwentwater

Catbells

Ludlow & the Shropshire Hills

Address: Ludlow ST8 1ES (ludlow.org.uk, shropshiretourism.co.uk)

Getting there: air (Birmingham, 42mi), rail (Ludlow, Transport for Wales), road (A49, B4361)

Highlights: Castle, Town Walls, medieval inns, St Laurence's Church, The Reader's House, Ludlow Museum, Millennium Green, fine dining, market

Nearby: Church Stretton, **Horeford**, Kidderminster, Leominster, **Shrewsbury**, **Worcester**

Sleep

- **Luxury:** Old Downton Lodge (5*), Downton-on-the-Rock, SY8 2HU (01568-771826).
- **Moderate:** Feathers Hotel (3*), 24-25 Bull Ring, SY8 1AA (01584-87526).
- **Budget:** Travelodge Ludlow (2*), Foldgate Ln, SY8 1LS (0871 984 6347).

A historic 'Marcher' market town in Shropshire at the confluence of the Rivers Teme and Corve, Ludlow is the gateway to the Shropshire Hills and Welsh Marches. The town boasts some 500 listed buildings, including many medieval, Tudor and Georgian buildings, and was described by Sir John Betjeman as 'probably the loveliest town in England'. Founded by the Normans in the late 11th century and originally called Dinham, the medieval walled town was centred on a small hill on the eastern bank of a bend of the River Teme. An important and prosperous town throughout the Middle Ages, when wool and cloth production were major industries (later glove-making), today its main sources of income are tourism (gastronomy), service industries and light engineering.

Eleventh-century **Ludlow Castle**, built on a promontory overlooking the River Teme, is one of the finest medieval ruins in England, which became crown property in 1461 and remained a royal castle for the next 350 years. It fell into ruin in the 18th century but has since been restored and is well worth a visit. Also of significance are Ludlow's **Town Walls** – built in the 13th century to repel marauding Welsh armies – two-thirds of which survive today, including **Broad Gate**, the sole surviving original gateway. Among the town's many important buildings is striking 11th-century **St Laurence's Church**, the parish church of Ludlow. Largely Perpendicular in style due to 15th-century renovations, it's dubbed the 'cathedral of the Marches' due to its size and grandeur, and is noted for its superb stonemasonry (beautiful reredos), chancel stalls, misericords and stained glass.

Ludlow Town & Castle

Shropshire Hills AONB

Designated an Area of Outstanding Natural Beauty (AONB) in 1958, the Shropshire Hills extend to 310mi^2, primarily in southwest Shropshire just north of Ludlow. The area encompasses a patchwork of hills, rolling farmland, woods and river valleys, providing a dramatic link between the Midlands and the Welsh mountains. They're located within the Welsh Marches, a medieval term used to describe the borderland between England and Wales. Especially noteworthy is the Long Mynd, a 7-mile long plateau affording wonderful views across Wales.

Other outstanding buildings include 16th-century **Reader's House**, once the official residence of the Bible Reader of Saint Laurence's Church; **Castle Lodge**, a medieval Tudor and Elizabethan transition period house close to Ludlow Castle; and the **Buttercross**, built in 1746 in Classical style, the upper rooms of which are home to **Ludlow Museum**, which traces the town's architecture and social history. Other notable buildings include half-timbered **Feathers Hotel**, constructed in 1619, with outstanding Jacobean furnishings; the **Bull**

Food & Drink

- **Fish House:** superb fish and seafood bar (Tolsey House, 51 Bull Ring, SY8 1AB, 01584- 879790, Wed-Sat 10am-2/4pm, closed Sun-Tue, £-££).

- **Mortimers:** fine dining restaurant offering modern British/French cuisine (17 Corve St, SY8 1DA, 01584-872325, Tue-Sat noon-4pm, 6.30pm-midnight, closed Sun-Mon, ££-£££).

- **Unicorn Inn:** attractive, timber-framed gastropub with riverside garden (66 Corve St, SY8 1DU, 01584-873555, daily noon-2pm, 6-11pm, ££).

Hotel set in a half-timbered coaching inn dating from the 12th century; the 13th-century **Rose and Crown;** and the early 17th-century timber-framed **Angel**.

Ludlow has a number of attractive green spaces, including **Ludlow Millennium Green** by the River Teme and Dinham Bridge, and expansive **Whitcliffe Common Nature Reserve**, while the town is surrounded by unspoilt countryside with a web of marked trails. Ludlow has an enviable gastronomic reputation and many excellent restaurants, cafés and pubs, which are showcased in September during the **Ludlow Food & Drink Festival**. The town is also noted for its wealth of independent shops, antiques emporiums, art galleries and 900-year-old general **Market** (daily except Tue and Sun).

Shropshire Hills

Portmeirion & Snowdonia

Address: Portmeirion LL48 6ER (portmeirion. wales, visitsnowdonia.info)

Getting there: air (Anglesey, 46mi), rail (Minffordd, 1mi), road (A487)

Highlights: fairytale architecture, gardens, beaches, rivers, mountain railways, coastline

Nearby: Criccieth, Ffestiniog, Harlech, Porthmadog

A holiday village in Gwynedd (North Wales) on the estuary of the River Dwyryd, stunning Portmeirion was designed and built by Welsh architect Sir Clough Williams-Ellis (1883-1978) between 1925 and 1975 in the style of an Italian village (influenced by the Italian village of Portofino). The village – the location for the 1960s cult TV series, *The Prisoner* – is the perfect base to explore **Snowdonia National Park** (see box on page 192).

Williams-Ellis incorporated parts of demolished buildings into his village – including a medieval castle (Castell Deudraeth) that was developed in the 1850s – along with works by a number of other architects, endangered buildings and unwanted artefacts from around the globe. The result is a bizarre, tongue-in-cheek combination of medieval, Italian, Georgian and Arts & Crafts architecture, with a bit of Art Deco design thrown in too. The result

Sleep

• **Luxury:** Hotel Portmeirion (4*), Penrhyndeudraeth LL48 6ER (01766-772440).

• **Moderate:** Royal Sportsman (3*), 131 High St, Porthmadog LL49 9HB (01766-512015).

• **Budget:** Golden Fleece Inn, 8 Market Sq, Porthmadog LL49 9RB (01766-514421).

is a fantastical Mediterranean resort plonked in wildest North Wales with a piazza, grand porticoes, plazas, loggias, domed, terracotta-roofed houses (painted in bright pastel colours) and narrow winding streets. Allow some time to admire the Gothic Pavilion, Bristol Colonnade, Hercules Hall and Belvedere, where statues, corbels and whimsical details fill every nook and cranny with interest. Williams-Ellis firmly believed that buildings didn't need to be serious and stern, and aimed to create something playful and enchanting – and succeeded brilliantly!

Portmeirion

Snowdonia National Park

Established in 1951, rugged Snowdonia National Park (Welsh: *Parc Cenedlaethol Eryri*) was the third National Park in Britain after the Peak and Lake Districts. It extends to 827mi^2 with 37 miles of coastline in the counties of Gwynedd and Clwyd, containing the highest peaks in the UK outside Scotland, including Mt Snowdon (3,560ft). Looming over the village of Llanberis, Snowdon is part of a group of jagged peaks offering views of Snowdonia, Anglesey, Pembrokeshire and Ireland. If you fancy a hike there are eight paths up to the summit: Crib Goch, Llanberis Path, Miners' Track, Pyg Track, Rhyd Ddu Path, Snowdon Ranger Path, South Ridge and the Watkin Path (see walkupsnowdon.co.uk).

temples and breathtaking views. Here you'll discover an exotic Japanese garden with a pagoda and lily-covered lake, an Oriental Garden and 'secret' sites such as the Dog Cemetery, Tangle Wood, Ghost Garden and Shelter Valley.

Portmeirion is owned by a charitable trust and has always been run as a hotel, employing most of the village's buildings as hotel rooms or self-catering cottages, together with shops, a café, tea-room and restaurant. Today, it's one of Wales's premier attractions – welcoming over 200,000 visitors a year (there's an admission fee for day visitors) – and one of the most successful British architectural projects of the 20th century.

Also worth a visit is nearby **Porthmadog** and the pretty beachside village of **Borth-y-Gest** (opposite Portmeirion) on the **Glaslyn Estuary** and **Black Rock Sands**; the lovely seaside resort of **Criccieth** (nine

Allow some time to explore the surrounding area and **Portmeirion Gardens**, the *Gwyllt* ('wildwood' in Welsh), a 70-acre sub-tropical forest with 20 miles of paths, featuring splendid trees, secret gardens, hidden lakes, coastal coves,

miles west of Portmeirion); and beautiful **Harlech Beach** a few miles south, along with **Harlech** town and its splendid 13th-century castle.

If you're up for adventure then Snowdonia

lays claims to being the UK's 'adventure capital' with **Zip World**, the world's fastest zip wire (Penrhyn Quarry, Bethesda); **Adventure Parc Snowdonia** at Dolgorrag,

Portmeirion village & gardens

Harlech Beach

the world's first inland surfing lagoon; the **National White Water Centre** (Canolfan Tryweryn, Fron-goch), the only commercially rafted stretch of water in the UK; **Coed y Brenin** (Ganllwyd, Dolgellau), the UK's first specialist mountain bike centre; and **Traws Lake** (Llyn Trawsfynydd), a 1,200-acre lake created in the 1920s for the Maentwrog hydro-electric power station, which is renowned for its trout fishing and birdlife.

Food & Drink

- **Hotel Portmeirion:** award-winning Art Deco restaurant with great views (Portmeirion, LL48 6ER, 01766-770000, telephone for meal times, ££-£££).

- **Castel Deudraeth Brasserie:** restaurant specialising in Welsh fare (Minffordd, LL48 6ER, 01766-772400, daily 10am-11pm, £-££).

- **Town Hall Café & Bar:** retro, 50's-style licensed diner serving hot meals and snacks (Portmeirion, LL48 6ER, 01766-770000, daily 10am-4.30pm, £).

Mountain Railways

The summit of Snowdonia can be reached by the narrow gauge rack and pinion **Snowdon Mountain Railway** from Llanberis (4.7mi), while the narrow-gauge **Ffestiniog Railway** is a major tourist attraction running 13½ miles from the harbour at Porthmadog (close to Portmeirion) to the historic slate mining town of Blaenau Ffestiniog through magnificent forests and mountainous scenery. Porthmadog is also the southern terminus of the **Welsh Highland Railway** to Caernarfon (25mi) and home to the **Welsh Highland Heritage Railway**, a reconstructed heritage steam railway.

Snowdonia National Park

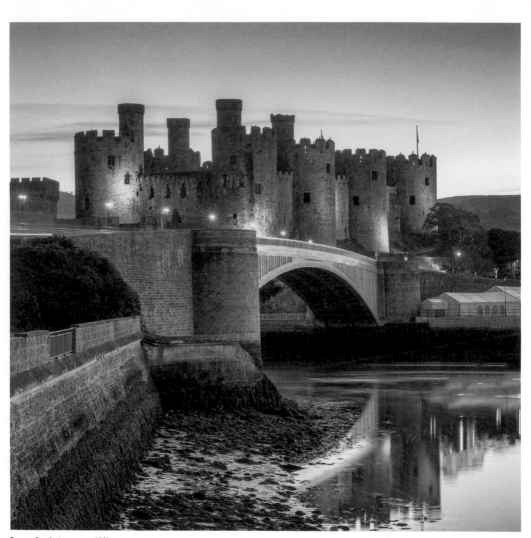

Conwy Castle (see page 198)

5.
Coastal Delights

The UK is home to a wealth of lovely seaside resorts, so many in fact that it's difficult to choose those most worthy of a weekend bolthole. Those featured include ever-popular Brighton in West Sussex with its magnificent pier and genteel Rye in East Sussex; regal Ramsgate in Kent and its splendid harbour and bustling Cowes (Isle of Wight) and its yachting fraternity; the charming historic Welsh towns of Conwy and Tenby; Oban in Scotland, 'Gateway to the Isles', and Yorkshire's dramatic port of Whitby; fabulous Falmouth in Cornwall with its vast natural harbour and whimsical Southwold with its delightful pier and colourful beach huts, the jewel in the crown of Suffolk's seaside resorts.

Brighton

Address: Brighton BN2 1TW (visitbrighton.com)

Getting there: air (Gatwick, 28mi), rail (Brighton, Southern Rail), road (M23/A23, A27)

Highlights: Royal Pavilion, Palace Pier, Museum & Art Gallery, Brighton Dome, Brighton Beach, Sea Life, Marina, Brighton Centre, The Lanes, seafood

Nearby: Chichester, Eastbourne, Lewes, Newhaven, **Portsmouth**, Worthing

Sleep

- **Luxury:** The Grand (4*), 97-99 King's Rd, BN1 2FW (01273-224300).

- **Moderate:** * (4*), King's Rd, BN1 2GS (01273-206700).

- **Budget:** Ibis (3*), 88-92 Queen's Rd, BN1 3XE (01273-201000).

Located in West Sussex on the south coast, 74 miles south of London, bohemian Brighton is one of the UK's most popular seaside resorts, renowned for its diverse culture, vibrant music and arts scene, quirky shopping areas and large LGBT population (it's the unofficial 'gay capital of the UK'). The town's origins date back to the Neolithic period, with Roman, Anglo-Saxon and Norman settlements. Its importance grew in the Middle Ages, but it wasn't until the 18th century that Brighton's star soared, when its handsome Georgian terraces were built and the Prince Regent became a regular visitor. The arrival of the railway in 1841 brought the town within reach of day trippers from London, and many of its attractions were constructed during the Victorian era.

Among the town's must-see sights is the amazing **Royal Pavilion** (see box opposite) and **Pavilion Gardens**, the adjoining **Brighton Museum & Art Gallery**, which houses a wide-ranging collection of art and artefacts, and the **Brighton Dome**, built in 1803-6 as the Prince Regent's stables and now the south coast's leading arts venue. Other attractions include the 1,722ft **Palace Pier**, which opened in 1899 and features a funfair, restaurants and arcade halls; it's one of the UK's finest piers attracting some five million visitors a year. Some 100 yards to the west are the ruins of the **West Pier** (1866), destroyed by fire in 2003.

Palace Pier

Also worth seeking out is **St Nicholas Church**, Brighton's oldest building, dedicated in the 14th century to St Nicholas of Myra; **St Peter's Church** (1824-28), one of the UK's finest examples of pre-Victorian Gothic Revival architecture; **Brighton Clock Tower**, built in 1888 to commemorate Queen Victoria's Golden Jubilee; **Volk's Electric Railway** (opened 1883) which runs along the seafront and is the world's oldest operating electric railway; and the 21st-century **British Airways i360** (2016), an observation tower perched 531ft above the old West Pier entrance, affording panoramic views of the town and coastline.

The town's endless list of entertainments includes the **Brighton Centre** for music, comedy and events; the **Theatre Royal**, founded in 1807; **Sea Life Brighton**, built in 1872 and the world's oldest aquarium; and a host of museums. There's also **Brighton Marina**, some beautiful parks and gardens and – not least – the town's 5½-mile sand and shingle **Beach** and surfeit of watersport options. For avid shoppers, **The Lanes** is a must-visit, a series of narrow pedestrianised streets and

Food & Drink

- **Gingerman:** intimate modern European restaurant with seasonal menus (21A Norfolk Sq, BN1 2PD, 01273-326688, Tue-Sat noon-2.30pm/6.30-10pm, Sun noon-3pm, closed Mon, ££).
- **Riddle & Finns:** highly acclaimed seafood restaurant in The Lanes (12b Meeting House Ln, BN1 1HB, 01273-821218, daily 11.30am/noon-11pm, ££).
- **Redroaster Café:** café in former post office serving creative brunch/lunch dishes (1D St James's St, BN2 1RE, 01273-686668, Sun-Tue 8am-5pm, Wed-Sat 8.30am-11pm, £).

alleys in the town's historic 16th-century centre, packed with a surfeit of independent boutiques, jewellers, antiques stores, restaurants, cafés and bars. When you're peckish, Brighton offers a world of gastronomic delights to suit every palate and pocket, including many superb seafood restaurants and classic fish and chips. Don't forget to check the latest events when you're planning to visit – Brighton Pride (Jul/Aug) being one of the biggest celebrations of the year.

Royal Pavilion

A bizarre seaside pleasure palace designed by Henry Holland and built (1787-1823) for the future George IV, the Royal Pavilion is based on Indo-Saracenic architecture prevalent in India at the time. Its exotic appearance – with its riot of domes and minarets – is the work of John Nash, who extended the building from 1815, and its interior is just as bizarre and extravagant.

View from British Airways i360

Conwy

Address: Conwy LL32 8LD (conwy.com)

Getting there: air (Anglesey, 35mi), rail (Conwy, TfW), road (A55, A470)

Highlights: Castle, Town Walls, Quay, Church of St Mary's & All Saints, Aberconwy House, Plas Mawr, Guildhall, beaches, coastline, bridges, seafood

Nearby: Bangor, Bodnant Gardens, Colwyn Bay, Gwydir Forest Park, Llandudno, Snowdonia

Sleep

- **Luxury:** Quay Hotel & Spa (4*), Deganwy Quay, Deganwy, LL31 9DJ (01492-564100).
- **Moderate:** Castle Hotel (4*), High St, LL32 8DB (01492-582800).
- **Budget:** Glan Heulig B&B (4*), Woodlands, LL32 8LT (01492-593845).

A walled market town (and county borough) on the north coast of Wales, charming Conwy (pronounced 'konwi', Conway in English) lies on the River Conwy estuary, some 45 miles west of Chester. One of Britain's best-preserved medieval towns, it was founded by Edward I in 1283 as one of a chain of forts in newly invaded North Wales. It was the site of Cistercian Aberconwy Abbey founded by Llywelyn the Great (1173-1240), which Edward I expropriated and moved down Conwy Valley to Maenan.

There wasn't a bridge over the River Conwy until 1826, when a suspension bridge (now pedestrian only) designed by Thomas Telford opened – one of the first suspension bridges in the world – prior to which the only way to cross the river was by ferry. In 1849, Robert Stephenson constructed a railway bridge over the river, but a new road bridge wasn't built until 1958, which was joined by the Conwy Road Tunnel (2,330ft) in 1991, the first immersed tube tunnel built in the UK. The bridges and railway opened up Conwy to travellers and the town's economy is now based almost entirely on tourism.

Dramatic **Conwy Castle** and the **Town Walls** – 30ft high and several feet thick, strengthened by 21 towers and three gates – were built between 1283 and 1289. It's the most intact in Europe and considered to be one of 'the finest examples of late 13th-century and early 14th-century military architecture in Europe', classed as a UNESCO World Heritage Site. There are stunning views from the battlements, with the

Conwy Castle

Conwy Bridges

Food & Drink

- **Alfredos:** traditional family restaurant serving authentic Italian cuisine (9-10 Lancaster Sq, LL32 8DA, 01492-592381, daily 5-9.30pm, £).
- **Signatures:** restaurant & bar serving contemporary British cuisine (Aberconwy Resort & Spa, LL32 8GA, 01492-583513, Wed-Sun noon-8/9pm, closed Mon Tue, ££).
- **Watson's Bistro:** family-run restaurant offering modern Welsh cuisine (Chapel St, LL32 8BP, 01492-596326, Wed-Thu 5.30-8.30pm, Fri-Sat noon-2pm, 5.30-9pm, Sun 5.45-8pm, closed Mon-Tue, ££).

mountains of Snowdonia in one direction and the Conwy Estuary in the other. The derelict castle was sold to Lord Conwy in 1627 and repaired and garrisoned during the English Civil War, when it was a Royalist stronghold, besieged in 1646 by the Parliamentary army, who (after its capture) damaged ('slighted') the castle to prevent the Royalists using it again.

The parish **Church of St Mary's & All Saints** was originally Aberconwy Abbey, completed in 1186 and moved to Maenan in 1283; much altered and enlarged over the centuries, it's the oldest building in Conwy. The church contains a number of interesting objects dating back to medieval times, while two windows in the nave's south aisle were made by the workshop of the Pre-Raphaelite artist, Edward Burne-Jones. Other important buildings in Conwy include **Aberconwy House** (National Trust), the town's only surviving 14th-century merchant's house and one of the first buildings built inside the walls of Conwy, and **Plas Mawr** ('great hall' in English), a fine Elizabethan townhouse built 1576-85 for the Wynn family. Later buildings of note include 19th-century **Vardre Hall** opposite the castle, erected in the 1850s (now a shop), and **Conwy Guildhall** completed in 1863

and enlarged in 1925. Just behind Plas Mawr is the **Royal Cambrian Academy**, a modern art gallery with monthly changing exhibitions.

Conwy has a number of green spaces, including the town's **Bonlondeb Park**, while opposite the castle is **RSPB Conwy**, a 114-acre nature preserve with

Town Square

Smallest House in Britain

Quay House, appropriately located on the Quay, is officially the smallest house in Britain, just ten feet high and six feet wide. It was in continuous occupation from the 16th century (even inhabited by a family at one point!) until 1900, when the owner (a 6ft fisherman, Robert Jones) was forced to vacate the house as it was too small for him to stand up in.

home to a number of national collections. A bit further south is **Adventure Parc Snowdonia** at Dolgarrog, the world's first inland surf lagoon. To the west of Conwy is **Conwy Mountain** (*Mynydd y Dref*), a popular hiking area, while further south is rugged **Gwydir Forest Park** (28mi^2) – on the edge of which, 13 miles south of Conwy, is 16th-century Gwydir Castle – and **Snowdonia National Park** (see page 191).

When you need to refuel, Conwy is renowned for its seafood restaurants, along with plenty of cafés, pubs (try the 1920s Albion Ale House) and bars, while its narrow streets are packed with quirky independent shops, including an award-winning chocolate shop (Baravelli's), a renowned butcher's shop (Edwards), antiques emporiums (including Drew Pritchard of *Salvage Hunters* TV fame) and galleries.

While visiting Conwy, allow some time to take in the charming neighbouring resort towns of Llandudno, with its splendid Victorian pier (the longest in Wales), and Colwyn Bay and its superb beaches.

grasslands, salt marsh & other habitats, while across the estuary in Llandudno is **Bodysgallen Hall**, which incorporates a medieval tower, possibly built as a watch tower for Conwy Castle. It's now a hotel and spa (owned by the National Trust) set in over 200 acres of parkland with beautiful gardens.

Six miles south of the town is glorious **Bodnant Garden** (National Trust), overlooking the Conway Valley towards the Carneddau mountains, noted for its laburnum arch (the longest in the UK) and

Conwy Mountain

Llandudno Bay

Cowes

Address: Cowes PO32 6RU (visitisleofwight.co.uk)

Getting there: air (Southampton, 38mi), ferry (Southampton, 23mi), road (Southampton, M3, M27)

Highlights: Sailing, Royal Yacht Squadron, harbour, River Medina, Osborne House, Norwood House, maritime museums, fish restaurants

Nearby: Coast Path, Farringford Historic House, The Needles, Newport, Ryde, Shanklin, Yarmouth

Sleep

- **Luxury:** Villa Rothsay Hotel (4*), 29 Baring Rd, PO31 8DF (01983-295178).
- **Moderate:** Woodvale Hotel (4*), 1 Prince's Esp, PO31 8LE (01983-292037).
- **Budget:** The Fountain Inn (3*), High St, PO31 7AW (01983-292397).

A seaport on the Isle of Wight – between two and five miles off the coast of Hampshire, separated by the Solent – regal Cowes is situated on the west bank of the River Medina estuary. One of the world's most famous yacht racing centres, it's home to its oldest regular regatta, **Cowes Week**, held annually in the first week of August. The town lies opposite the smaller town of East Cowes on the eastern bank of the estuary, linked by the **Cowes Floating Bridge** (a chain ferry, fee) There's a regular ferry service from Southampton on the mainland to Cowes, operated by the Red Funnel ferry company.

The first known settlements in the area were populated by Vikings, who during the 11th century used the River Medina as a base for raids along the south coast of England. The history of Cowes is steeped in its maritime heritage and it has a long and proud reputation for pioneer boat building, later diversifying into aircraft technologies and manufacturing, which continues to this day.

North of the town centre, the **Royal Yacht Squadron** (founded in 1815) clubhouse is located in Cowes Castle, built by Henry VIII in 1539. The yacht club inaugurated an annual racing regatta in 1826, now known as Cowes Week. South of the RYS HQ is **Northwood House** in Northwood Park, a country manor house built in 1799 for London businessman George Ward, now municipal offices, and its 26-acre public park. In the town centre is 18th-century **Westbourne House** (now a B&B), the former home to a collector of customs, where Dr Thomas Arnold, noted headmaster of Rugby School, was born in 1795. However, by far the most famous house in the area and a must-see is Queen Victoria's former home, **Osborne House** (see box on page 202).

Cowes Harbour

Osborne House

A former royal residence in East Cowes, Osborne House was built in 1845-51 for Queen Victoria and Prince Albert as a summer home and rural retreat. Prince Albert designed the house in the style of an Italian Renaissance palazzo, built by prominent London architect and builder, Thomas Cubitt. Queen Victoria died at Osborne House on 22nd January 1901, after which the house was given to the state (English Heritage).

Food & Drink

- **Gastronomy Cowes:** vibrant restaurant and bar serving delicious international cuisine (46-47, High St, PO31 7RR, 01983-200666, Tue-Fri 6pm-midnight, Sat-Sun 11am-midnight, closed Mon, £-££).
- **Mojac's:** restaurant offering innovative European dishes (10A Shooters Hill, PO31 7BG, 01983-281118, Tue-Sat 5-11pm, closed Sun-Mon, ££).
- **Murrays Seafood Restaurant:** local fish and seafood in a historic 18th-century building (106 High St, PO31 7AT, 01983-296233, daily noon-2.30/3pm, 6.30-8.30/9pm, £-££).

Cowes is home to a number of nautical-themed museums, including the **Sir Max Aitken Museum**, exhibiting historic and nautical artefacts in an 18th-century sailmaker's loft; **Cowes Maritime Museum & Library**, a local maritime museum located in the town's library; and – in East Cowes – the **Classic Boat Museum Gallery**, housing an array of classic boats and yachts, plus local maritime history exhibits; while three miles south is the **Wight Military & Heritage Museum** in Northwood. After you've seen the sights, take some time out to sample the town's array of cafés, restaurants and pubs, and perhaps indulge in a little retail therapy.

Other attractions worth visiting on the island include Carisbrooke Castle (Newport), Farringford Historic House (Tennyson's former home), the Isle of Wight Steam Railway (Wootton), the Needles (landmark chalk rocks, western tip of the island), Quarr Abbey (Ryde), Amazon World Zoo (Sandown) and Ventnor Botanic Garden.

Falmouth

Address: Falmouth TR11 2RT (falmouth.co.uk)

Getting there: air (Newquay, 20mi), rail (Falmouth Town, GWR), road (A39, A394)

Highlights: Pendennis Castle, King Charles the Martyr Church, National Maritime Museum, Art Gallery, harbour/docks, sailing, Gyllyngvase Beach

Nearby: Lizard & Roseland Heritage Coasts, Penryn, St Mawes, Trebah Garden, Trelissick Garden, Truro

Sleep

- **Luxury:** Greenbank Hotel (4*), Harbourside, TR11 2SR (01326-312440).
- **Moderate:** Falmouth Hotel (3*), Castle Beach, TR11 4NZ (01326-312671).
- **Budget:** Cutty Sark Inn (3*), 4 Grove Pl, TR11 4AU (01326-210861).

A port on the estuary of the River Fal in Cornwall, attractive Falmouth is noted for its deep natural harbour, the third largest in the world. Henry VIII built Pendennis Castle (see box on page 204) in 1540 to defend the estuary (called Carrick Roads). At the time the main town of the district (since the 13th century) was Penryn, and Falmouth wasn't officially created until around 1613 (granted a royal charter by Charles II in 1661). The town and port grew significantly in the late 17th century and from 1689-1851 was a Post Office Packet Station, responsible for shipping mail to and from the expanding British Empire, where news of Britain's victory and the death of Admiral Nelson at the Battle of Trafalgar first arrived in England. After the coming of the railway in 1863, Falmouth became a popular seaside resort, which it remains today.

The town's most prominent buildings include **Arwenack House**, a historic manor house partly destroyed in 1646 that was the home of the Killigrew family, who were responsible for the development of the town; the **Church of King Charles the Martyr**, built in 1662-64 and dedicated to Charles I; the cavernous **National Maritime Museum Cornwall**, which manages the National Small Boat Collection from the National Maritime Museum in Greenwich, in addition to its own collection; and the **Falmouth Art Gallery** on the upper floor of the Municipal Buildings, featuring everything from Old Masters to French Impressionists and leading Surrealists.

Falmouth & Carrick Roads

Pendennis Castle

The castle was built in 1540-42 – at the same time as **St Mawes Castle** on the opposite side of the estuary – to defend Carrick Roads against invasion from France and the Holy Roman Empire. The original, circular keep and gun platform was expanded at the end of the 16th century to cope with the increasing Spanish threat, with a ring of extensive stone ramparts and bastions constructed around the older castle.

Falmouth isn't particularly noted for its parks and gardens, but it does have a number of small parks and the pretty Fox Rosehill Gardens and Gyllyngdune Gardens. Around three miles southwest of the town are the renowned **Glendurgan Garden** (National Trust) and 26-acre, sub-tropical **Trebah Garden**, both equally spectacular, while further afield are the expansive Roseland and Lizard Heritage Coasts and splendid **Trelissick Garden** (National Trust). Falmouth is also a popular boating centre, from where you can tour the River Fal, visit Truro or explore Helford River. If beaches

Food & Drink

• **Fuel:** relaxing café and bar serving tasty homemade food (Arwenack St, TR11 3JG, 01326-314499, daily 8am-9pm, £).

• **Oliver's:** locally sourced seasonal food in bright venue (33 High St, TR11 2AD, 01326-218138, Tue 7-9pm, Wed-Sat noon-2pm, 6-9pm, Sun noon-4pm, closed Mon-Tue, ££).

• **Wheelhouse:** Highly rated fish and seafood restaurant on the harbour (Upton Slip, TR11 3DQ, 01326-318050, telephone for meal times, ££).

are more your scene, then Gyllyngvase is one of the best town beaches in the country.

When you've seen the sights, Falmouth has an abundance of restaurants and cafés where you can sample local oysters and Cornish pasties, and enjoy traditional award-winning ales and local gin in the town's many hostelries. If you fancy a spot of shopping, the town is noted for its galleries and craft shops and has a good selection of independent boutiques alongside the usual high street names.

Gyllyngvase Beach

Oban

Address: Oban PA34 4AW (oban.org.uk)

Getting there: air (Oban, 6mi), rail (Oban, Scotrail), road (A816, A85)

Highlights: Castles, War & Peace Museum, McCaig's Tower, Oban Distillery, Cathedrals, Oban Bay & harbour, fish & seafood, pubs

Nearby: Fort William, Glencoe, Hebridean islands Isle of Mull, Loch Lomond & Trossachs

- **Luxury:** Perle Oban Hotel (4*), Station Rd, PA34 5RT (01631-700301).

- **Moderate:** Royal Hotel (3*), Argyll Sq, PA34 4BE (01631-563021).

- **Budget:** Great Western Hotel (3*), Corran Esplanade, PA34 5PP (01631-563101).

A coastal resort town in Argyll & Bute in the west of Scotland, Oban is the unofficial capital of the West Highlands ('Gateway to the Isles'), known as 'the seafood capital of Scotland'. Human occupation in the area dates back to at least the Mesolithic period (10,000-8,000BC), although prior to the 19th century Oban was just a small village with minor fishing, trading, shipbuilding and quarrying industries. The modern town grew up around the distillery (est. 1794) in the 19th century and prospered with the arrival of the railway in 1880, which revitalised local industry and attracted tourists. Oban was an important naval base during World War Two in the Battle of the Atlantic. Since the '50s the principal industry has been tourism, while the town is the hub for ferries to the Inner and Outer Hebrides.

Just north of the town stands ruined **Dunollie Castle** on a site overlooking the main entrance to the bay, which has been fortified for over 1,000 years, although the existing castle dates largely from the 15th century. Three miles north of Oban is partially ruined **Dunstaffnage Castle**, one of Scotland's oldest stone castles dating from the 13th century and held by the Clan Campbell since the 15th century.

In town you can visit **Oban Distillery**, which offers tours and tastings, while just north of the distillery is the **Oban War & Peace Museum**, where you can learn about the town's history and its people. North of the town centre are the **Argyllshire Gathering Halls**, the

Oban

A prominent landmark to the east of town is **McCaig's Tower**, built in 1897 by local banker John Stuart McCaig to provide work for local stonemasons, from where there are spectacular views across Oban Bay to the Atlantic islands.

traditional home of the Argyllshire Gathering in Oban, the forerunner of Highland Games as we know them today. Oban is home to two cathedrals, the Scottish Episcopal **Cathedral Church of St John the Divine**, dating from 1864 – a grand scheme to enlarge it in 1906 was never finished – and **St Columba's Cathedral**, a Neo-Gothic Roman Catholic church designed by Sir Giles Gilbert Scott and completed in 1959.

Oban has a surfeit of small galleries, artists' studios and independent shops, and when it's time to refuel you can enjoy the town's award-winning restaurants and some of the best fish and seafood in the world, savour renowned Scottish venison and beef, and sample a wee dram in one of the town's many watering holes.

Oban is an excellent base from which to explore the Western Highlands and the Hebridean islands, such as Iona, Lismore, Mull and Staffa. North of Oban, the picturesque peninsulas of Benderloch and Appin offer

Food & Drink

• **Coast Restaurant:** modern Scottish fare, including seafood, fish and meat dishes (104 George St, PA34 5NT, 01631-569900, Mon-Sat noon-2pm, 5.30-10.30pm, Sun 5.30-10.30pm, ££).

• **Ee-usk:** local seafood in modern dining room with bay views (North Pier, PA34 5QD, 01631-565666, daily noon-3pm, 5.45-9pm, ££).

• **Waterfront Fishhouse:** informal seafood restaurant with water views (1 Railway Pier, PA34 4LW, 01631-563110, Wed-Sun noon-11pm, Closed Mon-Tue, £-££).

great walking and cycling, while closer to town is the island of Kerrera in Oban Bay, where you can explore the ruins of Gylen Castle.

Oban Bay

Ramsgate

Address: Ramsgate CT11 9FT (ramsgatetown.org)

Getting there: air (Gatwick, 70mi), rail (Ramsgate, Southeastern), road (A256, A299)

Highlights: Harbour/marina, Georgian architecture, St Augustine's church & abbey, St Laurence's church, Maritime Museum, Tunnels, beaches

Nearby: Broadstairs, Deal, Margate, Sandwich

Sleep

- **Luxury:** Albion House (4*), Albion Pl, CT11 8HQ (01843-606630).
- **Moderate:** Royal Harbour Hotel (3*), 10-12 Nelson Cres, CT11 9JF (01843-591514).
- **Budget:** Oak Hotel (2*), 66 Harbour Parade, CT11 8LN (01843-583686).

One of England's great 19th-century seaside resorts, Ramsgate on the Isle of Thanet in Kent (84 miles southeast of London) has one of the largest marinas on the south coast and glorious golden sands. The town started life as a hamlet dependent on fishing and farming, visited (or invaded) by Vikings, Anglo-Saxons, Romans and St Augustine, who landed here in AD507. Ramsgate was an associate member of the confederation of Cinque Ports (see box on page 210) as a 'limb' of Sandwich.

The town is noted for its elegant Georgian terraces and impressive Regency villas – it boasts some 900 listed buildings – alongside many fine Victorian buildings. The latter include the home of architect Augustus Pugin (1812-52), who designed the interiors of the Houses of Parliament. Pugin's home, **The Grange** (guided tours), which he built in 1843, lies next to gorgeous **St Augustine's Church** and shrine, designed by Pugin in 1847 and his final resting place. Pugin also built **St Augustine's Abbey**, across the road from the church. The oldest building in Ramsgate is pretty **St Laurence's Church**, aka St Laurence-in-Thanet, founded in 1062 and rebuilt after a lightning strike in 1439.

Ramsgate Harbour is England's only royal harbour – decreed by George IV in 1821 – and boasts its own Meridian line, five minutes and 41 seconds ahead of GMT, which you'll find in the **Maritime Museum**. Housed in the Clock House on the quayside, the museum tells the story of the town's rich heritage of fishing, lifeboats,

Ramsgate Harbour

Vincent Van Gogh

Ramsgate was briefly home to the Dutch artist Vincent Van Gogh, who moved to the town in 1876 at the age of 23. He boarded at 11 Spencer Square – identified by a blue plaque – and worked as a teacher at a local school.

shipbuilding and shipwrecks. The sheltered harbour was built between 1749 and 1850 as a response to the great storm of 1703, which saw the loss of much shipping and was the worst disaster to befall the Royal Navy in peacetime. During the Second World War, Ramsgate's residents sheltered from bombing in the **Ramsgate**

Food & Drink

- **Empire Room:** award-winning restaurant & bar in Royal Harbour Hotel (11 Nelson Cres, CT11 9JF, 01843-582511, Wed-Sun noon-2.30pm, Wed-Sat 6.30-9.30pm, Sun noon-2.30pm, closed Mon-Tue, ££).

- **La Magnolia:** Rustic Italian restaurant with a terrace overlooking the harbour (9-12 W Cliff Arcade, CT11 8LH, 01843-580477, Wed-Mon noon-9pm, closed Tue, £).

- **Royal Harbour Brasserie:** Seafood restaurant with unrivalled location on the harbour arm (Royal Harbour Parade, E Pier, CT11 8LS, 01843-599059, Mon, Wed-Thu noon-9pm, Fri-Sat noon-11pm, Sun 9am-9pm, closed Tue, £-££).

Tunnels, almost four miles long with a capacity of 60,000 (guided tours).

When you've enjoyed lunch at one of the town's harbourside restaurants, cafés or pubs, hop on a boat to see seals basking on the Goodwin Sands and discover beautiful beaches and bays. The town is at the centre of a network of clifftop walking trails, northeast to Broadstairs or south on the bracing Saxon Shore Way to Sandwich via Pegwell Bay Nature Reserve. If you fancy a spot of retail therapy, the old town is peppered with delightful shops and boutiques, while a few minutes away is **Petticoat Lane Emporium** on Dumpton Park Drive, with over 175 antiques, crafts and curios stalls.

Main Sands

Royal Viking Pavilion

Rye

> **Address:** Rye TN31 7HE (cometorye.co.uk, ryesussex.co.uk)
>
> **Getting there:** air (Gatwick, 42mi), rail (Rye, Southern), road (A259)
>
> **Highlights:** Castle, Landgate, St Mary's Church, half-timbered buildings, Rye Museum, Lamb House, coastline, historic inns, seafood
>
> **Nearby:** Dungeness, Great Dixter House & Gardens, Hastings, High Weald AONB, Rye Harbour

Sleep

- **Luxury:** The Mermaid Inn (3*), Mermaid St, TN31 7EY (01797-223065).

- **Moderate:** Rye Lodge Hotel (3*), E Cliff, TN31 7LD (01797-223838).

- **Budget:** Hope Anchor Hotel (3*), Watchbell St, TN31 7HA (01797-222216).

An ancient market town 77 miles southeast of London, picturesque Rye in East Sussex is situated at the confluence of three rivers: the Rother, the Tillingham and the Brede. It was part of the Saxon Manor of Rameslie, which was given to the Benedictine Abbey of Fécamp in Normandy by King Ethelred and remained in Norman hands until 1247. In the 18th century the town was one of the refuges of the notorious Hawkhurst Gang of smugglers, whose botholes included the town's Mermaid and Ye Olde Bell inns. Rye was once a seaport – it was a member of the renowned Cinque Ports (see box on page 210) – but the silting up of the River Rother stranded the town two miles inland. However, the town

still has a fishing fleet and is famous for its scallops.

Today, Rye is one of the best-preserved medieval towns in England, with a profusion of higgledy-piggledy, half-timbered

Mermaid Inn & Street (above)

Landgate

houses and a jumble of steep cobbled lanes. Notable buildings include the famous **Mermaid Inn** (see **Food & Drink**) with a history dating back to 1156 – the current building dates from 1420 but the cellars are the 12th-century originals – while the charming **Old Bell Inn** was built in 1390. Other highlights include **Oak Corner**, near the bottom of Mermaid Street, a private dwelling from 1377, rebuilt in 1490. The **Landgate** (dating from 1329) – the only survivor of the original four fortified entrances to the town – provides the only vehicular access to the medieval centre. A relative newcomer, the **Old Rye Grammar School** on the High Street was founded in 1636 as a free school and was in use until 1908.

Cinque Ports

The origins of the Cinque Ports can be traced back to Anglo-Saxon times, although it wasn't until 1100 that the term came into general use. In 1155, a royal charter established the ports to maintain ships ready for the crown in times of need. By the reign of Henry II (1154-1189), the towns of Hastings, New Romney, Hythe, Dover and Sandwich were known collectively as the Cinque Ports, while Rye and Winchelsea were known as 'Ancient Towns' and were added later.

One of the oldest buildings in Rye is **Ypres Tower**, aka Rye Castle. It was built in 1249 under Henry III as 'Baddings Tower' to defend the town from the French and later named after its owner, John de Ypres (pronounced 'Wipers' by locals!). Over the centuries it has been used for defence, a private home, a prison and a mortuary, and is now home to **Rye Museum**, where you can discover the town's rich history. Also well worth a visit is splendid 12th-century **St Mary's Church**, sometimes referred to as the 'cathedral of East Sussex'. The church has some beautiful stained-glass windows and one of the oldest functioning church turret clocks in the country installed around 1561-2 in the Quarter Boys clock tower, so called because it strikes the quarters but not the hours. You can climb the tower to see the clock mechanism and church bells, along with panoramic views of the surrounding countryside.

Rye has many literary and artistic connections, one of which is **Lamb House** (National Trust), built in 1722 by James Lamb. An early visitor was George I, when a storm drove his ship ashore at Camber in 1726. From 1897, Lamb House was the home of American author

Ypres Tower (Rye Castle)

Food & Drink

- **Mermaid Inn:** fine dining in characterful 15th-century smugglers' inn (Mermaid St, TN31 7EY, 01797-223065; daily noon-2.30pm, 6.30-9pm, ££).
- **Webbe's at the Fish Café:** lively brasserie serving local fish and seafood (17 Tower St, TN31 7AT, 01797-222210, daily noon-2/2.30pm, 5.30/6-9.30pm, ££).
- **Ypres Castle Inn:** cosy 17th century inn offering superb food and ales (Gungarden, TN31 7HH, 01797-223248, Thu-Sat noon-10pm, Sun noon-8pm, closed Mon-Wed, £).

Henry James, who wrote three novels while living there, and from 1918-40 was the base for English novelist E. F. Benson, who set his *Mapp & Lucia* novels in and around Rye. The handsome red-brick fronted house has an attractive walled garden and is wonderfully tranquil. The **Rye Heritage Centre**, housed in a 19th-century sail loft on the quayside, is home to the 'Story of Rye', a unique *son et lumière*, employing a scale model of Victorian Rye to bring to life over 700 years of history.

When you've had your fill of the town's gorgeous architecture and crave sustenance, Rye offers an abundance of fine restaurants (especially seafood), cosy inns, modern coffee shops and traditional tea rooms. If shopping is your bag, the town has a host of interesting independent shops, a weekly farmers' market, and a thriving antiques and art scene.

A couple of miles out of town, spectacular **Rye Harbour Nature Reserve** is worth a visit, encompassing 1,150 acres of wetlands, salt marshes and coastline, along with the ruins of 16th-century **Camber Castle** built by Henry VIII. One of Britain's most important conservation areas, the reserve is home to 4,500 different species, including some 300 bird varieties.

Rye rooftops

Rye Harbour

Southwold

Sleep

Address: Southwold IP18 6EF (visitsouthwold. co.uk, exploresouthwold.co.uk)

Getting there: air (Norwich, 42mi), rail (Lowestoft, 13mi), road (A12, A1095)

Highlights: Southwold Pier, Lighthouse, Southwold Museum, Adnams Brewery, Blackshore & harbour, beach & huts, Electric Picture Palace, St Edmund's Church, seafood restaurants, historic pubs

Nearby: Aldeburgh, Holy Trinity Blythburgh, Dunwich, Lowestoft, Minsmere RSPB Reserve, Suffolk Broads, Thorpeness, Waveney Valley

- **Luxury:** Swan Hotel (4*), Market Pl, IP18 6EG (01502-722186).
- **Moderate:** Crown Hotel (3*), 90 High St, IP18 6DP (01502-722275).
- **Budget:** Blyth Hotel (2*), Station Rd, IP18 6AY (01502-722632).

A small seaside resort on the East Anglian coast of Suffolk, delightful Southwold lies at the mouth of the River Blyth on the North Sea, 29 miles northeast of Ipswich and 31 miles southeast of Norwich. The town was listed in the *Domesday Book* (1086) as a fishing port but didn't receive its town charter until 1489 (from Henry VII). By the 16th century it was Suffolk's busiest fishing port (notably herrings), but in 1659 a devastating fire destroyed most of the town. The sheltered estuary provided a wide harbour for the king's fleet, which was wrecked in 1672 by the Dutch at the Battle of Sole Bay with an estimated 800 casualties. The battle, and the changing design of ships leading to a need for deeper harbours, saw Southwold's port dwindle in importance.

Today, Southwold is a peaceful haven and the jewel in the crown of East Suffolk's seaside resorts, a genteel backwater with a wealth of fine Georgian buildings, pink washed cottages and elegant townhouses. The town is arranged around a series of greens – on one of which, Gun Hill, are six 18-pound guns captured in 1746 at the

Southwold Beach

St Edmund's Church

Battle of Culloden (see page 185) – with a long sandy beach, traditional (eccentric and entertaining) pier and candy-coloured beach huts.

Among the town's most prominent landmarks is the parish church of **St Edmund's** (1460), on the site of a far older church dating from around 1200. One of Suffolk's finest churches, it has many outstanding features, including an imposing flint tower, magnificent screens, a 15th-century pulpit, an impressive font cover, richly wrought choir stalls and a splendid organ. The town's superb 101ft working **Lighthouse** (you can climb it) near East Green started operation in 1890 and was converted to electricity in 1938, while the **Old Water Tower**, built in 1896 with a capacity of 40,000 gallons, was replaced in 1937 by an Art Deco-style 150,000-gallon water tower. Another landmark is 620ft **Southwold Pier**, built in 1900 as a landing stage for steamships, which, following recent renovation is one of the finest piers in Britain and one of the town's main attractions, with whimsical arcade games, shops and cafés. On the High Street is William Denny's **Buckenham House**, built by a wealthy Tudor merchant and still displaying much evidence of its origins, having survived the 1659 fire.

Food & Drink

- **Coasters:** Smart restaurant with bar and modern British menu (12 Queen St, IP18 6EQ, 01502-724734, daily 9am-2.30pm, 6-9pm, ££).
- **Lord Nelson:** Nautical-themed pub with great food, beer and atmosphere (42 East St, IP18 6EJ, 01502-722079, daily noon-8pm, £-££).
- **Sole Bay Fish Company:** friendly, unpretentious shellfish restaurant on River Blyth (22E Blackshore, IP18 6ND, 01502-724241, daily 8am-3pm, £-££).

Southwold has a number of museums, including **Southwold Museum**, a quaint cottage museum dedicated to local and natural history, the **Alfred Corry Lifeboat Museum**, named after the *Alfred Corry* lifeboat (in service 1894-1918) – displayed in the museum – which in turn was named after its benefactor. Southwold is also home to the **Amber Shop & Museum**, the only museum in Britain dedicated to the history of amber. Another unusual attraction is the **Southwold Sailors'**

Beach Huts

Southwold Harbour

Dunwich

Located south along the coast (9 miles by road or a 3-mile walk along the beach), during the Anglo-Saxon period Dunwich was the capital of the Kingdom of the East Angles, which at its zenith was an international port similar in size to 14th-century London. Its decline began in 1286 when a storm surge hit the East Anglian coast followed by further great storms in 1287 and the following century, after which the harbour and most of the town was lost to coastal erosion. From a 'city' of 3,000 souls at the time of the *Domesday Book* in 1086, today Dunwich is a small coastal village with a population of around 200.

Reading Room, built in 1864 as a refuge for fishermen and mariners in an effort to keep them out of the pubs and encourage them in Christian ideals. Talking about pubs, Southwold is home to world-famous **Adnams Brewery**, one of the UK's oldest brewery sites dating back to Johanna de Corby in 1396 (Adnams was founded in 1872), which has helped keep the town prosperous (tours organised). Also worth a visit is the 70-seat Edwardian-style **Electric Picture Palace**, opened in 2002 by local resident Michael Palin.

Southwold Pier

When you've done the sights you can happily spend a few hours browsing the town's host of independent shops and boutiques, along with its many galleries and arts and crafts outlets. Southwold offers an array of eateries – from fine dining to traditional pubs, superb fresh fish and seafood to creative homemade café fare – and a host of historic pubs where you can sample Adnams' ales or gin. If you wish to commune with nature, just west of town is a vast nature reserve along the River Blyth estuary, extending to over 1,000 acres combining mudflats, meadows and marsh, and home to otters, deer and a wide variety of bird species.

After you've savoured all Southwold has to offer, the surrounding area is home to a host of lovely towns and villages just waiting to be discovered, such as idyllic Walberswick (reachable by rowboat ferry) just south of Southwold; Blythburgh and its 'cathedral of the marshes' (Holy Trinity church); the historic village ('lost city') of Dunwich (see box); charming Aldeburgh, where Benjamin Britten founded the Aldeburgh Festival (June) in 1948; beautiful Beccles on the River Waveney; Thorpeness and its watery wonderland, the Mere; and the historic market town of Saxmundham.

Tenby

> **Address:** Tenby SA70 7LS (tenbyvisitorguide.co.uk)
>
> **Getting there:** air (Cardiff, 100mi), rail (Tenby, TfW), road (A478)
>
> **Highlights:** St Mary's Church, Castle & Town Walls, Tudor Merchant's House, Tenby Museum & Art Gallery, Caldey Island, beaches, harbour
>
> **Nearby:** Carmarthen, Gower Peninsula, Laugharne, Milford Haven, Pembroke, St Davids

- **Luxury:** Trefloyne Manor (4*), Trefloyne Ln, SA70 7RG (01834-842165).
- **Moderate:** Giltar Hotel (3*), 9 Esplanade, SA70 7DU (01834-842507).
- **Budget:** Premier Inn (3*), White Lion St, SA70 7ET (0871-527 9514).

A walled seaside town on the western side of Carmarthen Bay in Pembrokeshire, Wales, enchanting Tenby – part of so-called 'Little England beyond Wales' – is one of the country's most picturesque towns with beautiful pastel-coloured houses, a natural sheltered harbour and some 2½ miles of glorious sandy beaches (Castle Beach was the *Sunday Times* 'Beach of the Year' 2019).

The earliest reference to a settlement at Tenby was in the 9th century. The town was invaded by the Normans in the 12th century but was repeatedly sacked by Welsh forces, which led to the construction of the castle and town walls in the late 13th century (see box on page 216). In the Middle Ages Tenby was an important port and trading centre. The English Civil War and a plague in 1650 led to the town's decline, until, in the early 19th century, it was re-born as a fashionable health and seaside resort, a recovery that gained pace with the arrival of the railway in 1863.

Tenby's historic buildings include 15th-century **St Mary's Church**, which contains some 13th-century features from an earlier Norman church and many interesting features; the 15th-century **Tudor Merchant's House** (National Trust), furnished and decorated as it would have been in 1500; and **Tenby Museum & Art Gallery**, the oldest independent museum in Wales (est 1878) with collections of local geology, biology, archaeology and maritime artefacts.

When you've seen the sights, soaked up the sun on the town's beaches, undergone a bit of retail therapy in Tenby's mix of independent boutiques and high street stores, and enjoyed the host of restaurants, cafés

Tenby Harbour

Tenby's Colourful Houses

and pubs, it's time to explore the surrounding area, commencing with a boat trip to monastic (Cistercian) **Caldey Island** or **St Catherine's Island**, a tidal island with 19th-century Palmerston Fort.

Three miles west of Tenby are the **Dinosaur Park** and **Manor Wildlife Park**, while further afield are 13th-century **Pembroke Castle**, where Henry VII was born; **St Davids** and its splendid Cathedral, the most westerly point in Wales; **Laugharne** – the home and last resting place of poet Dylan Thomas (1914-53) – and nearby **Pendine Sands**. The Sands hosted car and motorcycle races in the early 1900s and land speed record attempts in the 1920s by the likes of Malcolm Campbell and Welshman J.G. Parry-Thomas, who died in an accident here in 1927. If you fancy a hike, the magnificent

Town & South Beach

Food & Drink

- **Blue Ball Restaurant:** Locally sourced food including fresh seafood in stylish, rustic setting (10 Upper Frog St, SA70 7JD, 01834-843038, Mon-Sat 6-9pm, Sun 12.30-2.30pm, £-££).

- **Plantagenet House:** Modern British cuisine in period building with bar (1 Quay Hill, SA70 7BX, 01834-842350, Tue 6-9pm, Wed-Sun noon-2.30pm, 6-9pm, closed Mon, ££).

- **Stables Restaurant:** Relaxed venue serving British fare (S Parade, SA70 7DG, 01834-843318. Tue-Sat 6-11pm, closed Sun-Mon, £-££).

Pembrokeshire Coast Path is right on your doorstep; a popular stretch is north to Saundersfoot (4½mi), which offers fabulous views of Saundersfoot Bay from the headland at Monkstone Point.

Tenby Castle & Town Walls

The ruins of 13th-century **Tenby Castle** are situated on a headland (opposite Castle Beach) separated by an isthmus, while remnants of the medieval **Town Walls** are scattered around the town, including the semi-circular **Five Arches Gate**. There were originally four gates – the others were removed in the late 18th and early 19th centuries – and 24 towers, of which six survive.

Whitby

Address: Whitby YO21 1RE (visitwhitby.com)

Getting there: air (Durham, 33mi), rail (Whitby, Northern), road (A171)

Highlights: Abbey ruins, Captain Cook Memorial Museum, Whitby Museum, 199 Steps, Church of St Mary, brewery, River Esk, harbour, historic pubs

Nearby: Filey, North York Moors, Robin Hood's Bay, Scarborough, Staithes

Sleep

- **Luxury:** Raithwaite Estate (4*), Sandsend Rd, YO21 3ST (01947-661661).
- **Moderate:** The Angel (4*), 1 New Quay Rd, YO21 1DH (01947-824730).
- **Budget:** Resolution Hotel (3*), 1 Skinner St, YO21 3AH (01947-602085).

A popular seaside resort on the east coast of Yorkshire at the mouth of the River Esk, enchanting Whitby is 47 miles northeast of York and 31 miles southeast of Middlesbrough. The earliest record of a permanent settlement is in AD656, when the first abbey was founded. The town got its current name in the 11th century and in the Middle Ages was a small fishing settlement, which developed into an important port in the 18th and 19th centuries, with herring and whaling fleets, a major shipbuilding centre, alum mining and the manufacture of jet jewellery. Tourism began during the Georgian period (when Whitby was also a spa town) and accelerated with the arrival of the railway in 1839, enhanced by the town's proximity to the North York Moors (see box on page 218) and its heritage coastline.

For most visitors the first port of call is Whitby Abbey (see page 218), which can be reached from the town centre via **Whitby Bridge**, a swing bridge constructed in 1908. Close to the bridge is the **Captain Cook Memorial Museum**, housed in handsome Walker's

Whitby

House (1688), the former home of Captain John Walker to whom James Cook (1728-1779) was apprenticed in 1746, and where Cook lived and studied in the attic. The museum tells the story of Cook's life and epic voyages, and the work of the sailors, scientists and artists who sailed with him. After visiting the museum head north to the **Museum of Whitby Jet**, the home of jewellers W. Hamond, the world's oldest manufacturer and retailer of Whitby jet jewellery. The museum is located at the bottom of the **199 Steps**, aka Church Steps, that lead up the hill to the **Church of St Mary**, founded around 1110, although its interior dates mainly from the late 18th century. There are panoramic views over Whitby from the church, whose graveyard was famously a setting in Bram Stoker's 1897 novel, *Dracula*.

Nearby on East Cliff are the ruins of 13th-century Benedictine **Whitby Abbey** (English Heritage), which was destroyed during Henry VIII's Dissolution of the Monasteries in 1540 and further damaged by German shelling in 1914. Nearby is **Cholmley House** (aka Whitby Hall), built in 1672 by Sir Hugh Cholmley, who acquired the Abbey ruins and surrounding land after the dissolution. Today, it's a museum and visitor centre for

North York Moors

An upland area (554mi^2) in North Yorkshire encompassing one of the largest expanses of heather moorland in the UK, the North York Moors was designated a National Park in 1952. The moorland landscapes shelter tumbling waterfalls, characterful villages, coastal bays, moorland crags and a wealth of ancient sites, from Iron Age burial mounds to the haunting ruins of medieval abbeys, along with an abundance of flora and fauna.

the Abbey site. In the shadow of the Abbey is **Whitby Brewery**, where beer-lovers can join a tour.

Returning to the town centre, just south of Whitby Bridge is **The Endeavour Experience**, a life-size replica of Captain Cook's HM Bark *Endeavour* (built in Whitby), where you can discover what life was like for the 95 crew members during Cook's three-year voyage of discovery to Australia and New Zealand. Other museums worth a visit include **Whitby Museum & Pannett Art Gallery** – situated in the beautiful gardens of **Pannett Park** – a fascinating local history museum and gallery with an outstanding collection of 19th- and 20th-century paintings, and the **RNLI Whitby Museum** located close to Whitby Beach. Nearby is **Whalebone Arch**, a whale's jawbone erected in 1853 in recognition of the town's whaling history, while close by is a statue of Captain Cook, and the attractive **Whitby Pier Lighthouses** flanking Whitby's harbour entrance. The West Lighthouse marks the eastern end of **Whitby West Cliff Beach**, a superb (3-mile) sandy beach lined with gaily coloured beach huts just a few minutes' walk from the town centre. Just south of the beach is Victorian

Whitby Abbey

Whitby Pavilion (1878), where you can enjoy plays, traditional drama, pantomimes, musicals and comedy.

When you've done the sights, Whitby's meandering cobbled streets are packed with quirky independent shops and boutiques, along with **Whitby Open Market** (Tue, Sat-Sun), while the town is awash with restaurants, cafés and pubs, offering everything from fine dining to fast food, including an abundance of superb fish and seafood restaurants. Whitby has a lively nightlife, with a host of traditional pubs, bars, music venues, theatre and cinema - it's also the Goth capital of Britain (see whitbygothweekend.co.uk)!

It would be shame to visit Whitby and not spend some time exploring the surrounding region, not least the many pretty coastal villages such as **Robin Hood's Bay**, a picturesque fishing village five miles south; **Staithes** (10mi north), with its higgledy-piggledy cottages and winding streets; **Scarborough**, 20 miles south, a historic seaside resort with glorious beaches; and **Filey** (27mi south), a graceful fishing village offering simple, timeless pleasures. Then, of course, there are the spectacular **North York Moors** (see box opposite), which you can traverse on the heritage **North Yorkshire Moors Railway**, from Whitby to Pickering.

Food & Drink

- **Ditto Restaurant:** Homely, intimate restaurant serving meat and fish dishes (26 Skinner St, YO21 3AJ, 01947-601404, Wed-Sat 6.30-9pm, closed Sun-Tue, ££).

- **Harry's Lounge Bar & Brasserie:** Restaurant offering harbour views specialising in fish and steak dishes (10-11 Pier Rd, YO21 3PU, 01947-601909, 9am-11pm/midnight, Tue 8am-5pm, ££).

- **Magpie Café:** Yorkshire's most lauded seafood restaurant (14 Pier Rd, YO21 3PU, 01947-602058, daily 11.30am-9pm, £-££).

Robin Hood's Bay

North York Moors

London's Architectural Walks, 2nd edition

ISBN: 978-1-913171-01-8, 128 pages, softback, £9.99, Jim Watson

London's Architectural Walks is a unique guide to the most celebrated landmark buildings in one of the world's major cities. In thirteen easy walks, it takes you on a fascinating journey through London's diverse architectural heritage with historical background and clear maps. Some of the capital's most beautiful parks are visited, plus palaces, theatres, museums and some surprising oddities. The author's line and watercolour illustrations of all the city's significant buildings, make London's Architectural Walks an essential companion for anyone interested in the architecture that has shaped this great metropolis – and a great souvenir!

London's Secret Walks, 3rd edition

ISBN: 978-1-909282-99-5, 320 pages, softback, £10.99, Graeme Chesters

London is a great city for walking – whether for pleasure, exercise or simply to get from A to B. Despite the city's extensive public transport system, walking is often the quickest and most enjoyable way to get around – at least in the centre – and it's also free and healthy! Many attractions are off the beaten track, away from the major thoroughfares and public transport hubs, which favours walking as the best way to explore them, as does the fact that London is a visually interesting city with a wealth of stimulating sights in every 'nook and cranny'.

London's Waterside Walks

ISBN: 978-1-909282-96-4, 192 pages, softback, £9.99, David Hampshire

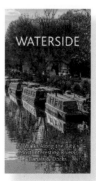

Most people are familiar with London's River Thames, but the city has much more to offer when it comes to waterways, including a wealth of canals, minor rivers (most are tributaries of the Thames), former docklands, lakes and reservoirs. London's Waterside Walks takes you on 21 walks along many of the city's lesser-known, hidden waterways, including the Rivers Brent, Lea and Wandle, and the Grand Union and Regent's Canals.

see citybooks.co

INDEX

Touring the Lake District

ISBN: 978-1-913171-22-3, 128 pages, softback, £9.99, Jim Watson

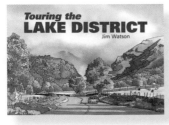

Touring the Lake District is a unique illustrated guide to exploring the area by car. Eight carefully planned tours take in the popular tourist centres plus a wealth of hidden gems many consider to be the 'Real Lakeland'. The tours visit most of the famous lakes, negotiate empty country lanes, cross open moorland and test your driving skills on mountain passes. With picturesque villages, award-winning restaurants, gastro pubs and rustic coffee shops to enjoy along the routes, this book will provide you with a comprehensive portrait of this varied and magnificent region.

Touring the Cotswolds

ISBN: 978-1-909282-91-9, 128 pages, softback, £9.99, Jim Watson

Touring the Cotswolds is a unique guide to exploring the best of the Cotswolds by car through eight carefully planned tours, taking in the heavyweight tourist centres plus a wealth of hidden gems (the 'Real Cotswolds'). You'll negotiate a maze of country lanes, high hills with panoramic views, lush woodlands and beautiful valleys, plus an abundance of picturesque villages, providing a comprehensive portrait of this varied and delightful area.

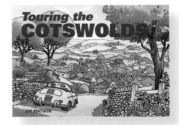

see citybooks.co

London's Green Walks

ISBN: 978-1-909282-82-7, 192 pages, £9.99, David Hampshire

London's Green Walks
20 Walks Around the City's Best Parks, Gardens & Waterways
David Hampshire

Green spaces cover almost 40 per cent of Greater London, ranging from magnificent royal parks and garden cemeteries, full of intrigue and history, to majestic ancient forests and barely tamed heathland; from elegant squares and formal country parks to enchanting 'secret' gardens. The 20 walks take in famous destinations, such as Hyde Park and Regent's Park, but also many smaller and lesser known – but no less beautiful – parks and gardens, all of which are free to explore.

London's Village Walks

ISBN: 978-1-909282-94-0, 192 pages, £9.99, David Hampshire

From its beginnings as a Roman trading port some 2,000 years ago, London has mushroomed into the metropolis we see today, swallowing up thousands of villages, hamlets and settlements in the process. Nevertheless, if you're seeking a village vibe you can still find it if you know where to look. Scratch beneath the surface of modern London and you'll find a rich tapestry of ancient villages just waiting to be rediscovered.

David Hampshire

London's Village Walks
20 Walks Around the City's Most Interesting Villages

Hidden London, 2nd Edition

David Hampshire
HIDDEN LONDON
2nd Edition
Discover over 100 of the City's Hidden Attractions

ISBN: 978-1-913171-20-9, 256 pages, £10.99, David Hampshire

London is one of the world's leading tourist destinations with a wealth of world-class sights. What aren't so well known are the city's numerous hidden – but no less worthy – attractions, most of which are neglected by the throngs who descend upon the tourist-clogged major sights. *Hidden London* includes over 100 largely undiscovered gems, including fascinating small museums and galleries; historic churches and other ancient buildings; captivating parks, gardens and cemeteries; cutting-edge art and design, and much more.

see citybooks.co

London Escapes

ISBN: 978-1-913171-00-1, 192 pages, softback, £10.99,
David Hampshire

London offers a wealth of attractions, but sometimes you just want to escape the city's constant hustle and bustle and visit somewhere with a gentler, slower pace of life. *London Escapes* offers over 70 days out less than two hours from the city, from historical towns and lovely villages to magnificent stately homes and gardens; beautiful, nostalgic seaside resorts and beaches to spectacular parks and nature reserves.

Peaceful London, 2nd edition

ISBN: 978-1-909282-84-1, 192 pages, softback, £9.99
David Hampshire

Whether you're seeking somewhere to recharge your batteries, rest your head, revive your spirits, restock your larder or refuel your body; a haven to inspire, soothe or uplift your mood; or you just wish to discover a part of London that's a few steps further off the beaten track, *Peaceful London* will steer you in the right direction.

Quirky London, 2nd edition

ISBN: 978-1-990282-98-8, 208 pages, softback, £9.99
Graeme Chesters

London is a city with a cornucopia of strange sights and stories, being ancient, vast and in a constant state of flux. Unlike most guide books, *Quirky London* takes you off the beaten path to seek out the more unusual places and tales that fail to register on the radar of both visitors and residents alike, while also highlighting unusual and often overlooked aspects and attractions of some of London's most famous tourist sites.

see citybooks.co